TRUSTING GOD

JERRY BRIDGES

A NavPress resource published in alliance
with Tyndale House Publishers, Inc.

NAVPRESS ⬤.

NavPress is the publishing ministry of The Navigators, an international Christian organization and leader in personal spiritual development. NavPress is committed to helping people grow spiritually and enjoy lives of meaning and hope through personal and group resources that are biblically rooted, culturally relevant, and highly practical.

For more information, visit www.NavPress.com.

Trusting God
Copyright © 1988, 2008 by Jerry Bridges. All rights reserved.

Trusting God Discussion Guide
Copyright © 1989, 2008 by Jerry Bridges. All rights reserved.

A NavPress resource published in alliance with Tyndale House Publishers, Inc.

NAVPRESS and the NAVPRESS logo are registered trademarks of NavPress, The Navigators, Colorado Springs, CO. *TYNDALE* is a registered trademark of Tyndale House Publishers, Inc. Absence of ® in connection with marks of NavPress or other parties does not indicate an absence of registration of those marks.

The Team:
Don Pape, Editor
David Zimmerman, Acquisitions Editor
Julie Chen, Designer

Author photograph by Steve Learned

For information about special discounts for bulk purchases, please contact Tyndale House Publishers at csresponse@tyndale.com or call 800-323-9400.

Library of Congress Cataloging-in-Publication Data

Names: Bridges, Jerry, author. | Bridges, Jerry, author. Trusting God.
Title: Trusting God with study guide : even when life hurts / Jerry Bridges.
Description: Colorado Springs : NavPress, 2016. | Includes bibliographical references.
Identifiers: LCCN 2016039826 (print) | LCCN 2016044451 (ebook) | ISBN 9781631467929 (softcover) | ISBN 9781631467936 (Apple) | ISBN 9781631467943 (E-Pub) | ISBN 9781631467950 (Kindle)
Subjects: LCSH: Providence and government of God—Christianity. | Trust in God—Christianity. | Providence and government of God—Christianity—Textbooks. | Trust in God—Christianity—Textbooks.
Classification: LCC BT96.3 .B755 2016 (print) | LCC BT96.3 (ebook) | DDC 231/.5—dc23
LC record available at https://urldefense.proofpoint.com/v2/url?u=https-3A__lccn.loc.gov_2016039826&d=DQIFAw&c=6BNjZEuL_DAs869UxGis0g&r=ZlF6A1J_SMm9xAyjgyDor34CB-fqQRaraBLNVSdnrVo&m=ZyQ3UGHQkcCey-cYZcMndiFSUnvDxuWy97BDVmpTEpk&s=KOQG-h2ZP_O1qIqpDUIUah0rBrK4xJf8iq_Vpd5Yvxs&e=

ISBN 978-1-63146-792-9

Printed in the United States of America

22   21   20   19   18   17   16
7   6   5   4   3   2   1

To our children, Kathy and Dan, who have
brought me much joy as a father.

CONTENTS

PREFACE

When I was fourteen years old, my mother died suddenly, without warning. I was in the adjoining room and rushed in just in time to see her gasp her last breath. I was stunned and devastated. My older brother was away at school, and my dad was too stricken with grief himself to be able to help me. Worst of all, I did not know how to turn to God in times of trouble. I was alone in my adversity.

That was not the first time adversity had struck in my life, and it was certainly not to be the last. As the Scripture says, "Yet man is born to trouble as surely as sparks fly upward" (Job 5:7). All of us experience adversity at different times and in varying degrees throughout our lives.

Learning to trust God in adversity has been a slow and difficult process for me. It is a process that is still under way. But several years ago, in an effort to strengthen my own trust in God, I began a lengthy Bible study on the subject of God's sovereignty in the affairs of His people. That study has helped me immeasurably, and it is the fruit of that study I now share with you.

During the time of the study, which actually covered a period of about four years, I encountered other believers who were struggling with some of the same issues I was: Does God actually control the circumstances of our lives, or do "bad" things just happen to us because we live in a sin-cursed world? If God really does control the circumstances of our lives, why did He allow my friend to get cancer? Can I truly trust God when the going gets tough in different areas of my life?

This book, then, was born out of the results of addressing needs in my own life and realizing that many other believers have similar questions and doubts. It is written from the perspective of a brother and companion to all those who are tempted at times to ask, "Can I really trust God?"

Trusting God has been a difficult book to write. For one thing, I have become much more aware of the widespread and frequent occurrences of adversity around me. I had not realized as acutely as I do now the pervasive nature of suffering and heartache, especially among believers. As a result of my heightened perception of suffering around me, I found myself frequently asking, "Do I truly believe what I am writing?"

Another difficulty for me has been the realization that many of my friends have experienced far greater adversity than I have. Who am I to seek to write words of instruction and encouragement to them when I have not experienced the measure of pain they have? My answer to that question is the realization that the truth of God's Word and the encouragement it is intended to give is not dependent upon my experience. I have not written this book about my experiences, which are not particularly unusual. I have written it as a Bible study about God and His sovereignty, wisdom, and love as they bear upon the adversities we all encounter.

Trusting God is written for the average Christian who has not necessarily experienced major catastrophe but who does frequently encounter the typical adversities and heartaches of life:

the pregnancy miscarriage, the lost job, the auto accident, the rebellious son or daughter, the unfair professor in college. These events do not make the "front page" of our lives; indeed, they are often buried within a broken or confused heart. Because of their low-keyness, they usually generate very little prayer support from our Christian friends.

I sincerely hope that none of the statements I make in the following chapters come across as glib and easy answers to the difficult problems of adversity and suffering. There are no easy answers. Adversity is difficult even when we know God is in control of our circumstances. In fact, that knowledge sometimes tends to aggravate the pain. "If God is in control," we ask, "why did He allow this to happen?"

The purpose of this book is twofold: First, I desire to glorify God by acknowledging His sovereignty and His goodness. Second, I desire to encourage God's people by demonstrating from Scripture that God is in control of their lives, that He does indeed love them, and that He works out all the circumstances of their lives for their ultimate good.

The reader will notice an abundance of quotations from other writers. This book, though, is not merely a synthesis of other people's views. The basic convictions stated in these chapters are the result of my own personal Bible study done over a long period of time. I acknowledge, however, my indebtedness to other writers for affirmation and, in some instances, clarification of my understanding of some of these truths.

I want to express my appreciation to a number of people who have contributed to the writing of this book. Don Simpson, my friend as well as editor, encouraged me, helped me, and sometimes challenged my conclusions as we worked through these chapters together. Dr. J. I. Packer graciously agreed to review some of the key chapters to check their theological accuracy—though he should not be held responsible for the final results. Jessie Halsell performed the very necessary and challenging task of transforming my handwritten pages to a typed manuscript. A special word of appreciation must go to Grace Peterson, a "senior saint," for her colaborship in prayer. Although a number of friends prayed for me during the eleven months of writing, Grace was always available when I sensed the need for that extra push of prayer to get over a difficult hurdle. Finally, I want to pay tribute to my first wife, Eleanor, now with the Lord, who herself experienced major adversity, even as I was writing this book, for her love and the sacrifices she made to allow me the time to study and write.

CHAPTER ONE

CAN YOU TRUST GOD?

And call upon me in the day of trouble;
I will deliver you, and you will honor me.

PSALM 50:15

The letter did not bring good news. A close relative, very dear to me, had just learned she had bone cancer. Malignant cells from a previous bout with cancer had lain dormant for eight years before invading the skeletal parts of her body. One hip was already almost destroyed; the doctor was amazed she was still able to walk. Such incidents are all too common these days. In fact, during the writing of this chapter I had seven friends, all with cancer, listed on my "urgent" prayer page.

But cancer or other physical ailments are obviously not the only source of anxiety. Over lunch a few weeks ago a business-man friend confided that his company is perilously close to bankruptcy; another friend experiences heartache over a spiritually rebellious teenager. The truth is, all of us face adversity in various forms and at different times. A best-selling book by a secular psychiatrist put it very well with this simple opening statement: "Life is difficult."

Adversity and its accompanying emotional pain come in many forms. There may be the heartache of an unhappy marriage or the disappointment of a miscarried pregnancy or grief over a spiritually indifferent or rebellious child. There is the anxiety of the family breadwinner who has just lost his job and the despair of the young mother who has learned she has a terminal illness.

Others experience the frustration of dashed hopes and unfulfilled dreams: a business that turned sour or a career that never developed. Still others experience the sting of injustice, the dull ache of loneliness, and the stabbing pain of unexpected grief. There is the humiliation of rejection by others, of demotion at work, and, worst of all, of failure that is one's own fault. Finally there is the despair of realizing that some difficult circumstances—a physical infirmity of your own or perhaps a severely handicapped child—will never change.

All of these circumstances and scores more contribute to the anxiety and emotional pain we all experience at various times and in varying degrees. Some pain is sudden, traumatic, and devastating. Other adversities are chronic, persistent, and seemingly designed to wear down our spirits over time.

In addition to our own emotional pains, we often are called upon to help bear the pain of others, either friends or relatives. None of the illustrations I've used in the preceding paragraphs are just imaginary. I could put names alongside each one. Most of them are on my personal prayer list. When friends and loved ones hurt, we hurt.

On a larger scale, we read in our daily newspapers or see on the evening news instances of grief, heartache, and pain on a massive scale. War, terrorism, earthquakes, famine, racial injustice, murder, and exploitation occur daily in various parts of the world. The threat of a nuclear holocaust hanging over our heads has caused this period of history to be called the age of anxiety. In such days when massive crises appear on our television screens almost daily, even the Christian is tempted to ask, "Where is God? Doesn't He care about the thousands who are starving in Africa or the innocent civilians who are being brutally murdered in many war-ravished countries around the world?"

On a much smaller scale, those whose lives are free from major pain still experience the frequently frustrating or anxiety-producing events of daily life, which momentarily grab our attention and rob us of our peace of mind. A long-planned vacation has to be cancelled because of illness, the washing machine breaks down the day company arrives, your class notes are lost or stolen the day before a major exam, you tear your favorite dress on the way to church, and on and on. Instances of this magnitude are numerous. Life is full of them.

It is true that such mundane events are only temporary and pale into insignificance alongside the truly tragic events of life. Yet, for most of us, life is filled with such little events, little frustrations, little anxieties, and little disappointments that tempt us to fret, fume, and worry. One author has aptly captured the flavor of how such little frustrations can cause us to doubt God in a devotional book for high schoolers entitled, *If God Loves Me, Why Can't I Get My Locker Open?* We may smile a little at the scene such a title brings to our imagination, but the fact is, this is the plane of adversity on which many of us live each day. And it is in the crucible of even this minor level of adversity that we are tempted to wonder, "Can I trust God?"

Even when life seems to be going our way and our daily path seems pleasant and smooth, we do not know what the future holds. As Solomon said, "[We] do not know what a day may bring forth" (Proverbs 27:1). Someone has described life as like having a thick curtain hung across one's path, a curtain that recedes before us as we advance, but only step by step. None of us can tell what is beyond that curtain; none of us can tell what events a single day or hour may bring into our lives. Sometimes the receding curtain reveals events much as we had expected them; often it reveals events most unexpected and frequently most undesired. Such events, unfolding in ways contrary to our desires and expectations, frequently fill our hearts with anxiety, frustrations, heartache, and grief.

God's people are not immune from such pain. In fact, it often seems as if theirs is more severe, more frequent, more unexplainable, and more deeply felt than that of the unbeliever. The problem of pain is as old as the history of man and just as universal. Even creation itself, Paul tells us, has been subjected to frustration and groans as in the pain of childbirth (see Romans 8:20-22).

So the question naturally arises, "Where is God in all of this?" Can you really trust God when adversity strikes and fills your life with pain? Does He indeed come to the rescue of those who seek Him? Does He, as the text at the beginning of this chapter affirms, deliver those who call upon Him in the day of trouble? Does the Lord's unfailing love surround the person who trusts in Him (see Psalm 32:10)?

Can you trust God? The question itself has two possible meanings before we attempt to answer it. Can you *trust* God? In other words, is He dependable in times of adversity? But the second meaning is also critical: Can *you* trust God? Do you have such a relationship with God and such a confidence in Him that you believe He is with you in your adversity even though you do not see any evidence of His presence and His power?

It is not easy to trust God in times of adversity. No one enjoys pain, and when it comes, we want it relieved as quickly as possible. Even the apostle Paul pleaded with God three times to take away the thorn in his flesh before he finally found God's grace to be sufficient. Joseph pleaded with Pharaoh's cupbearer to "get me out of this prison" (Genesis 40:14). And the writer of Hebrews very honestly states, "No discipline seems pleasant at the time, but painful" (Hebrews 12:11).

During the time I was working on this chapter I experienced one of those periods of adversity when I found it difficult to trust God. Mine happened to be a physical ailment that exacerbated a lifelong infirmity. It came at a very inconvenient time and for several weeks would not respond to any medical treatment.

During those weeks, as I continually prayed to God for relief, I was reminded of Solomon's words,

> Consider what God has done:
>   Who can straighten
>   what he has made crooked?
>
> ECCLESIASTES 7:13

God had brought a "crooked" event into my life, and I became acutely aware that only He could straighten it. Could I trust God whether or not He straightened my "crook" and relieved my distress? Did I really believe that a God who loved me and knew what was best for me was in control of my situation? Could I trust Him even if I didn't understand?

Further, could I encourage others to trust Him when they are in the throes of emotional pain? Is the whole idea of trusting God in adversity merely a Christian shibboleth that doesn't stand up in the face of the difficult events of life? Can you really trust God?

I sympathize with those who find it difficult to trust God in adversity. I have been there often enough myself to know something of the distress, the despair, and the darkness that fills our souls when we wonder if God truly cares about our plight. I have spent a good portion of my adult life encouraging people to pursue holiness, to obey God. Yet, I acknowledge it often seems more difficult to trust God than to obey Him. The moral will of God given to us in the Bible is rational and reasonable. The circumstances in which we must trust God often appear irrational and inexplicable. The law of God is readily recognized to be good for us, even when we don't want to obey it. The circumstances of our lives frequently appear to be dreadful and grim or perhaps even calamitous and tragic. Obeying God is worked out within well-defined boundaries of God's revealed will. Trusting God is worked out in an arena that has no boundaries. We do not know the extent, the duration, or the frequency of the painful, adverse circumstances in which we must frequently trust God. We are always coping with the unknown.

Yet it is just as important to trust God as it is to obey Him. When we disobey God, we defy His authority and despise His holiness. But when we fail to trust God, we doubt His sovereignty and question His goodness. In both cases we cast aspersions upon His majesty and His character. God views our distrust of Him as seriously as He views our disobedience. When the people of Israel were hungry, "they spoke against God, saying, 'Can God spread a table in the desert? . . . Can he supply meat for his people?'" The next two verses tell us, "When the Lord heard them, he was very angry . . . for they did not believe in God or trust in his deliverance" (Psalm 78:19-22).

In order to trust God, we must always view our adverse circumstances through the eyes of faith, not of sense. And just as the faith of salvation comes through hearing the message of the gospel (see Romans 10:17), so the faith to trust God in adversity comes through the Word of God alone. It is only in the Scriptures that we find an adequate view of God's relationship to and involvement in our painful circumstances. It is only from the Scriptures, applied to our hearts by the Holy Spirit, that we receive the grace to trust God in adversity.

In the arena of adversity, the Scriptures teach us three essential truths about God—truths we must believe if we are to trust Him in adversity. They are:

- God is completely sovereign.
- God is infinite in wisdom.
- God is perfect in love.

Someone has expressed these three truths as they relate to us in this way: "God in His love always wills what is best for us. In His wisdom He always knows what is best, and in His sovereignty He has the power to bring it about."

The sovereignty of God is asserted, either expressly or implicitly, on almost every page of the Bible. While doing the Bible study preparation for writing this book I never felt I completely finished compiling the list of verses on the sovereignty of God. New references to it kept appearing almost every time I opened my Bible. We are going to look at many of these passages in later chapters, but for now consider just one:

> Who can speak and have it happen
>   if the Lord has not decreed it?
> Is it not from the mouth of the Most High
>   that both calamities and good things come?

LAMENTATIONS 3:37-38

This passage of Scripture offends many people. They find it difficult to accept that both calamities and good things come from God. People often ask the question, "If God is a God of love, how could He allow such a calamity?" But Jesus Himself affirmed God's sovereignty in calamity when Pilate said to Him, "Don't you realize I have power either to free you or to crucify you?" Jesus replied, "You would have no power over me if it were not given to you from above" (John 19:10-11). Jesus acknowledged God's sovereign control over His life.

Because God's sacrifice of His Son for our sins is such an amazing act of love toward us, we tend to overlook that it was for Jesus an excruciating experience beyond all we can imagine. It was for Jesus in His humanity a calamity sufficient to cause Him to pray, "My Father, if it is possible, may this cup be taken from me" (Matthew 26:39), but He did not waver in His assertion of God's sovereign control.

Rather than being offended over the Bible's assertion of God's sovereignty in both good and calamity, believers should be comforted by it. Whatever our particular calamity or adversity may be, we may be sure that our Father has a loving purpose in it. As King Hezekiah said, "Surely it was for my benefit that I suffered such anguish" (Isaiah 38:17). God does not exercise His sovereignty capriciously but only in such a way as His infinite love deems best for us. Jeremiah wrote,

> Though he brings grief, he will show compassion,
>   so great is his unfailing love.
> For he does not willingly bring affliction
>   or grief to the children of men.
>
> LAMENTATIONS 3:32-33

God's sovereignty is also exercised in infinite wisdom, far beyond our ability to comprehend. After surveying God's sovereign but inscrutable dealings with His own people, the Jews, the apostle Paul bows before the mystery of God's actions with these words:

> Oh, the depth of the riches of the wisdom and
>   knowledge of God!
>   How unsearchable his judgments,
>   and his paths beyond tracing out!
>
> ROMANS 11:33

Paul acknowledged what we must acknowledge if we are to trust God. God's plan and His ways of working out His plan are frequently beyond our ability to fathom and understand. We must learn to trust when we don't understand.

In subsequent chapters we will explore these three truths—the sovereignty, love, and wisdom of God—in greater detail. But the primary purpose of this book is not to explore these wonderful truths. The primary purpose is for us to become so convinced of these truths that we appropriate them in our daily circumstances, that we learn to trust God in the midst of our pain, whatever form it may take. It does not matter whether our pain is trivial or traumatic, temporary or interminable. Regardless of the nature of the circumstances, we must learn to trust God if we would glorify God in them.

But there is one final thought before we begin our studies on the sovereignty, love, and wisdom of God. In order to trust God we must know Him in an intimate, personal way. David said in Psalm 9:10, "Those who know your name will trust in you, for you, LORD, have never forsaken those who seek you." To know God's name is to know Him in an intimate, personal way. It is more than just knowing facts about God. It is coming into a deeper personal relationship with Him as a result of seeking Him in the midst of our personal pain and discovering Him to be trustworthy. It is only as we know God in this personal way that we come to trust Him. As you read and study the following chapters and as you relate what you are learning about God to your own situations, pray that the Holy Spirit of God will enable you to get beyond the facts about God so that you will come to know Him better, and so be able to trust Him more completely.

CHAPTER TWO

IS GOD IN CONTROL?

*God . . . is the blessed controller of all things, the king
over all kings and the master of all masters.*

1 TIMOTHY 6:15, PH

In 1981 a widely acclaimed best-selling book swept the nation.
In literary reviews Rabbi Harold Kushner's book, *When Bad
Things Happen to Good People*, was described as touching, heart-
warming, wise, and compassionate, a book all humanity needs.
In the book, which is an attempt to make sense out of a tragedy
in his own family, Rabbi Kushner concludes that the author of
the book of Job, "forced to choose between a good God who is
not totally powerful, or a powerful God who is not totally good
. . . chooses to believe in God's goodness."[1] In Rabbi Kushner's
view of the teaching of Job, "God wants the righteous to live
peaceful, happy lives, but sometimes even He can't bring that
about. It is too difficult even for God to keep cruelty and chaos
from claiming their innocent victims."[2]

Rabbi Kushner, of course, is not alone in his denial of the
sovereign control of God over the events of our lives. Christians
as well as non-Christians frequently speak of misfortune and accidents, of circumstances beyond our (and presumably God's)
control, of things just happening by chance. Down through

the centuries, sickness, suffering, and sorrow have always raised questions about God's control and care of His creation.

The implicit assumption in the minds of many is: If God is both powerful and good, why is there so much suffering, so much pain, so much heartache in the world? God is either good and not all powerful, or He is powerful and not all good. You can't have it both ways.

THE PROVIDENCE OF GOD

The Bible teaches us we do have it both ways. God is sovereign (all powerful), and He is good. The Bible's teaching on this subject is categorized under a subject theologians call the providence of God. God's providence is a term we often use in Christian parlance to acknowledge God's seeming intervention in our affairs. For example, in giving my personal testimony, I frequently say something such as, "When I became aware that I could not live the Christian life in the Navy alone, God, in His providence, brought me into contact with The Navigators." In making such a statement I intend to say that God so controlled or arranged certain circumstances of my life that a specific result—in this case, coming into contact with The Navigators—was bound to occur.

There are two things wrong, however, with that way in which we refer to the providence of God. For one, we almost always use the expression "the providence of God" in connection with apparently "good" events. Coming into contact with The Navigators was a good event for me, so I'm quite happy to attribute it to the providence of God. But you almost never hear anyone say something such as, "In the providence of God I had an accident and was paralyzed from my waist down." Like Rabbi Kushner, we are reluctant to attribute "bad" things to the intervening hand of God.

The second problem with our popular use of the expression "the providence of God" is that we either unconsciously or deliberately imply that God intervenes at specific points in our lives but is largely only an interested spectator most of the time. When we think this way, even unconsciously, we reduce God's control over our lives to a stop-and-go, in-and-out proposition. Our unconscious attitude is that the rest of the time we are the "master of our fates" or conversely the victims of unhappy circumstances or uncaring people that cross our paths.

Historically, however, the church has always understood the providence of God to refer to His care of and governance over all of His creation at all times. Well-known theologian J. I. Packer defines providence as, "The unceasing activity of the Creator whereby, in overflowing bounty and goodwill, He upholds His creatures in ordered existence, guides and governs all events, circumstances, and free acts of angels and men, and directs everything to its appointed goal, for His own glory."[3] Note the absolute terms Packer uses: "unceasing activity," "all events . . . all acts," "directs everything." Clearly there is no concept of stop-and-go, part-time governance on God's part in this definition.

Packer's definition of God's providence is very complete and, I believe, very accurate according to Scripture. For my own sake, I have developed a slightly shorter definition that I can more easily remember: *God's providence is His constant care for and His absolute rule over all His creation for His own glory and the good of His people.* Again, note the absolute terms: constant care, absolute rule, all creation. Nothing, not even the smallest virus, escapes His care and control.

But note also the twofold objective of God's providence: His own glory and the good of His people. These two objectives are never antithetical; they are always in harmony with each other. God never pursues His glory at the expense of the good of His people, nor does He ever seek our good at the expense of His glory. He has designed His eternal purpose so that His glory and our good are inextricably bound together. What comfort and encouragement this should be to us. If we are going to learn to trust God in adversity, we must believe that just as certainly as God will allow nothing to subvert His glory, so He will allow nothing to spoil the good He is working out in us and for us.

In chapter 1 I asked the question, "Can you trust God?" and observed that the first meaning of the question is, "Is God trustworthy?" Can God always care for us (is He sovereign), and does He always care for us (is He good)? The doctrine of God's providence clearly affirms that we can trust God. God does care for us and He does constantly—not just occasionally—govern all the affairs of our lives.

In order to better understand and benefit from the biblical teaching of God's providence, we need to also consider another aspect of providence: the *sustaining* action of God in upholding and preserving His creation.

GOD SUSTAINS

The Bible teaches that God not only created the universe but that He upholds and sustains it day by day, hour by hour. Scripture says, "The Son is . . . sustaining all things by his powerful word" (Hebrews 1:3), and "in him all things hold together" (Colossians 1:17). As theologian A. H. Strong said,

> Christ is the originator and upholder of the universe.
> . . . In him it consists, or holds together, from hour to
> hour. The steady will of Christ constitutes the law of
> the universe and makes it a cosmos instead of a chaos,
> just as his will brought it into being in the beginning.[4]

All things are indebted for their existence to the continuous sustaining action of God exercised through His Son. Nothing exists of its own inherent power of being. Nothing in all creation stands or acts independently of the Lord's will. The so-called laws of nature are nothing more than the physical expression of the steady will of Christ. The law of gravity operates with unceasing certainty because Christ continuously wills it to operate. The chair I am sitting on while I write these words holds together because the atoms and molecules in the wood are held in place by His active will.

The stars continue in their courses because He keeps them there. Scripture says,

> He . . . brings out the starry host one by one,
>   and calls them each by name.
> Because of his great power and mighty strength,
>   not one of them is missing.

ISAIAH 40:26

God's sustaining action in Christ goes beyond the inanimate creation. The Bible says that He gives life to everything (see Nehemiah 9:6):

> He supplies the earth with rain
>   and makes grass grow on the hills.
> He provides food for the cattle
>   and for the young ravens when they call.

PSALM 147:8-9

God did not simply create and then walk away. He constantly sustains that which He created.

Further, the Bible teaches that God sustains you and me: "He himself gives all men life and breath and everything else. . . . 'For in him we live and move and have our being'" (Acts 17:25, 28).

He supplies our daily food (see 2 Corinthians 9:10). Our times are in His hands (see Psalm 31:15). Every breath we breathe is a gift from God, every bite of food we eat is given to us from His hand, every day we live is determined by Him. He has not left us to our own devices or the whims of nature or the malevolent acts of other people. No! He constantly sustains, provides for and cares for us every moment of every day. Did your car break down when you could least afford the repairs? Did you miss an important meeting because the plane you were to fly in developed mechanical problems? The God who controls the stars in their courses also controls nuts and bolts and everything on your car and on that plane you were to fly in.

When I was an infant I had a bad case of measles. The virus apparently settled in my eyes and in my right ear, leaving me with monocular vision and deafness in that ear. Was God in control of that virus, or was I simply a victim of a chance childhood disease? God's moment-by-moment sustaining of His universe and everything in it leaves me no choice but to accept that the virus was indeed under His controlling hand. God was not looking the other way when that virus settled in the nerve endings of my ear and the muscles of my eyes. If we are to trust God, we must learn to see that He is continuously at work in every aspect and every moment of our lives.

GOD GOVERNS

The Bible also teaches that God governs the universe, not only inanimate creation, but also the actions of all creatures, both men and animals. He is called "the ruler of all things" (1 Chronicles 29:12), "the blessed and only Ruler" (1 Timothy 6:15), the One apart from whose will the sparrow cannot fall to the ground (see Matthew 10:29). Jeremiah asks, "Who can speak and have it happen if the Lord has not decreed it?"

(Lamentations 3:37). The book of Daniel says, "[He] is sovereign over the kingdoms of men and gives them to anyone he wishes" (4:17) and:

> He does as he pleases
>> with the powers of heaven
>> and the peoples of the earth.
> No one can hold back his hand
>> or say to him: "What have you done?"
>
> DANIEL 4:35

No one can act outside of God's sovereign will or against it. Centuries ago, Augustine said, "Nothing, therefore, happens unless the Omnipotent wills it to happen: he either permits it to happen, or he brings it about himself."[5] Philip Hughes said, "Under God, however, all things are without exception fully controlled—despite all appearances to the contrary."[6] Nothing is too large or small to escape God's governing hand. The spider building its web in the corner and Napoleon marching his army across Europe are both under God's control.

As God's rule is invincible, so it is incomprehensible. His ways are higher than our ways (see Isaiah 55:9). His judgments are unsearchable, and His paths are beyond tracing out (see Romans 11:33). The sovereignty of God is often questioned because man does not understand what God is doing. Because He *does not* act as we think He should, we conclude He *cannot* act as we think He would.

GOD OR CHANCE?

This, then, is divine providence: God sustaining and governing His universe, bringing all events to their appointed end. This doctrine, however, is scarcely accepted among people today. The non-Christian, for the most part, has ruled out both the creating act of God and His providence. For him, all events are in the hands of fate or chance.

Such a view comes out matter-of-factly, if incidentally, in one book about managing crisis. The author says, "You should view and plan for the inevitability of a crisis . . . out of the strength that comes from knowing you are prepared to face life and play the hand that fate deals you. . . . Fate dealt me an interesting hand early in 1979."[7]

In Rabbi Kushner's book, *When Bad Things Happen to Good People*, Kushner asks, "Can you accept the idea that some things happen for no reason, that there is randomness in the universe?" Speaking of the direction a forest fire takes, he asks, "But is there a sensible explanation for why wind and weather combine to direct a forest fire on a given day toward certain homes rather than others, trapping some people inside and sparing others? Or is it just a matter of pure luck?"[8]

Elsewhere Rabbi Kushner reminds us that insurance companies refer to earthquakes, hurricanes, tornadoes, and various other natural disasters as "acts of God." Then he says, "I consider that a case of using God's name in vain. I don't believe that an earthquake that kills thousands of innocent victims without reason is an act of God. It is an act of nature. Nature is morally blind, without values. It churns along, following its own laws, not caring when or what gets in the way."[9]

Randomness, luck, chance, fate. This is modern man's answer to the age-old question, "Why?" Of course, if one dismisses the whole idea of God, as many do, then there is no other alternative. Many, while not dismissing the idea of God, have fabricated a God of their own speculation. Seventeenth-century deism constructed a God who created a universe and then walked away to leave it running according to its natural laws and man's devices. Many people today are practical deists.

Even Christians often think as deists today. Many accept the concept that God is sovereign but believe that He chooses not to exercise His sovereignty in the daily affairs of our lives. As one writer put it, "We know that God is sovereign, but we also know that, in His sovereignty, God has placed us in a world of sin and suffering from which we have no immunity," and again, "God's love . . . for us, does not place us in a protected position."[10] While I agree with the author's basic thesis in her article, that we shouldn't be asking *why*, I am troubled with what I understand her to be saying about God's exercise of His sovereignty and His care for His people.

In His well-known statement about sparrows, Jesus said, "Are not two sparrows sold for a penny? Yet not one of them will fall to the ground apart from the will of your Father. . . . So don't be afraid; you are worth more than many sparrows" (Matthew 10:29, 31). According to Jesus, God does exercise His sovereignty in very minute events—even the life and death of an almost worthless sparrow. And Jesus' whole point is: If God so exercises His sovereignty in regard to sparrows, most certainly He will exercise it in regard to His children. While it is certainly true that God's love for us does not protect us from pain and sorrow, it is also true that all occasions of pain and sorrow are under the absolute control of God. If God controls the circumstances of the sparrow, how much more does He control the circumstances that affect us? God does not walk away and leave us to the mercy of uncontrolled random or chance events.

A Christian husband flew in a private plane to another city to give his testimony at an evangelistic meeting, taking his son with him. On the way home they ran into an electrical storm that caused the plane to crash. Both the father and son were killed. A Christian friend, in an effort to comfort the bereaved wife and mother said, "One thing you can be sure of: God had no part in that accident." According to this friend, God was apparently looking the other way when the pilot got into trouble. A sparrow cannot fall to the ground without our Father's will but apparently a plane with Christians aboard can.

I read a blasphemous statement by someone who said, "Chance is the pseudonym God uses when He'd rather not sign His own name." A lot of Christians are doing that for God today. Often unwilling to accept the fact that God is working because they don't understand *how* He is working, they have chosen to substitute the doctrine of chance for the doctrine of divine providence.

GOOD BUT NOT SOVEREIGN

Along with the doctrine of chance, many Christians are also buying into the philosophy expounded by Rabbi Kushner that God is good but not sovereign. One Christian writer, for example, speaks of her pain as being utterly frustrating to God and gives thanks to God for being her devoted, caring, frustrated heavenly Father. Faced with the dilemma of how a loving, sovereign Father could allow her to experience such agonizing pain, she found relief in the belief that God was indeed frustrated about her pain, shedding tears with her, even as a mother may weep at the suffering of her child.

In fairness to this writer, she suffered excruciating pain for months. As one who has suffered less severe pain, and that only for several weeks at any one time, I realize I have not sat where she sat, I have not had to wrestle to the degree she has with the love of God in the midst of unbearable pain. But, as so often has been observed, we are to establish our beliefs by the Bible, not by our experiences. The Bible leaves us no doubt: God is never frustrated. "No one can hold back his hand or say to him: 'What have you done?'" (Daniel 4:35). It is true that God is involved in an invisible war with Satan and that the lives of God's people often are battlegrounds, as seen in the life of Job. But even then Satan must get permission to touch God's people (see Job 1:12; 2:6; and Luke 22:31-32). Even in this invisible war, God is still sovereign.

Author Margaret Clarkson, herself a lifelong sufferer, said, "That God is, indeed, both good and powerful is one of the basic tenets of Christian belief."[11] We admit that we are often unable to reconcile God's sovereignty and goodness in the face of widespread tragedy or personal adversity, but we believe that, although we often do not understand God's ways, He is sovereignly at work in all of our circumstances.

It is not easy to believe in the doctrine of the providence of God, especially in these days when it seems that doctrine has fallen upon hard times. As Professor G. C. Berkouwer said in his book *The Providence of God*,

> Raw reality assaults this comforting and optimistic confession. Could the catastrophic terrors of our century, with the improportionate sufferings they inflict on individuals, families, and peoples—could these be a reflection of the guidance of God? Does not pure honesty force us to stop seeking escape in a hidden, harmonious supersensible world? Does not honesty tell us to limit ourselves realistically to what lies before our eyes, and, without illusions, face the order of the day?[12]

All people—believers as well as unbelievers—experience anxiety, frustration, heartache, and disappointment. Some suffer intense physical pain and catastrophic tragedies. But that which should distinguish the suffering of believers from unbelievers is the confidence that our suffering is under the control of an all-powerful and all-loving God; our suffering has meaning and purpose in God's eternal plan, and He brings or allows to come into our lives only that which is for His glory and our good.

CHAPTER THREE

THE SOVEREIGNTY OF GOD

The LORD foils the plans of the nations;
he thwarts the purposes of the peoples.
But the plans of the LORD stand firm forever,
the purposes of his heart through all generations.

PSALM 33:10-11

In the year 1902, a young English boy came down to breakfast to find his father reading the newspaper, which carried news of preparations for the first coronation in Britain in sixty-four years. In the middle of breakfast the father turned to his wife and said, "Oh, I am sorry to see this worded like that." She said, "What is it?" "Why," he replied, "here is a proclamation that on a certain date Prince Edward will be crowned king at Westminster and there is no *Deo volente*, God willing." The words stuck in the young boy's mind for the very reason that on the appointed date the future Edward VII was ill with appendicitis and the coronation had to be postponed.[1]

At this time, at the end of Queen Victoria's reign, the political, economic, and military power of the British Empire was at its zenith. Yet for all its great might, Great Britain could not carry out its planned coronation on the appointed date.

Was the omission of "God willing" from the proclamation and the subsequent postponement of the coronation merely a coincidence, two events without any relation to one another?

23

Or did God cause Prince Edward to have appendicitis to show that He was "in control"? We don't know why the situation occurred as it did. One thing we do know, however: whether we acknowledge it with *Deo volente* or not, we cannot carry out any plan apart from God's will. The Bible leaves no doubt about that fact. James says it so clearly in the following passage:

> Now listen, you who say, "Today or tomorrow we will go to this or that city, spend a year there, carry on business and make money." Why, you do not even know what will happen tomorrow. What is your life? You are a mist that appears for a little while and then vanishes. Instead, you ought to say, *"If it is the Lord's will, we will live and do this or that."*
> JAMES 4:13-15, EMPHASIS ADDED

GOD'S ABSOLUTE CONTROL

God is in control; He is sovereign. He does whatever pleases Him and determines whether we can do what we have planned. This is the essence of God's sovereignty: His absolute independence to do as He pleases and His absolute control over the actions of all His creatures. No creature, person, or empire can either thwart His will or act outside the bounds of His will.

In chapter 1 I stated that, for us to trust God in times of adversity, we must believe in God's sovereignty, His love, and His wisdom. Of these three truths, the sovereignty of God seems to be questioned the most frequently and most stridently. It seems we will allow God to be anywhere except upon His throne ruling His universe according to His good pleasure and His sovereign will.

Even godly Christian writers whose books are helpful to many can, in their writings, take God off His throne. One of their most common statements is that God has voluntarily limited Himself to the actions of men in order to give man his freedom. For example, Andrew Murray wrote, "In creating man with a free will and making him a partner in the rule of the earth, *God limited himself. He made himself dependent on what man would do.* Man by his prayer would hold the measure of what God could do in blessing" (emphasis added).[2]

Other Christian writers fail to acknowledge the controlling hand of God—either directing or permitting—in every event of our lives. One writer, for example, speaks of suffering sometimes coming because of misfortune or accident, things "just happening," and pain coming our way, "due to circumstances beyond our control."

Our response to such statements is more than mere theological discussion. Confidence in the sovereignty of God in *all* that affects us is crucial to our trusting Him. *If there is a single event in all of the universe that can occur outside of God's sovereign control, then we cannot trust Him.* His love may be infinite, but if His power is limited and His purpose can be thwarted, we cannot trust Him. You may entrust to me your most valuable possessions. I may love you and my aim to honor your trust may be sincere, but if I do not have the power or ability to guard your valuables, you cannot truly entrust them to me.

Paul, however, said we can entrust our most valuable possession to the Lord. In 2 Timothy 1:12, he said, "That is why I am suffering as I am. Yet I am not ashamed, because I know whom I have believed, and *am convinced that he is able to guard what I have entrusted to him* for that day" (emphasis added). "But," someone says, "Paul is speaking there of eternal life. Without question, we can entrust our eternal destiny to God, but what about our problems in this life? They make me wonder about the sovereignty of God."

It should be evident, however, that God's sovereignty does not begin at death. As we will see in a later chapter, His sovereign direction in our lives even precedes our births. God rules as surely on earth as He does in heaven. He permits, for reasons known only to Himself, people to act contrary to and in defiance of His revealed will. But He never permits them to act contrary to His sovereign will.

In support of the statement I have just made—God never permits people to act contrary to His sovereign will—consider the following passages of Scripture:

> In his heart a man plans his course,
>> but the LORD determines his steps.
>
> PROVERBS 16:9

> Many are the plans in a man's heart,
>> but it is the LORD's purpose that prevails.
>
> PROVERBS 19:21

> There is no wisdom, no insight, no plan
>> that can succeed against the LORD.
>
> PROVERBS 21:30

> Consider what God has done:
>> Who can straighten
>> what he has made crooked?
>
> ECCLESIASTES 7:13

> Who can speak and have it happen
>> if the LORD has not decreed it?
>
> LAMENTATIONS 3:37

> You ought to say, "If it is the Lord's will, we will live
> and do this or that."
>
> JAMES 4:15

To the angel of the church in Philadelphia write:

These are the words of him who is holy and true, who holds the key of David. What he opens no one can shut, and what he shuts no one can open.

REVELATION 3:7

We make plans, but those plans can succeed only when they are consistent with God's purpose. No plan can succeed against Him. No one can straighten what He makes crooked or make crooked what He has made straight. No emperor, king, supervisor, teacher, or coach can speak and have it happen if the Lord has not first decreed to either make it happen or permit it to happen. No one can say, "I will do this or that," and have it happen if it is not part of God's sovereign will.

What an encouragement, what a stimulus to trusting God this aspect of God's sovereignty should be to us. Is someone "out to get you"? That person absolutely cannot execute his malicious plan unless God has first decreed it. I spoke with a military chaplain who had a confrontation with a more senior chaplain over an illegal act the senior chaplain proposed to do. As a result the senior chaplain wrote a very critical letter to the chief of chaplains that has seriously jeopardized my friend's career. Is my friend merely a victim of a cruel act of revenge? Not according to Scripture. The ungodly chaplain may write a dozen critical letters, but he absolutely cannot end my friend's military career unless God permits it. And if God permits it, it is because the ungodly action is part of God's plan for him. No one can speak and have it happen if the Lord has not decreed it (see Lamentations 3:37).

My friend's experience is not unique. Thousands of Christians have experienced similar injustices at the hands of teachers, coaches, fellow workers, and supervisors at work.

Perhaps you have, too. When these events occur, they always hurt. We cannot dismiss them with the glib expression, "God is in control." God is in control, but in His control He allows us to experience pain. The pain is very real. We hurt, we suffer. But in the midst of our suffering we must believe that God is in control, that He is sovereign.

As author Margaret Clarkson again so beautifully has written,

> The sovereignty of God is the one impregnable rock to which the suffering human heart must cling. The circumstances surrounding our lives are no accident: they may be the work of evil, but that evil is held firmly within the mighty hand of our sovereign God. . . . All evil is subject to Him, and evil cannot touch His children unless He permits it. God is the Lord of human history and of the personal history of every member of His redeemed family.[3]

Not only are the willful malevolent acts of other people under God's sovereign control, so also are the mistakes and failures of other people. Did another driver go through a red light, strike your car, and send you to the hospital with multiple fractures? Did a physician fail to detect your cancer in its early stages, when it would have been treatable? Did you end up with an incompetent instructor in a very important course in college, or an inept supervisor who blocked your career in business? All of these circumstances are under the controlling hand of our sovereign God, who is working them out in our lives for our good.

Neither the willful malicious acts nor the unintended mistakes of people can thwart God's purpose for us. "There is no wisdom, no insight, no plan that can succeed against the LORD"

(Proverbs 21:30). The Roman governor Felix left Paul in prison for over two years. Felix committed a totally unjust act because he wanted to grant a favor to the Jews (see Acts 24:27). Joseph was left in prison for two years because Pharaoh's cupbearer forgot him (see Genesis 40:14, 23; 41:1). These two godly men were left to languish in prison—one because of deliberate injustice and the other because of inexcusable forgetfulness—but both of their predicaments were under the sovereign control of an infinitely wise and loving God.

Nothing is so small or trivial as to escape the attention of God's sovereign control; nothing is so great as to be beyond His power to control it. The insignificant sparrow cannot fall to the ground without His will; the mighty Roman empire cannot crucify Jesus Christ unless that power is given to it by God (see Matthew 10:29; John 19:10-11). And what is true for the sparrow and for Jesus is true for you and me. No detail of your life is too insignificant for your heavenly Father's attention; no circumstance is so big that He cannot control it.

Within two days I received word of calamitous events in the lives of two of my friends. The wife of one friend was killed instantly when her car apparently stalled at a railroad crossing in the path of an oncoming train. The other friend is an independent over-the-road truck driver, struggling to get established in that business. On a recent trip, his truck broke down, necessitating expensive repairs on the road. The cost of the repairs completely wiped out the income he would have made from that trip.

The consequences of these two events, of course, cannot be compared. The struggling truck driver would agree that no amount of lost income can be compared with the loss of a precious wife. But what do we say to either of these men, each grappling with his own unique set of circumstances, about the sovereignty of God? Do we just speak to the one of a "tragic accident" and to the other about his "bad luck"?

Are we truly left to the mercy of stalled cars, of trucks that break down, of people who are in a position to do us harm and are intent on doing it? *No*, a thousand times no! We are in the hands of a sovereign God who controls every circumstance of our lives and who rejoices in doing us good (see Jeremiah 32:41).

GOD'S SOVEREIGNTY IS NOT ALWAYS APPARENT

One of our problems with the sovereignty of God is that it frequently does not appear that God is in control of the circumstances of our lives. We see unjust or uncaring or even clearly wicked people doing things that adversely affect us. We experience the consequences of other people's mistakes and failures. We even do foolish and sinful things ourselves and suffer the often bitter fruit of our actions. It is difficult to see God working through secondary causes and frail, sinful human beings. But it is the ability of God to so arrange diverse human actions to fulfill His purpose that makes His sovereignty marvelous and yet mysterious. No Bible-believing Christian has any difficulty believing that God can and has worked miracles—instances of His sovereign but *direct* intervention into the affairs of people. Regardless of our theological position regarding miracles occurring today, we all accept without question the validity of the miracles recorded in Scripture. But to believe in the sovereignty of God when we do not *see* His direct intervention—when God is, so to speak, working entirely behind the scenes through ordinary circumstances and ordinary actions of people—is even more important because that is the way God usually works.

A nineteenth-century writer, Alexander Carson, in his book, *Confidence in God in Times of Danger*, says, "For the wisdom of man cannot see how the providence of God can arrange human actions to fulfill his purpose without any miracle."[4] For example, one writer, commenting on an accident in which her car was struck by another that went through a red light, supposed that for God to have protected her, He would have made the other driver's car suddenly sprout wings so that it could fly over her car without impacting. What is implied in such a statement is the idea that God is suddenly confronted with a crisis in the life of one of His children and has no recourse but to work a miracle or let the crisis occur.

God did allow the crisis to occur in her situation, but it was not because He could not prevent it. In His sovereignty He could have changed the timing of either driver's arrival at the intersection, or even diverted one of them along another route had He chosen to do so. None of us knows of such events in our own lives (perhaps hundreds) when we have been unknowingly spared from adversity or tragedy by the unseen sovereign hand of God. As the psalmist said,

> He will not let your foot slip—
>   he who watches over you will not slumber;
> indeed, he who watches over Israel
>   will neither slumber nor sleep.

PSALM 121:3-4

Undoubtedly, one of the reasons the book of Esther is included in Scripture is to help us see the sovereign hand of God at work behind the scenes, caring for His people. One of the more arresting things about the book is that the name of God is never once mentioned. Yet the observant reader sees God's hand in every circumstance, bringing about the deliverance of His people just as surely as He brought about their deliverance from Egypt through mighty miracles centuries before. God was as sovereignly at work through ordinary circumstances in the time of Esther as He was through miracles in the time of Moses.

The pivot point of the book of Esther is chapter 6. Prior to the events of the night recorded in that chapter, the lives of all the Jews in the entire realm of the Persian King Xerxes were in danger due to the diabolical scheme of one wicked man, Haman, who had recently been elevated to a position higher than that of all the other nobles in the kingdom. But in chapter 6, events begin to turn, leading ultimately to the downfall and death of wicked Haman, the physical salvation of the Jews, and the elevation of Mordecai (the hero of the story) to the second highest position in the kingdom.

Because the series of events recorded in Esther chapter 6 reveals in a remarkable way how God sovereignly uses the most ordinary circumstances to accomplish His purpose, we will look at those circumstances in some detail.

On the fateful night, King Xerxes could not sleep, so he ordered the book of the chronicles of his reign to be brought in and read to him. In the course of the reading, it came to light that Mordecai, who was in danger of being hanged the next morning, had on an earlier occasion reported a plot to assassinate the king. The king asked what recognition had been given Mordecai and found that nothing had been done. So the king decided on the spot to honor Mordecai, and, as it turned out, the very man who had determined to hang Mordecai ended up carrying out the king's edict to publicly honor him.

Consider what had to happen to save Mordecai from the gallows. Why could the king not sleep that fateful night? Why, then, did he ask for a dry register of facts to be read to him rather than soothing music to lull him to sleep? And when the book of the chronicles of his reign was read, why did the reader happen to read from the particular section of the book where

Mordecai's actions were recorded? Were there not a thousand chances that the reader would have selected some other portion of the annals of the Persian empire to read?

The king heard about Mordecai's service and asked how he was rewarded. Why had the king not rewarded Mordecai at the time he had saved the king's life? Why did he suddenly determine to do something? And why did wicked Haman appear at that moment to ask the king's permission to hang Mordecai? Why did Xerxes ask Haman what should be done to honor the man in such a way as to conceal the object of his favor, causing Haman to think he himself was the one to be honored?[5]

The answer to all of these questions was that God was sovereignly orchestrating the events of that night to save His people. The question naturally arises, however, "Does God always orchestrate the events of *my* life for my good?" If we grant that the unusual outworking of events in Esther was due to the sovereign hand of God, are we justified in concluding that God *always* orchestrates the events of our lives to fulfill His purpose? According to Romans 8:28, the answer is a solid yes. That verse says, "We know that in *all* things God works for the good of those who love him, who have been called according to his purpose" (emphasis added). It is this assurance that God works in *all* events of our lives that gives sense to Paul's exhortation elsewhere to "give thanks in *all* circumstances" (1 Thessalonians 5:18, emphasis added). How could we possibly give thanks to God for all the circumstances of our lives if He were not at work in them for our good?

GOD DOES AS HE PLEASES

So no one can act and no circumstances can occur outside the bounds of God's sovereign will. But this is only one side of His sovereignty. The other side, which is just as important to our trusting Him, is that no plan of God's can be thwarted. God does as He pleases, and only as He pleases, and no one can frustrate His plans or hinder His purposes.

Again, since this is such a difficult concept to accept, and one which is so frequently disputed, it will be helpful to consider a number of Scripture passages on this subject.

I know that you can do all things;
    no plan of yours can be thwarted.

JOB 42:2

Our God is in heaven;
    he does whatever pleases him.

PSALM 115:3

For the LORD Almighty has purposed, and who can
    thwart him?
His hand is stretched out, and who can turn it back?

ISAIAH 14:27

Yes, and from ancient days I am he.
    No one can deliver out of my hand.
    When I act, who can reverse it?

ISAIAH 43:13

I make known the end from the beginning,
    from ancient times, what is still to come.
I say: My purpose will stand,
    and I will do all that I please.

ISAIAH 46:10

All the peoples of the earth
    are regarded as nothing.
He does as he pleases
    with the powers of heaven
    and the peoples of the earth.

No one can hold back his hand
   or say to him: "What have you done?"

DANIEL 4:35

In him we were also chosen, having been predestined
according to the plan of him who works out everything
in conformity with the purpose of his will.

EPHESIANS 1:11

No plan of God's can be thwarted; when He acts, no one
can reverse it; no one can hold back His hand or bring Him
to account for His actions. God does as He pleases, only as He
pleases, and works out every event to bring about the accomplishment of His will. Such a bare unqualified statement of the
sovereignty of God would terrify us if that were all we knew
about God. But God is not only sovereign, He is perfect in love
and infinite in wisdom.

As we saw in chapter 2, Rabbi Kushner ascribed a sort of
bare sovereignty to nature. He said, "Nature is morally blind,
without values. It churns along, following its own laws, not caring who or what gets in its way." But God does care. God exercises His sovereignty for His glory and the good of His people.

But how does this aspect of God's sovereignty (specifically,
God does as He pleases) relate to our trusting Him? Why is this
any more than merely an abstract statement about God to be
debated by the theologians, a statement that has little relevance
to our day-to-day lives?

The answer is that God does have a purpose and a plan for
you, and *God has the power to carry out that plan*. It is one thing
to know that no person or circumstance can touch us outside of
God's sovereign control; it is still another to realize that no person or circumstances can frustrate God's purpose for our lives.

God has an over-arching purpose for all believers: to conform us to the likeness of His Son, Jesus Christ (see Romans 8:29). He also has a specific purpose for each of us that is His unique, tailor-made plan for our individual life (see Ephesians 2:10). And God will fulfill that purpose. As Psalm 138:8 says, "The Lord will fulfill his purpose for me." Because we know God is directing our lives to an ultimate end and because we know He is sovereignly able to orchestrate the events of our lives toward that end, we can trust Him. We can commit to Him not only the ultimate outcome of our lives, but also all the intermediate events and circumstances that will bring us to that outcome.

Again it is difficult for us to appreciate the reality of God sovereignly doing as He pleases in our lives because we do not *see* God doing anything. Instead we see ourselves or other people acting and events occurring, and we evaluate those actions and events according to our own preferences and plans. We see ourselves influencing or perhaps even controlling or being controlled by the actions of other people, but we do not see God at work. But over all the actions and events of our lives, God is in control doing as He pleases—not apart from those events, or in spite of them, but *through* them. Joseph's brothers sold him into slavery—a malicious act in and of itself—but in due time Joseph recognized that through his brothers' actions God was acting. He could say to them, "So then, it was not you who sent me here, but God" (Genesis 45:8). Joseph recognized the hand of God in his life sovereignly directing all the events to bring about God's plan for him.

You and I may never have the privilege in this life of seeing an obvious outcome of God's plan for us, as Joseph did. But God's plan for us is no less firm and its outcome is no less certain than was God's plan for Joseph. God did not give us the story of Joseph's life just to inform us but to encourage us. "For everything that was written in the past was written to teach us, so that through endurance and the *encouragement of the Scriptures* we might have hope" (Romans 15:4, emphasis added). What God did for Joseph, He will do for us. But to derive the comfort and encouragement from this truth that God has provided, we must learn to trust God. We must learn to live, as Paul said, "by faith, not by sight" (2 Corinthians 5:7).

One of the passages of Scripture that has been very meaningful to me for several years is Jeremiah 29:11, "'For I know the plans I have for you,' declares the LORD, 'plans to prosper you and not to harm you, plans to give you hope and a future.'" Although those words were directed to the nation of Judah in its captivity, they express a principle about God, a principle affirmed elsewhere throughout the Bible: God has a plan for you. Because He has a plan for you, and because no one can thwart that plan, you too can have hope and courage. You, too, can trust God.

From our limited vantage point, our lives are marked by an endless series of contingencies. We frequently find ourselves, instead of acting as we planned, reacting to an unexpected turn of events. We make plans but are often forced to change those plans. But there are no contingencies with God. Our unexpected, forced change of plans is a part of His plan. God is never surprised; never caught off guard; never frustrated by unexpected developments. God does as He pleases, and that which pleases Him is always for His glory and our good.

Our lives are also cluttered with a lot of "if onlys." "If only I had done this," or "if only that had not happened." But again, God has no "if onlys." God never makes a mistake; God has no regrets. "As for God, his way is perfect" (Psalm 18:30). We *can* trust God. He is trustworthy.

Just as the book of Esther showed us God's sovereign care for His people, so the short book of Ruth shows us God at work to fulfill His plan for one of His people. In one sense, Ruth is more instructive than Esther because it gives us an insight into the sovereign working of God in more ordinary circumstances than those depicted in the book of Esther.

Ruth, you will recall, was the widowed daughter-in-law of Naomi who uttered those familiar words, "Where you go I will go, and where you stay I will stay. Your people will be my people and your God my God" (Ruth 1:16). To help us see God at work in Ruth's life, we need to read Ruth 2:1-10:

> Now Naomi had a relative on her husband's side, from the clan of Elimelech, a man of standing, whose name was Boaz.
>
> And Ruth the Moabitess said to Naomi, "Let me go to the fields and pick up the leftover grain behind anyone in whose eyes I find favor."
>
> Naomi said to her, "Go ahead, my daughter." So she went out and began to glean in the fields behind the harvesters. As it turned out, she found herself working in a field belonging to Boaz, who was from the clan of Elimelech.
>
> Just then Boaz arrived from Bethlehem and greeted the harvesters, "The LORD be with you!" . . .
>
> Boaz asked the foreman of his harvesters, "Whose young woman is that?"
>
> The foreman replied, "She is the Moabitess who came back from Moab with Naomi. She said, 'Please let me glean and gather among the sheaves behind the harvesters.' She went into the field and has worked steadily from morning till now, except for a short rest in the shelter."
>
> So Boaz said to Ruth, "My daughter, listen to me. Don't go and glean in another field and don't go away

from here. Stay here with my servant girls. Watch the field where the men are harvesting, and follow along after the girls. I have told the men not to touch you. And whenever you are thirsty, go and get a drink from the water jars the men have filled."

At this, she bowed down with her face to the ground. She exclaimed, "Why have I found such favor in your eyes that you notice me—a foreigner?"

To quickly conclude the story, Ruth marries Boaz and becomes the great-grandmother of King David and one of the four women listed in Matthew's record of the genealogy of our Lord (see Matthew 1:1-16).

Notice in the passage quoted, four key events that all had to come together to begin the process of Ruth's becoming Boaz's wife. As Ruth went out to glean in the fields, she could have ended up in anyone's field. Verse 3 says, "As it turned out, she found herself working in a field belonging to Boaz." God guided her to the right field. But she still must meet Boaz, so verse 4 says, "Just then Boaz arrived from Bethlehem." God, who controlled Ruth's direction so that she happened to go to Boaz's field, controlled Boaz's timing so that he happened to go to check on his harvest at just the time Ruth was there.

But still Ruth must gain Boaz's attention and favor.

Undoubtedly many of the poor gathered from Boaz's field since leaving the leftover grain was part of the Mosaic law (see Leviticus 19:9-10), and hence a common event in the life of Israel. We would suppose that a landowner such as Boaz would not normally notice one poor woman gathering up leftover grain. But Boaz notices Ruth, verse 5: "Boaz asked the foreman of his harvesters, 'Whose young woman is that?'" Finally we see Boaz responding favorably to Ruth, verses 8-10.

The right location, the right timing, being noticed, and gaining Boaz's favor were all key links in the chain of events that eventually resulted in Ruth's marriage to Boaz. None of the events were extraordinary, and all give the appearance of "just happening," nothing more than a coincidence in a romantic story. But the reverent reader of Scripture cannot fail to see the sovereign hand of God arranging those ordinary circumstances to accomplish His purpose. Naomi herself, though not at the time aware of God's future plan for Ruth and Boaz, ascribes the events to the hand of God (see Ruth 2:20).

The stories of Esther and Mordecai and of Ruth and Boaz both had happy endings. We can see God's hand at work in those events. But what about when the story does not have a happy ending? Is God sovereign then also? This is the crucial question. It's easy to trust God when a process of events turns out as we would desire, though even here our faith often falters during the process until we know the outcome.

Consider, for example, the stories of two apostles, James and Peter, as recorded in Acts 12. The close relationship of these two men predated their apostleship because they were partners in the fishing business (see Luke 5:10). They were called by Jesus to leave their business and to follow Him at the same time (see Matthew 4:18-22). Both were part of Jesus' inner circle—Peter, James, and John. But in Acts 12, radically different events happen to them. James is put to death, and Peter is miraculously spared the same fate.

Put yourself in the shoes of James's wife and then Peter's. One is grieving over the murder of her husband; the other rejoices over the miraculous deliverance of hers. Peter's wife rejoices in the sovereignty of God, but what does James's wife do? Was God any less sovereign in the death of James than He was in the deliverance of Peter? Is God sovereign only in the "good" circumstances of our lives? Is He not also sovereign in the difficult times, the times when our hearts ache with pain?

The Bible teaches us that God is sovereign over both the "good" and the "bad." Consider the following:

When times are good, be happy;
    but when times are bad, consider:
God has made the one
    as well as the other.
Therefore, a man cannot discover
    anything about his future.

ECCLESIASTES 7:14

I form the light and create darkness,
    I bring prosperity and create disaster;
    I, the LORD, do all these things.

ISAIAH 45:7

Is it not from the mouth of the Most High
    that both calamities and good things come?

LAMENTATIONS 3:38

These three passages clearly state what is taught in principle throughout the rest of the Bible. God controls both the good and the bad. God has not looked the other way or been caught by surprise when adversity strikes us. He is in control of that adversity, directing it to His glory and our good.

So let's go back to James's wife. She, too, must trust in God and in His sovereign control over her life and the death of her husband. Trusting in God does not mean she does not suffer grief, that her heart does not ache. It means that in the midst of her heartache and grief she can say something to the effect of, "Lord, I know You were in control of this dreadful event. I do not understand why You allowed it to happen, but I trust You."

I readily admit it is difficult to believe God is in control when we are in the midst of anxiety, heartache, or grief. I have struggled with this many times myself. Because of my schedule, most of my writing is done on an intermittent basis, a "few hours here and a few hours there." Because of that, this particular chapter was written and rewritten over a period of six weeks or more. During that time I had to work through God's sovereignty on two occasions myself. In each instance I realized I knew the truth regarding God's sovereignty. What I had to do was to decide if I would trust Him, even when my heart ached.

I realized anew that, just as we must learn to obey God one choice at a time, we must also learn to trust God one circumstance at a time. Trusting God is not a matter of my feelings but of my will. I never feel like trusting God when adversity strikes, but I can choose to do so even when I don't feel like it. That act of the will, though, must be based on belief, and belief must be based on truth.

The truth we must believe is that God is sovereign. He carries out His own good purposes without ever being thwarted, and He so directs and controls all events and all actions of His creatures that they never act outside of His sovereign will. We must believe this and cling to this in the face of adversity and tragedy, if we are to glorify God by trusting Him.

I will say this next statement as gently and compassionately as I know how. Our first priority in times of adversity is to honor and glorify God by trusting Him. We tend to make our first priority the gaining of relief from our feelings of heartache or disappointment or frustration. This is a natural desire, and God has promised to give us grace sufficient for our trials and peace for our anxieties (see 2 Corinthians 12:9; Philippians 4:6-7). But just as God's will is to take precedence over our will (in Matthew 26:39 Jesus Himself said, "Yet not as I will, but as you will"), so God's honor is to take precedence over our feelings. We honor God by choosing to trust Him when we don't understand what He is doing or why He has allowed some adverse circumstance to occur. As we seek God's glory, we may be sure that He has purposed our good and that He will not be frustrated in fulfilling that purpose.

A WORD OF CAUTION

The material in this chapter is "tough stuff." It should be read, studied, and prayed about when life is more or less routine. It should be stored up or hidden in our hearts (see Psalm 119:11) for the time of adversity when we must draw upon its truth.

Above all, we need to be very sensitive about instructing someone else in the sovereignty of God and encouraging that person to trust God when he or she is in the midst of adversity or pain. It is much easier to trust in the sovereignty of God when it is the other person who is hurting. We need to be like Jesus, of whom it was said, "A bruised reed he will not break" (Matthew 12:20). Let us not be guilty of breaking a bruised reed (a heavy heart) by insensitive treatment of the heavy doctrine of the sovereignty of God.

CHAPTER FOUR

GOD'S SOVEREIGNTY OVER PEOPLE

The king's heart is in the hand of the LORD;
he directs it like a watercourse wherever he pleases.

PROVERBS 21:1

Picture yourself in this situation: You've been working for someone all of your life, your boss has been extremely cruel, your wages have been barely at subsistence level, and you feel very downtrodden and oppressed. For all practical purposes, you are nothing more than a slave. Suddenly you are freed from that almost unbearable situation. You are free to leave and start life all over again. There is only one problem—you have no financial resources, no way to make the trip, no funds to start anew someplace else, no way to take advantage of this incredible opportunity.

So you go to your boss and ask him for money for the trip and for getting started after you reach your new location. As farfetched as it may sound, your boss gives you the money. He doesn't just give you a little, he gives you a lot; in fact, he gives you so much he impoverishes himself.

Sounds like make-believe, doesn't it; like a childhood happily-ever-after story, the kind that never happens in real life. Only this one did; not in the exact details I have used, but in principle. This story actually happened. It's recorded for us in the Bible in the book of Exodus. You know the story: The Israelites were the cruelly oppressed people, forced to "make bricks without straw." Suddenly God intervenes in their lives and Pharaoh says, "Get out!" But the Israelites had no resources for making the journey, for starting over again; they were poverty-stricken. God had foreseen this problem, however, and had made plans to overcome it. He had said to Moses:

> And I will make the Egyptians favorably disposed toward this people, so that when you leave you will not go empty-handed. Every woman is to ask her neighbor and any woman living in her house for articles of silver and gold and for clothing, which you will put on your sons and daughters. And so you will plunder the Egyptians.
> EXODUS 3:21-22

What God promised did indeed come to pass. Exodus 12:35-36 says,

> The Israelites did as Moses instructed and asked the Egyptians for articles of silver and gold and for clothing. The LORD had made the Egyptians favorably disposed toward the people, and they gave them what they asked for; so they plundered the Egyptians.

GOD PROMPTS PEOPLE

The Egyptians did something completely contrary to normal human behavior. They voluntarily and freely *gave* these hitherto downtrodden slaves what they asked for, so much so that the account says the Israelites "plundered" the Egyptians. The usual meaning of plunder is to rob or seize or take by force; yet the Egyptians actually plundered themselves. They did this because God had made them favorably disposed toward the Israelites.

How did God do this? We don't know. We only know what the text tells us. It is obvious that the Egyptians acted freely and voluntarily of their own wills. Yet they acted that way because as the text says, "the LORD had made [them] favorably disposed toward [the Israelites]." God in some mysterious way moved in their hearts so that they, of their own free choice, did exactly what He planned for them to do. God sovereignly intervened in the hearts—the desires and wills—of the Egyptians to accomplish His purpose for the Israelites.

All of us at times find ourselves and our futures seemingly in the hands of other people. Their decisions or their actions determine whether we get a good grade or a poor one, whether we are promoted or fired, whether our careers blossom or fold. I am not overlooking our own responsibility in these situations, but all of us know that even when we have, so to speak, done our best, we are still dependent upon the favor or frown of that teacher or boss or commanding officer. We are, from a human point of view, often at the mercy of other people and their decisions or actions.

Sometimes those decisions or actions are benevolent and good; sometimes they are wicked or careless. Either way they do affect us, often in a significant way. How are we to respond when we find ourselves seemingly in the hands of someone else, when we desperately need a favorable decision or a favorable action on that person's part? Can we trust God that He can and will work in the heart of that individual to bring about His plan for us?

Or consider the instance when someone is out to harm us, to ruin our reputation, or jeopardize our career: Can we trust God to intervene in the heart of that person so that he does not carry out his evil intent? According to the Bible, the answer in both instances is yes. We can trust God. He does sovereignly intervene in the hearts of people so that they make decisions and carry out actions that accomplish His purpose for our lives. Yet God does this in such a way that these people make their decisions and carry out their plans by their own free and voluntary choices.

I realize that such a bold statement about the sovereignty of God within the minds of people gets me into a theological sand trap. Many people are prepared to grant God's sovereignty over nature and impersonal circumstances such as, for example, a mechanical failure in an airplane. After all, nature does not have a will of its own. God is free to operate through His physical laws as He pleases. But we balk at the sovereignty of God over the decisions and actions of people. Such a concept of God's sovereignty seems to many people to destroy the free will of man and make him only a puppet on God's stage.

Christians have discussed and debated this subject down through the ages. I have no illusions of adding any new knowledge or insight to the subject, but we cannot ignore it. The subject of other people's controlling influence over our lives is simply too pervasive to omit it in a book on trusting God. If God is not sovereign in the decisions and actions of other people as they affect us, then there is a whole major area of our lives where we cannot trust God; where we are left, so to speak, to fend for ourselves.

So let's set aside the theological problem for the moment and examine the Scriptures. Do they give us a warrant for believing that God does in fact sovereignly intervene in the minds of people so that they decide or act in a certain way to accomplish His plan for us? Does God cause people to make decisions that favor us, and does God restrain people from making decisions that would harm us?

Perhaps the clearest biblical statement that God does sovereignly influence the decisions of people is found in Proverbs 21:1, "The king's heart is in the hand of the LORD; he directs it like a watercourse wherever he pleases." Charles Bridges, in his exposition of Proverbs, states, "The general truth [of God's sovereignty over the hearts of all people] is taught by the strongest illustration—his uncontrollable sway upon the most absolute of all wills—the *king's heart.*"[1]

In our day of limited monarchies in which kings and queens are largely figureheads, it may be difficult for us to appreciate fully the force of what Charles Bridges is saying when he speaks of the king's heart as the most absolute of all wills. But in Solomon's time the king was an absolute monarch. There was no separate legislative body to make laws he wouldn't like or a Supreme Court to restrain him. The king's word was law. His authority over his realm was unconditional and unrestrained.

Yet God controls the king's heart. The stubborn will of the most powerful monarch on earth is directed by God as easily as the farmer directs the flow of water in his irrigation canals. The argument, then, is from the greater to the lesser—if God controls the king's heart, surely He controls everyone else's. All must move before His sovereign influence.

We have already seen this demonstrated in the actions of the Egyptians toward the Israelites. We see it also in the account of Cyrus, king of Persia, when he issued a proclamation to allow the Jews to return to Jerusalem to rebuild the Temple. Ezra 1:1 says,

> In the first year of Cyrus king of Persia, in order to fulfill the word of the LORD spoken by Jeremiah, *the LORD moved the heart of Cyrus* king of Persia to make a proclamation throughout his realm and to put it in writing. (emphasis added)

The text clearly says that King Cyrus issued the proclamation because God moved his heart. The destiny of God's people was, humanly speaking, in the hands of the most powerful monarch of that day. In reality, though, their destiny was completely in

God's hand because He had the ability to sovereignly control the decisions of that monarch.

God, speaking through the prophet Isaiah, gives us another helpful insight into His working in Cyrus's heart:

> For the sake of Jacob my servant,
>   of Israel my chosen,
> I summon you by name
>   and bestow on you a title of honor,
>   *though you do not acknowledge me.* . . .
> I will strengthen you,
>   *though you have not acknowledged me.*
>
> ISAIAH 45:4-5, EMPHASIS ADDED

It is not necessary for a person to acknowledge God's sovereign control in his heart or to even acknowledge the existence of God. Neither the Egyptians nor Cyrus intended to obey any revealed will of God. They simply acted as their hearts directed them, but their hearts were directed by God.

While we are looking at Cyrus, we see another instance of God's moving in people's hearts in the response of the Jews to Cyrus's proclamation. Ezra 1:5 says, "Then the family heads of Judah and Benjamin, and the priests and Levites—everyone whose heart God had moved—prepared to go up and build the house of the LORD in Jerusalem." Cyrus could issue a proclamation, but there must still be a response of the Jews. Some of them must decide to leave the comforts of their established surroundings—they had been there seventy years, about two generations—and undertake the arduous and hazardous journey back to Jerusalem and commence the long and difficult task of rebuilding the Temple. How did God ensure that would happen? He moved in the hearts of some of the people. Some years later we find these people rejoicing because God "[changed] the attitude of the king of Assyria, so that he assisted them in the work on the house of God" (Ezra 6:22). This was a later king, King Darius. So God moved in the hearts of two kings, one to start the project and another to keep it going, and He moved in the hearts of some of the Jewish people to respond. God does move people to accomplish His purpose.

Still another illustration of God's influence in the heart of a heathen official is found in the life of Daniel. When Daniel had resolved not to defile himself with food from the king's table—food spiritually contaminated by being offered first to idols, and perhaps even prepared from animals the Jews were not to eat—he asked the chief official for permission not to defile himself that way. The Scripture then comments, "Now God had caused the official to show favor and sympathy to Daniel" (Daniel 1:9).

Daniel's request to the chief official was a difficult one—so difficult that the chief official's first concern was for his own life if he granted Daniel's request (see verse 10). Nevertheless, he granted the request. He granted it because God had first moved in his heart to show favor and sympathy to Daniel. He granted it because his heart was indeed in God's hand, who directed it as He pleased.

One final instance from Scripture will suffice to show that God moves sovereignly in the lives of both Christians and non-Christians. Paul said of his colaborer Titus, "I thank God, who put into the heart of Titus the same concern I have for you. For Titus not only welcomed our appeal, but he is coming to you with much enthusiasm and on his own initiative" (2 Corinthians 8:16-17). Titus's actions are attributed by Paul to both God, who put a concern for the Corinthians into Titus's heart, and to Titus, who acted with enthusiasm and on his own initiative. Titus acted freely, yet under the mysterious sovereign impulse of God.

GOD RESTRAINS PEOPLE

We have seen that God can and does move in the hearts of people to show favor to us when that favor will accomplish His purpose. But there is still another important dimension to His sovereignty in the hearts of people; when necessary, God restrains people from decisions or actions that would harm us. An incident from the life of Abraham illustrates this.

In fear of his own life, Abraham lied about his wife, Sarah, saying she was his sister. As a result Abimelech moved to take Sarah as his wife. God, however, kept Abimelech from carrying out his plan. He said to Abimelech, "So I have kept you from sinning against me. That is why I did not let you touch her" (Genesis 20:6). God did not physically or circumstantially restrain Abimelech. He restrained him through his mind. For some reason, which probably Abimelech himself didn't understand, he simply did not proceed to consummate a physical relationship with Sarah. God sovereignly intervened and protected the moral purity of Sarah, who was to be the mother of the promised son of Abraham. God could have intervened circumstantially to preserve Sarah's purity, but He chose to do so through moving in some way upon Abimelech's mind. He restrained Abimelech through moving upon his will.

Was Abimelech conscious that God was restraining him? No, the Scripture simply says that he had not gone near her (see verse 4). Abimelech chose of his own free will not to be with Sarah, but his choosing was under the sovereign control of God. This incident is even more amazing when we consider that Abraham had put Sarah in this difficult position through his own unbelief and sin. God did not excuse Abraham's sin, but He did not let that stop Him from intervening in Abimelech's mind to prevent the serious consequences of the sin.

On another occasion Abraham's grandson Jacob set out with his family to move from Shechem to Bethel. Two of Jacob's sons had just committed a heinous act against the people of the land, and it would be expected the people would have sought revenge. But Genesis 35:5 says, "Then they set out, and the terror of God fell upon the towns all around them so that no one pursued them."

Terror or fear is a state of the mind usually induced by some external circumstances. In this case there do not appear to be any external circumstances to cause such terror. In fact, just the opposite was true. Just a few verses prior to Genesis 35:5, Jacob himself had said, "We are few in number, and if they join forces against me and attack me, I and my household will be destroyed" (Genesis 34:30). There was no reason why the Canaanites should not have swooped down upon Jacob and his family to avenge the crime of Jacob's sons except that God restrained them through a fear that could not be rationally explained.

Returning again to the Temple builders we looked at previously in the book of Ezra, we find still another instance of God's restraining hand. Before King Darius issued his decree that the rebuilding of the Temple was not to be stopped but even assisted from the royal treasury (see Ezra 6:6-10), the territorial governor and other officials had questioned the authority of the Jews to rebuild the Temple. They could have stopped the rebuilding progress until word was received from the king, but they did not. Why? The Scripture says, "But the eye of their God was watching over the elders of the Jews, and they were not stopped until a report could go to Darius and his written reply be received" (Ezra 5:5).

One of the strongest illustrations of God's restraint of people is given to us in an almost passing comment in Exodus 34:23-24. God says in that passage:

Three times a year *all your men* are to appear before the Sovereign LORD, the God of Israel. I will drive out nations before you and enlarge your territory, and *no one will covet your land* when you go up three times each year to appear before the LORD your God. (emphasis added)

God commanded *all* the men to drop their normal activities three times a year to appear before Him. To appreciate the significance of this command, that would be equivalent today to our nation shutting down all its commerce, all its educational activities, and most crucial of all, furloughing all its military personnel simultaneously, and gathering all those people into one giant assembly three times a year. We can easily see how totally vulnerable and defenseless our nation would be before hostile powers on those three occasions each year.

Yet that is what God commanded Israel to do. But along with the command He promised them that no one would covet their land during those times when they were utterly defenseless. Not only would no other nations attack them, *they would not even desire to do so*. Covetousness—the evil desire for something belonging to another—is one of the most deeply rooted emotions in the human heart. The apostle Paul, who as a Pharisee could speak of his faultless outward observance of God's Law (see Philippians 3:6), is finally exposed as a sinner by the command, "You shall not covet" (see Romans 7:7-8). He could refrain from stealing, but he could not of himself refrain from coveting.

Yet God said that no other nation would covet the land of the Israelites, even during their vulnerable and defenseless times. God can restrain not only people's actions, but even their most deeply rooted desires. No part of the human heart is impervious to God's sovereign but mysterious control.

I have used a number of illustrations from Scripture to document that God does move in the hearts of people—either positively to cause them to do His will or negatively to restrain them from doing what is contrary to His will. Too often, however, we tend to read these accounts merely as biblical history without relating them to our lives and our situations. But, as we have seen previously, Paul said, "For everything that was written in the past was written to teach us, so that through endurance and the encouragement of the Scriptures we might have hope" (Romans 15:4). The stories of God moving the Egyptians to provide for the Israelites and restraining the surrounding nations from invading Israel are meant to teach us and encourage us. These stories are meant to teach us that God is sovereign over people and to encourage us by the knowledge that God exercises His sovereignty for our good.

DOES GOD PERMIT EVIL?

Of course, God does not always restrain the wicked and harmful actions of others toward His people. We see this even in the account of the rebuilding of the Temple. There was a period of perhaps ten years when the project was stopped due to opposition from the enemies of the Jews (see Ezra 4:6-24). We do not know why God allowed the enemies of His people to prevail at one time and restrained them at another. It is enough to know that God can and does restrain the harmful acts of others toward us when that is His sovereign will. Furthermore, God, in His infinite wisdom and love, intends that good ultimately comes from those harmful acts.

The classic, oft-quoted story of Joseph illustrates this truth so well. When Joseph's brothers decided to sell him into slavery, God did not restrain them. Neither did He restrain Potiphar's wife when she maliciously and unjustly accused him. But in

God's time He turned those circumstances around. God was orchestrating the wicked acts of people exactly as He planned in order to accomplish His purpose through Joseph. In the end, Joseph could look back over all the difficult events and say to his brothers, "You intended to harm me, but God intended it for good to accomplish what is now being done, the saving of many lives" (Genesis 50:20).

Commenting on Joseph's story, Professor Berkouwer said,

> Joseph's brothers devise and execute their plans; aroused by jealousy they gradually commit themselves irrevocably to their chosen course. . . . Their evil plan achieves historical realization, but the historical events are products of the Divine activity. God's good intents follow the mischievous path of the brothers or, rather, the brothers unwittingly follow the path that God has blazed. They work in His service. The purpose of God lights up the horizon of evil, jealous, malicious activity.[2]

Commenting on the same events, Alexander Carson said,

> From the history of Joseph we may see that the same thing may be from man, in one point of view, and from God, in another; and that what man may do sinfully to the injury of the people of God, God may effect through them for the good of his people. It is man's work, yet it is, in another view, God's work.[3]

Sometimes, according to the Bible, God even moves in the hearts of some people to act stubbornly. "But Sihon king of Heshbon refused to let us pass through. For the LORD your God had made his spirit stubborn and his heart obstinate in order to give him into your hands, as he has now done" (Deuteronomy 2:30). And again, "For it was the LORD himself who hardened their hearts to wage war against Israel, so that he might destroy them totally, exterminating them without mercy, as the LORD had commanded Moses" (Joshua 11:20).

There are admittedly some difficult things to understand in both of these passages. My purpose is not to attempt an explanation but rather to exhibit once again the Bible's consistent teaching that God is able and does move upon the hearts and minds of people to accomplish His purposes. Yet it also seems equally clear from these passages that God does this without violating or coercing their wills, but rather that He works in His mysterious way *through* their wills to accomplish His purposes. There is no doubt that Sihon and the Canaanite kings *wanted* to do exactly what the Scriptures say God caused them to do.

God is never at a loss because He cannot find someone to cooperate with Him in carrying out His plan. He so moves in the hearts of people—either Christians or non-Christians, it makes no difference—that they willingly, of their own free will carry out His plans. Do you need the good favor of a certain professor in order to get a good recommendation for a job? If that job is God's plan for you, God is able to and will move in the heart of that professor to give you a good recommendation.

Are you dependent upon your boss (or your commanding officer) for advancement in your career? God will move in the heart of your boss or commander one way or the other, depending on God's plan for you.

No one from the east or the west
   or from the desert can exalt a man.
But it is God who judges:
   He brings one down, he exalts another.
PSALM 75:6-7

Your promotion, or lack of it, is in the hand of God. Your superiors are simply His agents to carry out His will. They are not conscious of doing His will and never intended to (unless, of course, they are Christians prayerfully seeking to do the will of God), but that does not alter the result in your life. You can trust God in all the areas of your life where you are dependent upon the favor or frown of another person. God will move in that person's heart to carry out His will for you.

THE PROBLEM OF GOD'S SOVEREIGNTY

Earlier I asked you to set aside for the moment the problem that is raised by the assertion of God's sovereignty over people. We will now look at it briefly. As we do so, it will be helpful to keep in mind that the biblical writers never seemed to be aware of the problem, except for one statement by Paul in Romans 9:19-21. And Paul's statement seems to raise more problems for us than it solves. So while the Bible asserts both God's sovereignty and people's freedom and moral responsibility, it never attempts to explain their relationship. As we seek to examine this question, there are three truths we need to consider.

The first is that God is infinite in His ways as well as His being. A finite mind simply cannot comprehend an infinite being beyond what He has expressly revealed to us. Because of this, some things about God will forever remain a mystery to us. The relationship of the sovereign will of God to the freedom and moral responsibility of people is one of those mysteries.

Basil Manly, one of the founding fathers of the Southern Baptist Convention, while commenting on this difficult subject in one of his sermons, said, "The Scriptures do not undertake to explain mysteries. They leave them unexplained. There is a difference between difficulties, and mysteries:—difficulties may be removed;—mysteries cannot, without a new revelation, or the bestowment of a higher intellect."[4]

I believe one of our problems in dealing with this subject is that we tend to view the interaction between God and man on the same level as the interaction between man and man. In Psalm 50:21 God says, "You thought I was altogether like you." While the context of those words is completely different from our subject, the statement is appropriate to it. We tend to think of God as being like us. We tend to think that God can act upon the human mind only in the same way we can. We can argue, persuade, or even coerce, but we cannot move a person's will. Yet the Scriptures teach that God does move a person's will, but in such a way that the person acts freely and voluntarily. Furthermore, sovereignty on a human plane suggests force and coercion, people doing things against their wills as in the subjection of slaves to masters, but the Scriptures never portray God's sovereignty in this manner.

The second truth we must keep in mind is that God is never the author of sin. Though people's sinful intents and actions serve the sovereign purpose of God, we must never conclude that God has induced anyone to sin. "When tempted, no one should say, 'God is tempting me.' For God cannot be tempted by evil, nor does he tempt anyone; but each one is tempted when, by his own evil desire, he is dragged away and enticed" (James 1:13-14). It is frequently asserted in the Scriptures that God uses the sinful actions of men to accomplish His purposes (see, for example, Genesis 50:20; Acts 4:27-28; Revelation 17:17). But the fact that people's sinful intents and actions serve the sovereign purpose of God does not make God the author of their sin nor make them any less culpable for their actions. God judges people for the very sins that He uses to carry out His purpose. This truth is taught in such passages as Isaiah 10:5-16 (we will look at this passage in another chapter).

The third truth to keep before us is that the Bible consistently portrays people as making real choices of their own will. There is never any suggestion in Scripture of people being mindless puppets moved by divine strings. Furthermore, the choices people make are moral choices; that is, people are held accountable by God for the choices they make. The actions of Judas, Herod, and Pilate were wicked acts even though done under the sovereign appointment of God. The selling of Joseph into slavery was a malicious, wicked act by his brothers, even though the act accomplished the sovereign purpose of God.

The Bible teaches both the sovereignty of God and the free moral choices of men with equal emphasis. Richard Fuller, the third president of the Southern Baptist Convention, said, "It is impossible for us to reject either of these great truths, and it is equally impossible for our minds to reconcile them."[5]

But just as we must not misconstrue God's sovereignty so as to make people mere puppets, so we must not press man's freedom to the point of limiting God's sovereignty. Professor Berkouwer again helps us when he says:

> He who does injustice to this freedom [of the creature] does injustice to the Word of God, which already in paradise places man at a crossroad and gives him the choice of which road he will take. But in the light of Scripture, it is decisive that this creaturely freedom poses no threat or limitation to the sovereign and almighty Divine enterprise. . . . We are forced to direct ourselves to the Divine revelation which reveals to us the almighty activity of God and, at the same time, teaches human responsibility. . . . And anyone who does not take both this Divine ruling and human responsibility seriously can never rightly understand history.[6]

OUR RESPONSE

How shall we respond to the fact that God is able to and does in fact move in the minds and hearts of people to accomplish His will? Our first response should be one of trust. Our careers and destinies are in His hands, not the hands of bosses, commanding officers, professors, coaches, and all other people who, humanly speaking, are in a position to affect our futures. No one can harm you or jeopardize your future apart from the sovereign will of God. Moreover, God is able to and will grant you favor in the eyes of people who are in a position to do you good. You can entrust your future to God.

We should then look to God in prayer in all those situations where some aspect of our futures lies in the hands of another individual. As Alexander Carson said, "If we need the protection of men, let us first ask it from God. If we prevail with him, the power of the most mighty and of the most wicked must minister to our relief."[7] When Queen Esther was to go before King Xerxes without being summoned—an act that would normally result in her being put to death—she asked Mordecai to gather all of the Jews together to fast (and presumably to pray) that the king would grant her favor. Esther did not presume to know God's will—she said, "If I perish, I perish" (Esther 4:16)—but she certainly knew that God controlled the king's heart. Obviously we do not always know how God will answer our prayers, or if He will move in the heart of another individual, but it is enough to know that our destiny is in His hands, not those of other people.

Confidence in God's sovereignty in the lives of people should also keep us from becoming resentful and bitter when we are treated unjustly or maliciously by others. Bitterness usually stems not so much from the other person's actions as from the effects of those actions on our lives. Consider the following scenario in your life.

You have just been unjustly fired from your job for some reason entirely unrelated to your performance. After a couple of months of fruitless job hunting, you find yourself standing in the unemployment line. As you stand there you brood over the injustice perpetrated on you by your former boss. You are resentful and bitter.

Now suppose on the day you are unjustly fired, as you walk out the door, you meet a man looking for someone with your skill and experience who offers you a better job at twice the salary. There is one additional qualification: You must have had the experience of being unjustly fired. You gladly accept the job and thoroughly enjoy your new position. Do you ever become bitter? No, you think something such as, "I'm sure glad old Jones fired me. If he hadn't, I would never have gotten this great job." You see, it is the effects of your being fired, not the act itself, that determines whether you are tempted to become bitter.

Now God sometimes allows people to treat us unjustly. Sometimes He even allows their actions to seriously affect our careers or our futures viewed on a human plane. But God never allows people to make decisions about us that undermine His plan for us. God is for us, we are His children, He delights in us (see Zephaniah 3:17). And the Scripture says, "If God is for us, who can be against us?" (Romans 8:31). We can put this down as a bedrock truth: God will never allow any action against you that is not in accord with His will for you. And His will is always directed to our good.

Why then do we suffer such disappointment when the hoped for favor that we needed from another person doesn't materialize? Why do we struggle with resentment and bitterness when someone else's decision or action adversely affects us? Is it not because it is *our* plans that have been dashed, or our pride that has been wounded?

I once attended a seminar on the subject of Christians and stress. One of the speaker's main points was that if we want to live less stressful lives, we must learn to live with a single agenda: God's agenda. He pointed out that we tend to live under two agendas, ours and God's, and that the tension between them sets up stress.

I think his expression—a single agenda—aptly applies to our discussion of trusting God in the arena of other people's decisions in our lives. God is sovereign over people. He will move their hearts to cause them to do His will, or He will restrain them from doing anything contrary to His will. But it is His will, His agenda for our lives that God will guard, protect, and advance. We must learn to live by His agenda if we are to trust Him.

WORDS OF CAUTION

Before leaving this subject, there are some words of caution we need to consider lest we wrongly use the doctrine of God's sovereignty over people.

First, we should never use the doctrine as an excuse for our own shortcomings. If you failed to get the promotion you had hoped for, or worse yet, you are fired from your job or fail an important exam, you need to first examine your life to see if perhaps the reason lay in your own performance. Though God rescued Abraham and Sarah from the folly of Abraham's sin, He had not obligated Himself to do so. God has not promised to work in the heart of another individual just to make up for our shortcomings.

Second, we should not allow the doctrine of God's sovereignty to cause us to respond passively to the actions of other people that affect us. We should take all reasonable steps within the will of God to protect and advance our situation. I say within the will of God because there may be other reasons, for the sake of God's kingdom, why we should not take those steps. But the doctrine of God's sovereignty, considered by itself, should never be used to promote passivity.

Third, we must never use the doctrine of God's sovereignty to excuse our own sinful actions or decisions that hurt another person. We must never say, "Well, I made a mistake, but it's okay because God is sovereign." God is indeed sovereign in that other person's life, and He may choose to use our sinful actions to accomplish His will. But He will still hold us accountable for our harmful decisions and sinful actions.

A Scripture passage that can help us keep the doctrine of God's sovereignty in perspective is Deuteronomy 29:29, "The secret things belong to the LORD our God, but the things revealed belong to us and to our children forever, that we may follow all the words of this law." We do not know what God's sovereign will is. We do not know how He will work in the heart of another individual, whether favorably or unfavorably from our viewpoint. That is in the realm of the "secret things" that are not revealed to us. We do know He will work to accomplish His purpose, which is ultimately for our good.

Our duty, then, is to obey the "things revealed," that is, the will of God as revealed in Scripture for every area of life. Scripture teaches us to be prudent, conscientious, and responsible, and to do our jobs or our studies as best we can. If we find that, in spite of our best efforts, a superior or a teacher regards us unfavorably, we must then trust God for the eventual outcome of that relationship. Sometimes God will change the person's attitude toward us. At other times, He may even allow it to grow worse. In either case, the person's heart is in God's hands. He will direct it according to His sovereign purpose for His glory and our good.

CHAPTER FIVE

GOD'S RULE OVER
THE NATIONS

*O LORD, God of our Fathers, are you not the God who is in
heaven? You rule over all the kingdoms of the nations.
Power and might are in your hand, and no one
can withstand you.*

2 CHRONICLES 20:6

In a sermon entitled "God's Providence," C. H. Spurgeon said,

> Napoleon once heard it said, that man proposes and
> God disposes. "Ah," said Napoleon, "but I propose
> and dispose too." How do you think he proposed
> and disposed. He proposed to go and take Russia;
> he proposed to make all Europe his. He proposed to
> destroy that power, and how did he come back again?
> How had he disposed it? He came back solitary and
> alone, his mighty army perished and wasted, having
> well-nigh eaten and devoured one another through
> hunger. Man proposes and God disposes.[1]

As we trace the sovereignty of God through the Bible, one
of the most frequent references to it concerns His sovereignty
over nations and governments. I listed almost forty references
to God's rule over the nations without attempting to compile
an exhaustive list. God is Lord over all of human history, and
He is working out all the details of that history, as Paul said in

Ephesians 1:11, "in conformity with the purpose of his will." That is, God makes all events of history; all the decisions of rulers, kings, and parliaments; and all the actions of their governments, armies, and navies serve His will.

A RELEVANT ISSUE

In terms of our trusting God, the sovereignty of God over the nations can at first glance seem theoretical and remote from our daily lives. In the West, especially, we don't often consciously feel the actions of government impacting our lives from day to day. The laws of the land, for the most part, are reasonable and favorable to us, and we live each day unconscious of the multitude of laws and governmental decisions that affect us.

For most of the world, however, God's sovereignty over the ruling powers is a crucial issue. It is commonly said that more Christians were martyred for their faith in the twentieth century than during all the rest of church history. Christians are viewed unfavorably in much of the world today and in many countries face outright persecution from hostile governments. The freedom to publicly practice biblical Christianity, taken for granted in most Western countries, is not available to more than half of the world's population. For Christians living in these countries, the assurance that God rules over the governments that rule over them should give courage and confidence to them in times of harassment or persecution.

Those of us living in countries where religious freedom is allowed should regularly give thanks to God for that freedom. It is not an accident of history, or due merely to the foresight of our founding fathers, but rather to the sovereign hand of God working in and through our governments. We cannot take such liberty for granted. Alexander Carson stated it well when he said, "As God can protect his people under the greatest despotism, so the utmost civil liberty is no safety to them without the immediate protection of his Almighty arm. I fear that Christians in this country have too great a confidence in political institutions . . . [rather] than of the government of God."[2]

It is not just religious freedom we are concerned about. Our lives are affected daily by the decisions of legislative bodies and government officials. Government bodies at all levels are increasingly telling us what we must or must not do. Sometimes these decisions are directly apparent; sometimes we are unconscious of them. Sometimes they are good decisions, at least from our point of view; sometimes they are bad decisions. At all times, those decisions, apparent or not, good or not, are under the control of our sovereign God. We should put our trust in God, not in the decision-making powers of politicians, government officials, and even supreme courts.

An Iranian Christian wrote of the time, years ago, when the Iranian government issued a decree to close all foreign primary schools, a decision that affected the Christian school where he was enrolled. His principal went to the government and obtained permission to allow the school to remain partially open so that the fifth and sixth grade students could finish their primary education at the school. For us that is not a particularly striking event, but for a Muslim country to allow a Christian school to remain open when others were closed was indeed unusual. Why would such permission be granted?

This man wrote, "I think it was in God's plan for me that this permission was given, so that I might finish my primary education in a Christian school. Is not this the right way for a Christian to look at history, seeing the hand of God in all events weaving the pattern of the life of nations and individuals?"[3]

This Iranian brother had a correct perception of the sovereignty of God in the decrees and decisions of governments. He saw the hand of God ruling in the affairs of governments and through those governments in the affairs of us as individuals. Just as we saw in chapter 4 that God is sovereign in the hearts of individuals, whose decisions and actions affect us, so God is also sovereign in the decisions and actions of government as they affect us. As Margaret Clarkson wrote, "God is the Lord of human history and of the personal history of every member of His redeemed family."[4] We cannot separate the history of a nation from the people of that nation.

SOVEREIGNTY NOT USUALLY APPARENT

The fact that God is sovereign over our rulers is usually not evident to us as we view their decisions and actions on a human plane. For the most part, governmental officials and legislative bodies do their work quite apart from any intent to carry out the will of God. We see this amply demonstrated in the life and death of the Lord Jesus Christ.

Caesar Augustus issued a decree that a census should be taken. This required Joseph and Mary to go to the town of Bethlehem to register at just the right time for the Messiah to be born in Bethlehem in fulfillment of Micah's prophecy (see Micah 5:2). Caesar certainly did not intend to be an instrument to fulfill any Jewish prophecy, yet that is exactly what he was.

Matthew records several instances in the early life of Jesus where governmental action directly affected Jesus and in each instance makes the observation that through those actions certain prophecies were fulfilled (see Matthew 2:14-15, 17-18, 21-23). In each case, the people involved acted freely, doing what they intended to do, yet, in each instance, they did exactly what God planned for them to do.

In the apostles' prayer in Acts 4, they said concerning the death of Jesus,

Indeed Herod and Pontius Pilate met together with the
Gentiles and the people of Israel in this city to conspire
against your holy servant Jesus, whom you anointed.
They did what your power and will had decided beforehand
should happen.   ACTS 4:27-28, EMPHASIS ADDED

Obviously Herod, Pilate, and the Jewish leaders did exactly
what they wanted to do, yet they did exactly what God planned
that they do. What Solomon said of individuals in Proverbs
16:9—"In his heart a man plans his course, but the LORD determines his steps"—applies when men act not only in their private
capacities, but also when they act as officials and rulers of nations.

John Newton (1725–1807), converted slave trader, Anglican
minister, and author of the familiar hymn "Amazing Grace," wrote:

The kings of the earth are continually disturbing the
world with their schemes of ambition. They expect
to carry every thing before them, and have seldom
any higher end in view, than the gratification of their
own passions. But in all they do they are but servants
of this great King and Lord, and fulfill his purposes,
as the instruments he employs to inflict prescribed
punishment upon transgressors against him, or to open
a way for the spread of his Gospel. . . . They had one
thing in view, he had another.[5]

Although we may not perceive the hand of God in the affairs
of nations as we view them today, His rule is no less sovereign
today than it was in the days of the prophets or the apostles.
Professor Berkouwer is again helpful:

This does not mean that the work of God is always
evident in the interlacing of Divine and human
activity. . . . Yet it is striking to observe how often

the purpose of God is reached without radical intervention. On the surface there may be nothing to see except human activity creating and defining history on a horizontal level.[6]

It is only in the biblical revelation that we see the hand of God ruling over and guiding the activities of the nations and the effects of those activities on His people. The events that Matthew recorded as happening in the fulfillment of Old Testament prophecies all happened as a result of human decisions and were worked out in the course of ordinary human circumstances. Were it not for the inspired commentary by Matthew, we would have no more reason to see the sovereign hand of God in them than we do in the most mundane occurrences reported in our daily newspapers.

That being true, then, we should likewise see in those affairs reported in our daily paper the sovereign hand of God just as much as we see it in the Bible. Of course, we don't have the advantage of the divinely revealed explanation of today's events, as we do of those recorded in the Bible, but that does not make God's sovereign rule today any less certain. God recorded in His Word specific instances of His sovereign rule over history in order that we might trust Him in the affairs of history as they unfold before us today. We should remember that, for those experiencing the events recorded in the biblical narratives, God's hand was no more apparent to them in those events than His hand is apparent to us today in ours.

GOD ORDAINS RULERS

As we turn to the Scriptures to determine their teaching on the sovereignty of God over the nations, there are several specific truths that stand out. First, *God in His sovereignty has estab-*

lished government for the good of all people—believer as well as unbeliever. Paul said, "There is no authority except that which God has established. The authorities that exist have been established by God. . . . For [the ruler] is God's servant to do you good" (Romans 13:1, 4). Admittedly the statement, "the ruler is God's servant to do us good," seems difficult to accept when we see some of our brothers and sisters in Christ persecuted and perhaps killed because of their Christian commitment. We should remember again that God in His infinite wisdom and sovereignty and for reasons known only to Himself, allows rulers to act contrary to His revealed will. But the evil actions of those rulers against God's children are never beyond the bounds of His sovereign will. And we should remember that God works in history from an eternal perspective, whereas we tend to view the outworking of history from a temporal perspective.

Because God has ordained rulers for our good, and because He sovereignly rules over their actions, we should pray that they will rule for our good. Paul urges that prayers be made "for kings and all those in authority, that we may live peaceful and quiet lives in all godliness and holiness" (1 Timothy 2:2). Prayer is the most tangible expression of trust in God. If we would trust God for our persecuted brothers and sisters in other countries, we must be diligent in prayer for their rulers. If we would trust God when decisions of government in our own country go against our best interests, we must pray for His working in the hearts of those officials and legislators who make those decisions. The truth that the king's heart is in the hand of the Lord is meant to be a stimulus to prayer, not a stimulus to a fatalistic attitude.

Next we see that in addition to establishing government, *God determines who rules in those governments.* "The Most High is sovereign over the kingdoms of men and gives them to anyone he wishes and sets over them the lowliest of men" (Daniel 4:17, see also verse 32). When we consider some of the evil tyrants and dictators that have reigned, as well as some of the weak and foolish men who have held high office, even in this century, we are amazed to learn that they have ruled in the sovereign will of God. But that is what Scripture tells us.

Once again, we must view this truth from God's eternal perspective. Psalm 76:10, in the King James Version, says, "Surely the wrath of man shall praise thee: the remainder of wrath shall thou restrain." While more recent translations vary from that particular rendering, it is a truth supported by the whole tenor of Scripture. God will allow people, whether strong-willed tyrants or weak-kneed politicians, to do only what ultimately results in His glory. How sin and evil ultimately redound to God's glory is a mystery, but it is a truth affirmed throughout Scripture.

Just as God determines who rules in the nations, *He also determines their time of ruling*. Isaiah 40:23-24 says:

> He brings princes to naught
> and reduces the rulers of this world to nothing.
> No sooner are they planted,
> no sooner are they sown,
> no sooner do they take root in the ground,
> than he blows on them and they wither,
> and a whirlwind sweeps them away like chaff.

We see this most vividly illustrated in the life of the powerful Babylonian monarch, Nebuchadnezzar. At the height of his power, Nebuchadnezzar's sanity was taken from him, and he was driven away from his people to eat grass like cattle. Seven years later, his sanity was restored to him, his advisors and nobles sought him out, and he was restored to his throne and became even greater than before (see Daniel 4:33-36). From the greatest monarch of his time to a madman living like a wild beast to an even greater monarch, all in just over seven years, is a roller coaster series of events that could only be orchestrated by a sovereign God. And the God who ruled absolutely in the life and fortunes of the most powerful monarch of that time still rules in the fortunes and destinies of governments today. No government or dictator is so powerful as to be beyond the sway of His sovereign rule over all the nations of the earth.

GOD CONTROLS DECISIONS

God not only determines who governs, *He also rules in the decisions that they make.* Proverbs 16:33 says, "The lot is cast into the lap, but its every decision is from the LORD." The practice of casting lots was often used to determine important matters of state. Officials were chosen, tasks determined, dates selected, and disputes were settled by casting lots (see 1 Chronicles 24:5; Esther 3:7; Proverbs 18:18; Luke 1:9). The king of Babylon determined military strategy by casting lots (see Ezekiel 21:18-22). And Solomon tells us that every decision from casting lots was from God, that is, God controlled the decisions that kings and government officials made through this method.

Not every decision in biblical times was made from casting lots. Some were made, as is often true today, after seeking advice and counsel from others. In these cases, God rules in the advice given and the extent to which that advice is received and acted upon so that His sovereign will is always accomplished. Two instances recorded in the Old Testament bear this out.

David's son Absalom had mounted a rebellion against his father with the result that David and a few loyal followers fled Jerusalem. One of David's trusted counselors, Ahithophel, had entered into the conspiracy with Absalom. In seeking to determine how to consolidate his initial success, Absalom sought the advice of first Ahithophel and then another counselor, Hushai, who was secretly still loyal to David.

After hearing contradictory advice from Ahithophel and Hushai, Absalom and his men chose the advice of Hushai, which was secretly intended to favor David. The scriptural account of this incident tells us that "in those days the advice Ahithophel gave was like that of one who inquires of God" (2 Samuel 16:23). Yet Absalom chose to follow Hushai's advice instead of Ahithophel's. Why? The Scripture says, "For the LORD had determined to frustrate the good advice of Ahithophel in order to bring disaster on Absalom" (2 Samuel 17:14). So we see that the advice Ahithophel gave on this occasion was good, yet Absalom chose to disregard it because God caused him to do so.

A similar event occurred in the life of David's grandson Rehoboam. When he came to the throne, the men of Israel asked him to lighten the harsh labor and the heavy yoke Solomon, his father, had put on them. Rehoboam first consulted the elders who had served his father. They advised him to give the people a favorable answer. But Rehoboam rejected the advice of the elders and consulted the young men who had grown up with him. They advised him to answer the people harshly. As a result, ten tribes of Israel revolted against Rehoboam, splitting the kingdom.

Why did Rehoboam make such a foolish decision? The Scripture says, "So the king did not listen to the people, for this turn of events was from the LORD, to fulfill the word the LORD had spoken" (1 Kings 12:15). Two foolish decisions were made; in two instances good advice was rejected and harmful or foolish advice was followed. Both instances are attributed to the sovereign work of God guiding the minds of the kings to accomplish His will.

What observations can we make from these events recorded in Scripture? First, God *can* and *does* work in the hearts and minds of rulers and officials of government to accomplish His sovereign purpose. Their hearts and minds are as much under His control as the impersonal physical laws of nature. Yet their every decision is made freely—most often without any thought or regard to the will of God.

The second observation we can make is that God sometimes *causes* government leaders or officials to make foolish decisions in order to bring judgment upon a nation. Alexander Carson said,

> Why does folly often prevail over wisdom in the counsels of princes, and in houses of legislators? God has appointed the rejection of good counsel in order to bring on nations that vengeance that their crimes call down from heaven. God rules the world by Providence, not by miracle. See that grave senator. He rises and pours forth wisdom. But if God has determined to punish the nation, some prating speculatist will impose his sophisms on the most sagacious assembly.[7]

At the time of this writing, the government of the United States has just made what appears to be a series of incredibly foolish and naive decisions in the arena of foreign affairs. Viewed in the light of the exploding moral decadence of our American society, one cannot help but wonder if this is evidence of God's hand of judgment upon our nation. If so, believers as well as unbelievers will suffer the consequences of those decisions. Historically, God has not spared the righteous when He judges a nation (though He is well able to do so if He chooses; see Exodus 9:5-7).

If these apparently foolish decisions are allowed to run their course, and believers are caught up in the disastrous consequences of those decisions, then we must still continue to trust God even in those difficult times. We must believe both that God is sovereignly in control of those events and that the care and welfare of His children in those events has not been forgotten.

Third, as has been observed earlier in this chapter, we should take more seriously our responsibility to pray for the leaders of our government that they will make wise decisions. Although we may suspect that some of the more disastrous decisions are evidence of God's judgment, we do not know that. We do know God has instructed us to pray for leaders. Our duty, then, is to pray for wise decisions, but to trust when foolish and harmful decisions are made.

GOD DETERMINES MILITARY VICTORIES

In addition to ruling in the decisions of governments, *God also rules in the victories and defeats between nations on the battlefield.* The truth stated in Proverbs 21:31, "The horse is made ready for the day of battle, but victory rests with the LORD," is one of the most frequently stated truths about the sovereignty of God in all of the Old Testament. Consider the following few passages of many that could have been selected (emphasis added in each quotation):

> The LORD said to Gideon, "You have too many men *for me to deliver Midian into their hands.* In order that Israel may not boast against me that her own strength has saved her, announce now to the people, 'Anyone who trembles with fear may turn back and leave Mount Gilead.'" . . .
> When the three hundred trumpets sounded, *the LORD caused the men throughout the camp to turn on each other with their swords.* The army fled to Beth Shittah toward Zererah as far as the border of Abel Meholah near Tabbath.
> JUDGES 7:2-3, 22

Jonathan said to his young armor-bearer, "Come, let's go over to the outpost of those uncircumcised fellows. Perhaps the LORD will act in our behalf. *Nothing can hinder the LORD from saving, whether by many or by few.*" . . .

Then panic struck the whole army—those in the camp and field, and those in the outposts and raiding parties—and the ground shook. It was a panic sent by God. . . .

Then Saul and all his men assembled and went to the battle. They found the Philistines in total confusion, striking each other with their swords.   1 SAMUEL 14:6, 15, 20

The man of God came up and told the king of Israel, "This is what the LORD says: 'Because the Arameans think the LORD is a god of the hills and not a god of the valleys, *I will deliver this vast army into your hands*, and you will know that I am the LORD.'"

For seven days they camped opposite each other, and on the seventh day the battle was joined. The Israelites inflicted a hundred thousand casualties on the Aramean foot soldiers in one day.   1 KINGS 20:28-29

Now Naaman was commander of the army of the king of Aram. He was a great man in the sight of his master and highly regarded, *because through him the LORD had given victory to Aram.* He was a valiant soldier, but he had leprosy.   2 KINGS 5:1

Judah turned and saw that they were being attacked at both front and rear. Then they cried out to the LORD. The priests blew their trumpets and the men of Judah raised the battle cry. At the sound of their battle cry, *God routed Jeroboam and all Israel before Abijah and Judah.* The

Israelites fled before Judah, and *God delivered them into their hands.* 2 CHRONICLES 13:14-16

Because of this clear statement of God's sovereignty in war, we as Christians should put our trust in God, not in our nation's armaments. As Psalm 20:7 says, "Some trust in chariots and some in horses, but we trust in the name of the LORD our God." Or as another psalm says,

> No king is saved by the size of his army;
>> no warrior escapes by his great strength.
> A horse is a vain hope for deliverance;
>> despite all its great strength it cannot save.
>
> PSALM 33:16-17

To restate those truths from Psalms in modern-day language we could say, "Some trust in nuclear warheads and large armies, but we trust in God, because no country is saved by the size of its military forces or the power of its military armament. Instead, victory comes from God."

The debate between politicians over the size of our nuclear arsenal and the number of aircraft carriers and submarines our navy should have is, in a sense, a futile debate. Both sides are ultimately trusting in military muscle; they only differ in how much is necessary. The Christian, however, must trust in God, not military might of any size.

This does not mean our country should discharge all our military personnel and mothball our ships and tanks. It means we should not trust in them. The psalmist said, "I do not trust in my bow, my sword does not bring me victory" (Psalm 44:6). He did not trust in his bow or sword but neither did he discard them. He recognized that an army must fight but that God gives the victory in warfare to whomever He wills.

In Isaiah 5, at the end of a series of woes pronounced upon wicked Judah, the prophet predicts the forthcoming invasion of the Assyrian army, at the response to God's summoning "whistle" (verse 26). Isaiah describes the battle ready condition of this army in such terms as,

> They come,
>> swiftly and speedily!
> Not one of them grows tired or stumbles,
>> not one slumbers or sleeps.
>
> ISAIAH 5:26-27

Then he adds a rather amazing statement, "Not a sandal thong is broken" (verse 27). In modern-day language we would say, "Not a single shoelace [of any soldier] is broken."

We see in this statement not only an affirmation of the absoluteness of God's sovereignty, but also the thoroughness with which His sovereignty penetrates down to the last minute detail. Nothing is left to chance, not even the brokenness of a sandal thong or shoelace. We have all heard the old statement, "For want of a nail, the shoe was lost; for want of a shoe, the horse was lost; for want of a horse, the rider was lost; for want of a rider, the battle was lost." Details are important, and God is just as sovereign over the details as He is over the so-called "big picture." In Isaiah 5, the prophet assures us that, in the sovereignty of God over the battlefield, the missing nail that ultimately leads to defeat will not be lost. Victory belongs to the Lord and to the nation He chooses.

Because of God's sovereignty in warfare, we can also take courage regarding the threat of a nuclear holocaust. Such a disaster cannot happen apart from the sovereign will of God. Obviously none of us knows what the sovereign will of God is in this matter, so we cannot rule out the possibility of widespread nuclear destruction. What we can rule out is the possibility of that happening purely by the *uncontrolled* hand of some madman or some careless military officer. God controls the hand of both the mad tyrant and the careless officer.

As Christians we should not fall prey to the nuclear anxiety of our day. Rather we should trust in the sovereign control of God and pray to Him for protection from a possible holocaust.

This whole subject of God's sovereignty in warfare is a tricky business because of our innate tendency to think our country is always right. We assume that God will bless our side with victory. The Bible does not support such a view. In fact, according to biblical history, *God sometimes uses an evil nation to punish another one, then in turn punishes the first nation for its sin.*

God used the Assyrian army to punish Judah, calling Assyria, "the rod of my anger, in whose hand is the club of my wrath," and saying, "I send him against a godless nation, I dispatch him against a people who anger me" (Isaiah 10:5-6). God states very clearly that He is sending Assyria against Judah; one ungodly nation against another. Further, the Scripture is very clear that the king of Assyria did not consider himself as God's agent of punishment:

> But [God's will] is not what [the king of Assyria] intends,
>   this is not what he has in mind;
> his purpose is to destroy,
>   to put an end to many nations.
>
> ISAIAH 10:7

Therefore, God said, "When the Lord has finished all his work against Mount Zion and Jerusalem, he will say, 'I will punish the king of Assyria for the willful pride of his heart and the haughty look in his eyes. For he says: "By the strength of my hand I have done this, and by my wisdom, because I have understanding"'" (Isaiah 10:12-13).

The so-called sovereign nations of the world are not truly sovereign. They are nothing more than instruments in the hand of God to accomplish His will: sometimes to protect His people, sometimes to open doors for advancement of the gospel, and sometimes to be His instrument of judgment against ungodliness. As God looks down upon the nations that accomplish His purpose, even while rebelling against Him, He sees them as nothing more than His instruments. He says:

> Does the ax raise itself above him who swings it,
>> or the saw boast against him who uses it?
> As if a rod were to wield him who lifts it up,
>> or a club brandish him who is not wood!

ISAIAH 10:15

These mighty nations, even those of our own contemporary time, are nothing more than the ax or the saw in the hand of God. They may boast of their might and power, but that power is only as effective as God sovereignly determines.

We see that God is firmly in control of history and of the nations and rulers that, from our human point of view, determine history. God establishes governments, determines who will govern and for how long, rules in the councils of state, causes officials to make both wise and foolish decisions, grants victory or defeat in war, and uses ungodly nations to carry out His will.

As suggested by our Iranian brother, history is like a giant piece of fabric with very intricate and complex patterns. During the limited span of our lifetimes we see only a tiny fraction of the pattern. Furthermore, as has been observed by others, we see the pattern from the underside. The underside of a weaving usually makes no sense. Even the upper side makes little sense if we view just a tiny piece. Only God sees the upper side, and only He sees the entire fabric with its complete pattern. Therefore, we must trust Him to work out all the details of history to His glory, knowing that His glory and our good are bound up together.

ENLARGING OUR HORIZONS

Most of us as Christians tend to think of the sovereignty of God only in terms of its immediate effect upon us, or our families or friends. We're not too interested in the sovereignty of God over the nations and over history unless we are consciously and personally affected by that history. We are only vaguely interested in the political turmoil and wars of distant nations unless, for example, a missionary friend of ours can't get an entrance visa to his country of ministry.

But we must remember that God promised to Abraham and to his seed that all nations will be blessed through Christ (see Genesis 12:3; 22:18; Galatians 3:8). Someday that promise will be fulfilled for, as recorded in Revelation 7:9, John saw "a great multitude that no one could count, from every nation, tribe, people and language, standing before the throne and in front of the Lamb." God has a plan to redeem people from all nations and to bless all nations through Christ.

However, as we look around the world today what do we see? We see over one-half of the world's population living in countries whose governments are hostile to the gospel, where missionaries are not allowed, and where national Christians are severely hindered from proclaiming Christ. How do we trust God for the fulfillment of His promises when the current events and conditions of the day seem so directly contrary to their fulfillment?

We can take a lesson from the example of Daniel. Daniel understood from the Scriptures in the prophecy of Jeremiah that the desolation of Jerusalem would last seventy years, and realizing that seventy years was almost complete, Daniel set himself to pray (see Daniel 9). He recognized that his people were in exile because of their sins, and he recognized that a sovereign God, and only a sovereign God, could restore them from their exile. He trusted in the sovereignty and faithfulness of God, therefore he prayed. We might say he pleaded God's promise to Jeremiah. Neither God's sovereignty nor His promise to restore the exiles caused Daniel to lapse into a fatalistic, do-nothing attitude.

Daniel realized that God's sovereignty and God's promise were intended to stimulate him to pray. Because God is sovereign, He is able to answer. Because He is faithful to His promises, He will answer. Daniel prayed and God answered. As we saw in chapter 4, God moved the heart of the Persian king to permit and even encourage all the exiles who wanted to, to return to Jerusalem to rebuild the Temple.

As we look at the condition of the world today, so utterly hostile to the gospel, we must also look at the sovereignty of God and at His promises. He has promised to redeem people from every nation, and He has commanded us to make disciples of all nations. We must, then, trust God by praying. Some will go to those nations as God opens doors, but *all* of us must pray. We must learn to trust God, not only in the adverse circumstances of our individual lives, but also in the adverse circumstances of the church as a whole. We must learn to trust God for the spread of the gospel, even in those areas where it is severely restricted.

God is sovereign over the nations. He is sovereign over the officials of our own government in all their actions as they affect us, directly or indirectly. He is sovereign over the officials of government in lands where our brothers and sisters in Christ suffer for their faith in Him. And He is sovereign over the nations where every attempt is made to stamp out true Christianity. In all of these areas, we can and must trust God.

CHAPTER SIX

GOD'S POWER OVER NATURE

Do any of the worthless idols of the nations bring rain?
Do the skies themselves send down showers?
No, it is you, O LORD our God.
Therefore our hope is in you,
for you are the one who does all this.

JEREMIAH 14:22

In September 1985, an earthquake struck Mexico City, killing some 6,000 people and leaving more than 100,000 homeless. A friend of mine wanted to use the event to teach his young children a simple science lesson so he asked them,

"Do you know what caused the earthquake?" He planned to answer his question with a simple explanation of fault lines and shifting rocks in the earth's crust.

His seismology lesson quickly turned into a theological discussion, however, when his eight-year-old daughter replied, "I know why. God was judging those people." Though my friend's child had jumped to an unwarranted conclusion about God's judgment, she was theologically correct in one sense. God was in control of that earthquake. Why He allowed it to happen is a question we cannot answer (and should not try to), but we can say, on the testimony of Scripture, that God did indeed allow it or cause it to happen.

GOD CONTROLS THE WEATHER

All of us are affected by the weather and the forces of nature at various times to one degree or another. Most of the time we are merely inconvenienced by weather—a delayed airplane flight, a cancelled Fourth of July picnic, or something else on that order. Frequently some people somewhere are drastically affected by the weather or the more violent forces of nature. A prolonged drought withers the farmer's crop, or a hailstorm destroys it within an hour. A tornado in Texas leaves hundreds homeless, and a typhoon in Bangladesh destroys thousands of acres of crops.

Whenever we are affected by the weather—whether it is merely an inconvenience or a major disaster—we tend to regard it as nothing more than the impersonal expression of certain fixed meteorological or geological laws. A low pressure system settles over my hometown, bringing a huge snowstorm, and closing our airport the day I am to leave for a ministry engagement. Forces within the earth continually bend its crust until one day it snaps, causing a major earthquake. Whether it is trivial or traumatic, we tend to think of the expressions of nature as "just happening" and ourselves as the "unlucky" victims of whatever nature brings forth. In practice, even Christians tend to live and think like the deists I mentioned in an earlier chapter who conceived of God as the One who created the universe and then walked away to leave it running according to its own natural laws.

But God has not walked away from the day-to-day control of His creation. Certainly He has established physical laws by which He governs the forces of nature, but those laws continuously operate according to His sovereign will. A Christian TV meteorologist has determined that there are over 1,400 references to weather terminology in the Bible.[1] Many of these references attribute the outworking of weather directly to the hand of God. Most of these passages speak of God's control over *all* weather, not just His divine intervention on specific occasions.

Consider the following Scriptures:

> He unleashes his lightning beneath the whole heaven
> > and sends it to the ends of the earth. . . .
> He says to the snow, "Fall on the earth,"
> > and to the rain shower, "Be a mighty downpour." . . .
> The breath of God produces ice,
> > and the broad waters become frozen.
> He loads the clouds with moisture;
> > he scatters his lightning through them.
> At his direction they swirl around
> > over the face of the whole earth
> > to do whatever he commands them.
> He brings the clouds to punish men,
> > or to water his earth and show his love.
>
> JOB 37:3, 6, 10-13

> He covers the sky with clouds;
> > he supplies the earth with rain
> > and makes grass grow on the hills. . . .
> He spreads the snow like wool
> > and scatters the frost like ashes.
> He hurls down his hail like pebbles.
> > Who can withstand his icy blast?
> He sends his word and melts them;
> > he stirs up his breezes, and the waters flow.
>
> PSALM 147:8, 16-18

> When he thunders, the waters in the heavens roar;
> > he makes clouds rise from the ends of the earth.

He sends lightning with the rain
and brings out the wind from his storehouses.

JEREMIAH 10:13

I also withheld rain from you
when the harvest was still three months away.
I sent rain on one town,
but withheld it from another.
One field had rain;
another had none and dried up.

AMOS 4:7

Note how all these Scriptures attribute all expressions of weather—good or bad—to the direct controlling hand of God. The insurance companies refer to major natural disasters as "acts of God." The truth is, *all* expressions of nature, *all* occurrences of weather, whether it be a devastating tornado or a gentle rain on a spring day, are acts of God. The Bible teaches that God controls all the forces of nature, both destructive and productive, on a continuous, moment-by-moment basis.

Whether the weather is nice or bad, we are never the victims or even the beneficiaries of the impersonal powers of nature. God, who is the loving heavenly Father of every true Christian, is sovereign over the weather, and He exercises that sovereignty moment by moment. As G. C. Berkouwer stated, "The believer is never the victim of the powers of nature or fate. Chance is eliminated."[2]

COMPLAINING OR THANKSGIVING

Complaining about the weather seems to be a favorite American pastime. Sadly, we Christians often get caught up in this ungodly habit of our society. But when we complain about the weather, we are actually complaining against God who sent us our weather. We are, in fact, sinning against God (see Numbers 11:1).

Not only do we sin against God when we complain about the weather, we also deprive ourselves of the peace that comes from recognizing our heavenly Father is in control of it. Alexander Carson said, "Scripture represent[s] all physical laws as having their effect from the immediate agency of Almighty Power. . . . Christians themselves, though they recognize the doctrine [of divine providence], are prone to overlook it in practice, and consequently to be deprived, in a great measure, of that advantage which a constant and deep impression of this truth is calculated to give."[3] Whether the weather merely disrupts my plans or destroys my home, I need to learn to see God's sovereign and loving hand controlling it.

The fact is, for most of us, the weather and the effects of nature are usually favorable. The tornado, the drought, even the snowstorm that delays our flight are the exception, not the rule. We tend to remember the "bad" weather and take for granted the good. However, when Jesus spoke about the weather, He spoke about the goodness of God: "He causes his sun to rise on the evil and the good, and sends rain on the righteous and the unrighteous" (Matthew 5:45).

Though God sometimes uses the weather and other expressions of nature as instruments of judgment (see Amos 4:7-9), He most often uses weather as an expression of His gracious provision for His creation. Both saint and sinner alike benefit from God's gracious provision of weather. And, according to Jesus, this provision is not merely the result of certain fixed, inexorable physical laws. God controls those laws. He *causes* His sun to rise, He *sends* the rain.

God has indeed established certain physical laws for the operation of His universe; yet moment by moment those laws operate according to His direct will. Again Alexander Carson put it so well when he said, "The sun and the rain minister to the nourishment and comfort equally of the righteous and the wicked, not from the necessity of general laws, but from the immediate providence of Him who, in the government of the world, wills this result."[4]

We as Christians need to stop complaining about the weather and instead learn to give thanks for it. God, our heavenly Father, sends us each day what He deems best for all of His creation.

NATURAL DISASTERS

What about the natural disasters that occur frequently in various parts of the world? Many sensitive Christians struggle over the multitude of large-scale natural disasters around the world—an earthquake in one place, famine in another, typhoons and floods somewhere else. Thousands of people are killed immediately, others slowly starve to death. Entire regions are devastated, crops are ruined, homes destroyed. "Why does God allow all this?" we may ask. "Why does God permit all those innocent children to starve?"

It is not wrong to wrestle with these issues, as long as we do it in a reverent and submissive attitude toward God. Indeed, to fail to wrestle with the issue of large-scale tragedy may indicate a lack of compassion toward others on our part. However, we must be careful not to, in our minds, take God off His throne of absolute sovereignty or put Him in the dock and bring Him to the bar of our judgment.

While working on this chapter, I watched the evening news on television one night. One of the top stories was about several powerful tornados that swept across central Mississippi, killing seven people, injuring at least 145 more, and leaving nearly

500 families homeless. As I watched the scenes of people sifting through the rubble of what had been their homes, my heart went out to them. I thought to myself, "Some of those people are undoubtedly believers. What would I say to them about God's sovereignty over nature? Do I really believe it myself at a time such as this? Wouldn't it be easier to just accept Rabbi Kushner's statement that it is simply an act of nature—a morally blind nature that churns along following its own laws? Why bring God into chaos and suffering such as this?"

But God brings Himself into these events. He said in Isaiah 45:7,

> I form the light and create darkness,
>> I bring prosperity and create disaster;
>> I, the LORD, do all these things.

God Himself accepts the responsibility, so to speak, of disasters. He actually does more than *accept* the responsibility; He actually *claims* it. In effect, God says, "I, and I alone, have the power and authority to bring about both prosperity and disaster, both weal and woe, both good and bad."

This is a difficult truth to accept as you watch people sift through the rubble of their homes or—more to the point—if you are the one sifting through the rubble of *your* home. But as the late Dr. Edward J. Young commented on Isaiah 45:7, "We gain nothing by seeking to minimize the force of the present verse."[5] We must allow the Bible to say what it says, not what we think it ought to say.

We obviously do not understand why God creates disaster, or why He brings it to one town and not to another. We recognize, too, that just as God sends His sun and rain on both the righteous and the unrighteous, so He also sends the tornado, or the hurricane, or the earthquake on both. I have friends, fellow staff members of The Navigators, who were in the middle of the 1985 earthquake in Mexico City. God's sovereignty over nature does not mean that Christians never encounter the tragedies of natural disasters. Experience and observation clearly teach otherwise.

God's sovereignty over nature does mean that, whatever we experience at the hand of the weather or other forces of nature (such as plant diseases or insect infestation of our crops), all circumstances are under the watchful eye and sovereign control of our God.

PHYSICAL AFFLICTIONS

Illness and physical affliction is another area in which we struggle to trust God. Babies are born with major birth defects. Cancer strikes people who have apparently done everything possible to guard against it. Others experience continuous pain for years without any medical relief. Even those who are normally healthy and strong often experience sicknesses at the most inopportune times. Is God sovereign over this aspect of nature? Is He in control of the diseases and physical infirmities that affect us?

When God called Moses to lead the Israelites out of Egypt, Moses protested his inadequacy, including the fact that he was slow of speech. God's reply to Moses is very instructive to us in this area of physical affliction, for God said, "Who gave man his mouth? Who makes him deaf or mute? Who gives him sight or makes him blind? Is it not I, the LORD?" (Exodus 4:11). Here God specifically ascribes to His own work the physical afflictions of deafness, muteness, and blindness. These physical afflictions are not merely the products of defective genes or birth accidents. Those things may indeed be the immediate cause, but behind them is the sovereign purpose of God. Doctor Donald Grey Barnhouse, one of the great Bible teachers of the mid-twentieth century, once said, "No person in this world was ever blind that God had not planned for him to be blind; no person was ever deaf in this world that God had not planned for that person to be deaf. . . . If you do not believe that, you have a strange God who has a universe which has gone out of gear and He cannot control it."[6]

When Jesus encountered a man blind from birth, His disciples asked Him, "Rabbi, who sinned, this man or his parents, that he was born blind?" (John 9:2). Jesus replied, "Neither this man nor his parents sinned, . . . but this happened so that the work of God might be displayed in his life" (verse 3). Jesus didn't respond that it was merely a birth defect that caused the man's blindness. Rather, it happened in the plan of God so that God might be glorified. God was in control of that man's blindness.

This God who is the God of deafness, muteness, and blindness is also the God of cancer, arthritis, Down's syndrome, and all other afflictions that come to us or our loved ones. None of these afflictions "just happen." They are all within the sovereign will of God. Such a statement immediately brings us into the problem of pain and suffering. Why does a sovereign God who loves us allow such pain and heartache?

The answer to that question is beyond the scope of this book. Briefly, we know that all creation has been subjected to frustration because of the sin of Adam (see Romans 8:20). So we can say that the ultimate cause of all pain and suffering must be traced back to the Fall. God's weal and woe are not arbitrary or capricious, but His determined response to man's sin. The sovereign God who subjected creation to frustration still rules over it, pain and all. The laws of genetics and disease are as much under His control as are the laws of meteorology. My purpose is not to deal with the problem of pain theologically but to help us deal with it on the level of faith, of trust in God. The first thing we have to do in order to trust God is determine if God is in control, if He is sovereign over the physical area of our lives. If He is not—if illness and afflictions "just happen"—then, of course, there is no basis for trusting God. But if God is sovereign in this area, then we can trust Him without understanding all the theological issues involved in the problem of pain.

CHILDLESSNESS

Another common arena of struggle with trusting God is in the area of childlessness. Many couples pray for years without any results for children to be born of their marriage. Here again, however, the Bible consistently affirms that God is in control. It was said of Hannah that "the LORD had closed her womb" (1 Samuel 1:5), while He opened the womb of Leah (see Genesis 29:31). Sarah, Abraham's wife, said, "The LORD has kept me from having children" (Genesis 16:2). The angel of the Lord said to Samson's mother before his birth, "You are sterile and childless, but you are going to conceive and have a son" (Judges 13:3). The angel of the Lord also said to Zechariah, "Your prayer has been heard. Your wife Elizabeth will bear you a son" (Luke 1:13).

All of these Scripture passages teach us that God controls the conception of children. In fact Psalm 139:13 goes a step further and says that "[God] knit me together in my mother's womb." God not only controls the conception, He even superintends the formation of that little one in his or her mother's womb. Truly God exercises a sovereign and loving control over all the works of His creation, including that which happens to our physical bodies.

How then can we trust Him in the midst of the pain of affliction or disease, or the heartache of barrenness or of a child born with a major birth defect? If God is in control, why does

He allow these things to happen? In chapter 1, I said that in order to trust God in adversity we must believe that God is completely sovereign, perfect in love, and infinite in wisdom. We have not yet studied the love and wisdom of God, but for now consider just one passage of Scripture.

> For men are not cast off
>   by the Lord forever.
> Though he brings grief, he will show compassion,
>   so great is his unfailing love.
> For he does not willingly bring affliction
>   or grief to the children of men.
> LAMENTATIONS 3:31-33

God does not willingly bring affliction or grief to us. He does not delight in causing us to experience pain or heartache. He always has a purpose for the grief He brings or allows to come into our lives. Most often we do not know what that purpose is, but it is enough to know that His infinite wisdom and perfect love have determined that the particular sorrow is best for us. God never wastes pain. He always uses it to accomplish His purpose. And His purpose is for His glory and our good. Therefore, we can trust Him when our hearts are aching or our bodies are racked with pain.

Trusting God in the midst of our pain and heartache means that we *accept* it from Him. There is a vast difference between acceptance and either resignation or submission. We can resign ourselves to a difficult situation, simply because we see no other alternative. Many people do that all the time. Or we can submit to the sovereignty of God in our circumstances with a certain amount of reluctance. But to truly accept our pain and heartache has the connotation of willingness. An attitude of acceptance says that we trust God, that He loves us and knows what is best for us.

Acceptance does not mean that we do not pray for physical healing, or for the conception and birth of a little one to our marriage. We should indeed pray for those things, but we should pray in a trusting way. We should realize that, though God can do all things, for infinitely wise and loving reasons, He may not do that which we pray that He will do. How do we know how long to pray? As long as we can pray trustingly, with an attitude of acceptance of His will, we should pray as long as the desire remains.

As I have written this chapter, I well realize that I myself have never experienced the tragedies I am writing about. I have never stood as a farmer and watched the hail destroy my crop, nor have I sifted through the rubble of a house destroyed by a tornado. I have never experienced intense physical pain over a prolonged time, nor have I sorrowed over a child born with an incurable birth defect. The physical infirmities I do have—such as my partial deafness and my vision problem—are minor compared to the infirmities of others. So I am admittedly writing beyond my experience.

But I know that God does not need my experience to validate the truthfulness of His Word. The fact of His sovereign control over nature was affirmed in His Word long before I arrived on the scene and will still stand secure long after I have departed. Our trust in God must be based, not on someone else's experience, but upon what God has told us about Himself in His Word.

Many hundreds of years ago, the prophet Habakkuk struggled with the question of "Where is God?" in all the evil that he saw around him. He finally came to the conclusion that, though he did not understand what God was doing, he would trust Him. His affirmation of trust, couched in the language of a world falling apart around him, would be a fitting example for us to follow as we struggle with God's sovereignty over nature. Habakkuk said:

> Though the fig tree does not bud
> and there are no grapes on the vines,
> though the olive crop fails
> and the fields produce no food,
> though there are no sheep in the pen
> and no cattle in the stalls,
> yet I will rejoice in the Lord,
> I will be joyful in God my Savior.

HABAKKUK 3:17-18

CHAPTER SEVEN

GOD'S SOVEREIGNTY AND OUR RESPONSIBILITY

But we prayed to our God and posted a guard day and night to meet this threat.

NEHEMIAH 4:9

As we have examined the Scriptures to see what they teach us about the sovereignty of God, I have occasionally injected a word of caution about the dangers of misusing or abusing the teaching of His sovereignty. In this chapter, we want to address that problem in greater detail lest we unconsciously begin to think that God's sovereignty negates any responsibility of ours to live responsible and prudent lives.

There is an old story about a man who carried the doctrine of God's sovereignty to such an extreme that he drifted into a sort of divine fatalism. One day, walking down a flight of stairs, he carelessly stumbled and fell headlong to the bottom of the staircase. Picking himself up, he gingerly felt his bruises and said to himself, "Well, I'm glad that one is over."

You and I, if we are not careful, can, like the foolish man in the story, drift into a fatalistic attitude about the sovereignty of God. A student who fails an important exam tries to excuse himself by saying, "Well, God is sovereign, and He determined that I should fail that exam." A driver can cause an auto accident and, in his own mind, evade his carelessness by attributing the accident to the sovereignty of God. Obviously both attitudes are unbiblical and foolish, yet we can easily drift into them.

SOVEREIGNTY AND PRAYER

In the last chapter we looked at God's sovereign control over the weather and other forces of nature. As a frequent air traveler, I have been affected many times by weather unsuitable for flying. One afternoon, driving home in a snowstorm, I was reflecting on the fact that our airport was closed because of the storm and that I was scheduled to leave the next morning to speak at a weekend conference. But I said to myself and to God, "God, I know that You are in control of this storm, and You are also in control of the conference I am to speak at. If you want me to be at that conference tomorrow night, You will move this storm out so our airport can reopen tomorrow morning. I'm not going to be anxious about it."

Now, I have to admit that such an attitude of refusing to be anxious was progress for me in coping with adverse flying weather. After arriving home, I announced to my wife my decision not to be anxious about whether I would be able to leave on schedule the following morning. She looked at me with a smile and said, "Don't be anxious, but pray about it."

I thought to myself, *How foolish I was.* I had been concentrating so strongly on God's sovereignty over the weather that I completely neglected His express command to pray. He does indeed say to us, "Do not be anxious about anything," but then immediately follows that with, "but in everything, by prayer and petition, with thanksgiving, present your requests to God" (Philippians 4:6).

God was certainly in sovereign control of the snowstorm that had closed our airport. But the knowledge of His sovereignty is meant to be an encouragement to pray, not an excuse to lapse into a sort of pious fatalism.

The fourth chapter of Acts tells about Peter and John being threatened by the Jewish Sanhedrin and commanded not to speak or teach at all in the name of Jesus. When Peter and John reported this to the other believers, they raised their voices together in prayer:

> "Sovereign Lord," they said, "you made the heaven and
> the earth and the sea, and everything in them. . . . They
> [Herod, Pontius Pilate, the Gentiles, and Jews] did what
> your power and will had decided beforehand should
> happen. Now, Lord, consider their threats and enable
> your servants to speak your word with great boldness."
> ACTS 4:24, 28-29

The disciples believed in the sovereignty of God. But God's sovereignty to them was a reason and an encouragement to pray. They believed because God was sovereign He was able to answer their prayers. They acknowledged God's sovereign purpose in events past (for example, the Crucifixion), but they did not presume to know the divine decree about future events. They only knew Christ had commanded them to be His witnesses in Jerusalem, and in all Judea and Samaria, and to the ends of the earth. So they prayed, confident that the sovereign God, who had commanded them to be witnesses, was able to clear away the obstacles to their obedience.

Prayer assumes the sovereignty of God. If God is not sovereign, we have no assurance that He is able to answer our prayers. Our prayers would become nothing more than wishes. But while God's sovereignty, along with His wisdom and love, is the foundation of our trust in Him, prayer is the expression of that trust.

The Puritan preacher Thomas Lye, in a sermon entitled "How Are We to Live by Faith on Divine Providence?" said, "As prayer without faith is but a beating of the air, so trust without prayer [is] but a presumptuous bravado. He that promises to give, and bids us trust his promises, commands us to pray, and expects obedience to his commands. He will give, but not without our asking."[1]

The apostle Paul, while imprisoned in Rome, wrote to his friend Philemon, "Prepare a guest room for me, because I hope to be restored to you in answer to your prayers" (Philemon 1:22). Paul did not presume to know God's secret will. He *hoped* to be restored. He did not say, "I will be restored." But he did know that God in His sovereignty was well able to effect his release, so he asked Philemon to pray. Prayer was the expression of his confidence in the sovereignty of God.

John Flavel was another Puritan preacher and a prolific writer (six volumes of collected works). He wrote a classic treatise entitled *The Mystery of Providence*, first published in 1678.[2] It is instructive to note that Flavel begins this treatise on the sovereign providence of God with a discourse on Psalm 57:2, "I cry out to God Most High, to God, who fulfills his purpose for me." That is, Flavel says to us, because God is sovereign, we should pray. God's sovereignty does not negate our responsibility to pray, but rather makes it possible to pray with confidence.

SOVEREIGNTY AND PRUDENCE

Just as God's sovereignty does not set aside our responsibility to pray, it also does not negate our responsibility to act prudently. To act prudently, in this context, means to use all legitimate, biblical means at our disposal to avoid harm to ourselves or others and to bring about what we believe to be the right course of events.

An illustration of using all proper means to avoid harm is seen in the life of David as he continually evaded Saul while Saul was determined to kill him. David had already been anointed to succeed Saul as king (see 1 Samuel 16:13). And as we have just seen in Psalm 57:2, David was confident that God would fulfill His purpose for him. Yet David took all the precautions he could to avoid being killed by Saul. He did not presume upon the sovereignty of God but rather acted prudently in dependence upon God to bless his efforts.

We see in Paul's life an illustration of prudent action to bring about the right course of events. The story involves Paul's trip to Rome and the shipwreck that occurred on the island of Malta, recorded in Acts 27. After many days of being battered by a storm of hurricane force, and when everyone had given up all hope of being saved, Paul stood before them and said:

> But now I urge you to keep up your courage, because not one of you will be lost; only the ship will be destroyed. Last night an angel of the God whose I am and whom I serve stood beside me and said, "Do not be afraid, Paul. You must stand trial before Caesar; and God has graciously given you the lives of all who sail with you." So keep up your courage, men, for I have faith in God that it will happen just as he told me. Nevertheless, we must run aground on some island. ACTS 27:22-26

Paul not only trusted in the sovereignty of God, he had an express revelation from heaven that no life would be lost in the shipwreck. Yet some time later, when he saw the sailors trying to escape from the ship with the lifeboat, he said to the Roman centurion, "Unless these men stay with the ship, you cannot be saved" (Acts 27:31). Paul apparently realized that the presence of the skilled sailors was necessary for the safety of the passengers, even at that point. Therefore, he took prudent action to bring about that which God by divine revelation had already promised would certainly come to pass. He did not confuse God's sovereignty with his responsibility to act prudently.

Paul did not consider God's sovereign purpose a reason to neglect his duty even though, in that instance, God's purpose had been revealed to him by an angel from heaven. In our circumstances today, we do not know what God's sovereign purpose is in a specific situation. We should be even more aware not to use God's sovereignty as an excuse to shirk the duties that He has commanded in the Scriptures. God usually works through means, and He intends that we use the means He has placed at our disposal.

When Nehemiah was rebuilding the wall around Jerusalem, he and his people faced the threat of an armed attack from their enemies (see Nehemiah 4:7-8). Nehemiah's response was to pray and post a guard—prayer and prudence (see verse 9). In addition the text says, "From that day on, half of my men did the work, while the other half were equipped with spears, shields, bows and armor." Not only that but, "Those who carried materials did their work with one hand and held a weapon in the other, and each of the builders wore his sword at his side as he worked" (verses 16-18).

Nehemiah trusted in the sovereignty of God. He said, "Our God will fight for us!" (verse 20). But he also used all available means, believing that God in His sovereignty would bless those means.

One of the most basic means of prudence that God has given to us is prayer. We must not only pray for His overruling providence in our lives as David did (see Psalm 57:2), but we must also pray for wisdom to rightly understand our circumstances and use the means He has given us. When the Gibeonites sought to deceive Joshua and the men of Israel, they came with worn clothing and dried-out bread, pretending to have come from far away. The Scripture says, "The men of Israel sampled their provisions but did not inquire of the LORD" (Joshua 9:14). As a result they were deceived by the Gibeonites and made a treaty with them, when they should have destroyed them. They were not prudent because they did not pray and ask God for wisdom and insight to understand the situation.

Another means of prudence God has given us is the opportunity to seek wise and godly counsel. Proverbs 15:22 says, "Plans fail for lack of counsel, but with many advisers they succeed." However, Proverbs 16:9 tells us that a person's plans succeed only within the sovereign will of God. All the wise counsel in the world cannot enable our plans to succeed contrary to the sovereign will of God. But God uses the wise counsel of others to bring our plans into line with His sovereign will. Once again, we must not confuse duty—in this case, to seek wise counsel—with God's sovereign will.

PRAYER AND PRUDENCE

Earlier, I referred briefly to Nehemiah's use of prayer and prudence, "But we prayed to our God and posted a guard day and night to meet this threat" (Nehemiah 4:9). Prayer is the acknowledgment of God's sovereignty and of our dependence upon Him to act on our behalf. Prudence is the acknowledgment of our responsibility to use all legitimate means. We must not separate these two. We see this beautifully illustrated for us in the following passage of Scripture:

> The Reubenites, the Gadites and the half-tribe of Manasseh had 44,760 men ready for military service— able-bodied men who could handle shield and sword,

who could use a bow, and who were trained for battle. They waged war against the Hagrites, Jetur, Naphish and Nodab. They were helped in fighting them, and God handed the Hagrites and all their allies over to them, because they cried out to him during the battle. He answered their prayers, because they trusted in him.

1 CHRONICLES 5:18-20

The warriors described in this passage were able-bodied and well-trained. They were prudent; they had taken all precautions to be able to fight when they needed to. But they did not trust in their ability and training. They cried out to God, and He answered their prayers because they trusted in Him. God sovereignly intervened. He handed all their enemies over to them because they prayed.

All of our plans, all of our efforts, and all of our prudence are of no avail unless God prospers those means. Psalm 127:1 says,

Unless the LORD builds the house,
    its builders labor in vain.
Unless the LORD watches over the city,
    the watchmen stand guard in vain.

In this passage there is the concept of both offensive and defensive efforts—of both building for progress and watching against destruction. In a sense, the verse sums up all of our responsibilities in life. Whether it be in the physical, the mental, or the spiritual, we should always be building and watching. And Psalm 127:1 says none of those efforts will prosper unless God intervenes in them.

Note how strongly the psalmist described the necessity of God's intervention in our efforts. He does not say, "Unless God *blesses* or *helps* the builders and the watchmen, their efforts are in vain." Rather he speaks in terms of God Himself building the house and watching over the city. At the same time, there is, of course, no suggestion in the text that God *replaces* the builders and the watchmen. The obvious meaning is that in every respect we are dependent upon God to enable us and prosper our efforts.

We must depend upon God to do *for* us what we cannot do for ourselves. We must, to the same degree, depend on Him to *enable us* to do what we must do for ourselves. The farmer must use all of his skills, experience, and resources to produce a harvest. Yet he is utterly dependent upon forces outside of himself. Those forces of nature—moisture, insects, sun—are, as we have already seen, under the direct sovereign control of God. The farmer is dependent upon God to control nature so that his crop will grow. But he is just as dependent upon God to enable him to plow, plant, fertilize, and cultivate properly. From where did he get his skills, his ability to learn from his experience, the financial resources to buy the equipment and fertilizer he uses? Where does even his physical strength to do his tasks come from? Are not all these things from the hand of God who "gives all men life and breath and everything else" (Acts 17:25)? In every respect, we are utterly dependent upon God.

There are times when we can do nothing, and there are times when we must work. In both instances we are equally dependent upon God. When the Israelites were in the desert, they were consciously dependent upon God for both food and water. Moses said to them, "He humbled you, causing you to hunger and then feeding you with manna . . . to teach you that man does not live on bread alone but on every word that comes from the mouth of the LORD" (Deuteronomy 8:3). The Israelites had to learn that they could not simply dig into their food supplies to eat whenever they desired. God reduced them to a conscious dependence upon His daily provision.

The time would come, however, when they would be in "a land where bread will not be scarce and you will lack nothing" (Deuteronomy 8:9). Then, Moses warned them, they were not to trust in their own ability as farmers, saying to themselves, "My power and the strength of my hands have produced this wealth for me." Rather he warned them to "remember the LORD your God, for it is he who gives you the ability to produce wealth" (Deuteronomy 8:17-18).

Sometimes, God reduces us to a *conscious*, utter dependence upon Him. A loved one is desperately ill, beyond the expertise and skill of medical service. Unemployment has persisted to the point that the cupboard is bare and no job prospects are in sight. At such times we readily recognize our dependence and cry out to God for His intervention. But we are just as dependent on God when the physician diagnoses a routine illness and prescribes a successful medication. We are just as dependent when the paycheck comes regularly and all our material needs are met.

At the same time we are responsible. The Bible never allows us to use our utter dependence on God as an excuse for indolence. Ecclesiastes 10:18 says, "If a man is lazy, the rafters sag; if his hands are idle, the house leaks." And again, "A sluggard does not plow in season; so at harvest time he looks but finds nothing" (Proverbs 20:4). We are absolutely dependent upon God, but, at the same time, we are responsible to diligently use whatever means are appropriate for the occasion.

The man in our story at the beginning of the chapter should have been more careful walking down the stairs. He might have paid attention to the "please use the handrail" notice. He cannot blame a divine fatalism for his fall. Neither can the student who fails her exam, nor the worker who loses his job for lack of diligence, nor the person who becomes ill because of poor health habits. Our *duty* is found in the *revealed* will of God in the Scriptures. Our *trust* must be in the *sovereign* will of God, as He works in the ordinary circumstances of our daily lives for our good and His glory.

There is no conflict between trusting God and accepting our responsibility. Thomas Lye, the Puritan preacher quoted earlier in the chapter, said, "Trust . . . [uses] such means as God prescribes for the bringing about his appointed end. . . . God's means are to be used, as well as God's blessing to be expected."[3]

And Alexander Carson made a similar observation when he said, "Let us learn . . . that as God has promised to protect us and provide for us, it is through the means of his appointment, vigilance, prudence, and industry, that we are to look for these blessings."[4]

OUR FAILURES AND GOD'S SOVEREIGNTY

We have seen that God's sovereignty does not do away with our duty to act responsibly and prudently on all occasions. But what about the other side of the question? Does failure on our part to act prudently frustrate the sovereign plan of God? The Scriptures never indicate that God is frustrated to any degree by our failure to act as we should. In His infinite wisdom, God's sovereign plan includes our failures and even our sins.

When Mordecai asked Queen Esther to intercede with King Xerxes on behalf of the Jews, she demurred with the explanation that she could enter the king's presence unbidden only on the threat of death (see Esther 4:10-11). However, Mordecai sent word back to her, "For if you remain silent at this time, relief and deliverance for the Jews will arise from another place, but you and your father's family will perish. And who knows but that you have come to royal position for such a time as this?" (Esther 4:14). The key phrase in Mordecai's response is "relief and deliverance for the Jews will arise from another place."

God, in His infinite wisdom and resources, was not limited to Esther's response. The options available to God to bring about deliverance for the Jews were as infinite as His wisdom and power. He literally did not need Esther's cooperation. But in this instance, He chose to use her. Mordecai's closing argument to Esther, "And who knows but that you have come to royal position for such a time as this?" assumes that God uses people and means to accomplish His sovereign purpose.

As subsequent events proved, God had indeed raised up Esther to accomplish His purpose. But He could just as easily have raised up someone else or used an altogether different means. God usually works through ordinary events (as opposed to miracles) and the voluntary actions of people. But He always provides the means necessary and guides them by His unseen hand. He is sovereign, and He cannot be frustrated by our failure to act or by our actions, which in themselves are sinful. We must always remember, however, that God still holds us accountable for the very sins that He uses to accomplish His purpose.

As we conclude these studies on God's sovereignty and turn our attention to His wisdom and love, we need to realize once again that there is no conflict in the Bible between His sovereignty and our responsibility. Both concepts are taught with equal force and with never an attempt to "reconcile" them. Let us hold equally to both, doing our duty as it is revealed to us in the Scriptures and trusting God to sovereignly work out His purpose in us and through us.

CHAPTER EIGHT

THE WISDOM OF GOD

Oh, the depth of the riches of the wisdom and knowledge
of God! How unsearchable his judgments,
and his paths beyond tracing out!

ROMANS 11:33

"At 9:15 a.m., just after the children had settled into their first lesson on the morning of 21 October 1966, a waste tip from a South Wales [coal mine] slid into the quiet mining community of Aberfan. Of all the heartrending tragedies of that day, none was worse than the fate of the village Junior School. The black slime slithered down the man-made hillside and oozed its way into the classrooms. Unable to escape, five teachers and 109 children died.

"A clergyman being interviewed by a BBC reporter at the time of [the tragedy, in response] . . . to the inevitable question about God [said], 'Well . . . I suppose we have to admit that this is one of those occasions when the Almighty made a mistake.'"[1]

True Christians will be appalled at the clergyman's flippant and blasphemous statement about God. But do we not sometimes wonder, when calamity of some kind strikes us, if God has not made a mistake in our lives? I think of another statement—not flippant but heartfelt—made by a sincere Christian watching a child struggle with cancer: "I sure hope God knows what

He's doing in this." Anyone who has dealt deeply with adversity can probably identify with the doubts this person struggled with.

When we stop and think about it, we know in our heart of hearts that God does not make any mistakes in our lives or in the villages of South Wales or anywhere else. God does know what He is doing. God is infinite in His wisdom. He always knows what is best for us and what is the best way to bring about that result.

Wisdom is commonly defined as good judgment or the ability to develop the best course of action or the best response to a given situation. We all recognize that human wisdom at its best is fallible. The wisest men or women simply do not have all the facts of a given situation, nor are they able to predict with certainty the results of a given course of action. All of us from time to time agonize over some important decisions, trying to determine the best course of action.

But God never has to agonize over a decision. He does not even have to deliberate within Himself or consult others outside of Himself. His wisdom is intuitive, infinite, and infallible: "His understanding has no limit" (Psalm 147:5).

Nineteenth-century theologian J. L. Dagg described wisdom "as consisting in the selection of the best end of action, and the adoption of the best means for the accomplishment of this end." He then said, "God is infinitely wise, because he selects the best possible end of action . . . [and] because he adopts the best possible means for the accomplishment of the end which he has in view."[2]

The best possible end of all of God's actions is ultimately His glory. That is, all that God does or allows in all of His creation will ultimately serve His glory. As John Piper says in his book *Desiring God*, "The chief end of *God* is to glorify God and enjoy himself forever."[3] One has only to thumb through the New Testament looking at passages with the word *glory* in them to agree with John Piper that the chief end of God is His own glory. (Just for starters look up John 15:8; Romans 1:21; 11:36; 1 Corinthians 10:31; Ephesians 1:12, 14; Revelation 4:11; 5:13; 15:4.)

Everything that is included in the concept of God's glory is a mystery we cannot fully comprehend. But we do know that it involves a display of all His grandeur and His wondrous perfections, including the perfection of His wisdom.

BEAUTY OUT OF ASHES

As we watch tragic events unfolding, or more particularly as we experience adversity ourselves, we often are prone to ask God *why*. The reason we ask is because we do not see any possible good to us or glory to God that can come from the particular adverse circumstances that have come upon us or our loved ones. But is not the wisdom of God—thus the glory of God— more eminently displayed in bringing good out of calamity than out of blessing?

The wisdom of the chess player is displayed more in winning over a capable opponent than over a novice. The wisdom of the general is displayed more in defeating a superior army than in subduing an inferior one. Even more so, the wisdom of God is displayed when He brings good to us and glory to Himself out of confusion and calamity rather than out of pleasant times.

There is no question that God's people live in a hostile world. We have an enemy, the Devil, who "prowls around like a roaring lion looking for someone to devour" (1 Peter 5:8). He wants to sift us like wheat as he did Peter (see Luke 22:31), or make us curse God as he tried to get Job to do. God does not spare us from the ravages of disease, heartache, and disappointment of this sin-cursed world. But God is able to take all of these elements—the bad as well as the good—and make full use of every one.

As someone years ago said, "A lesser wisdom than the Divine would feel impelled to forbid, to circumvent or to resist the outworking of these hellish plans. It is a fact that often God's people try to do this themselves, or cry unceasingly to the Lord that He may do it. So it is that prayers often seem to lie unanswered. For we are being handled by a wisdom which is perfect, a wisdom which can achieve what it [intends] by taking hold of things and people which are meant for evil and making them work together for good."[4]

God's infinite wisdom then is displayed in bringing good out of evil, beauty out of ashes. It is displayed in turning all the forces of evil that rage against His children into good for them. But the good that He brings about is often different from the good we envision.

HOLINESS OUT OF ADVERSITY

Romans 8:28, "And we know that in all things God works for the good of those who love him, who have been called according to his purpose," is an oft-quoted verse. But we often fail to note that the following verse helps us understand what the "good" of verse 28 is. Verse 29 begins with the word *for*, indicating that it is a continuation and amplification of the thought of verse 28. It says, "For those God foreknew he also predestined to be conformed to the likeness of his Son, that he might be the firstborn among many brothers."

The good that God works for in our lives is conformity to the likeness of His Son. It is not necessarily comfort or happiness but conformity to Christ in ever-increasing measure in this life and in its fullness in eternity.

We see this same thought in Hebrews 12:10, "Our fathers

disciplined us for a little while as they thought best; but God disciplines us for our good, that we may share in his holiness." To share in God's holiness is an equivalent expression to being conformed to the likeness of Christ. God knows exactly what He intends we become and He knows exactly what circumstances, both good and bad, are necessary to produce that result in our lives.

Note the contrast the author of Hebrews draws between the finite, fallible wisdom of human parents and the infinite, infallible wisdom of God. He says, "Our fathers disciplined us for a little while as they thought best." As a father, I can readily identify with the phrase "as they thought best." Sometimes in rearing our children we agonized over the proper discipline, both in kind and amount. And even when we thought we knew what was best, there were many times when we erred.

But, the writer says without qualification, God disciplines us for our good. There is no agonizing by God, no hoping He has made the right decision, no wondering what is really best for us. God makes no mistakes. He knows infallibly with infinite wisdom what combination of good and bad circumstances will bring us more and more into sharing His holiness. He never puts too much of the "salt" of adversity into the recipe of our lives. His blending of adversity and blessing is always exactly right for us.

The author of Hebrews readily admits that discipline is painful (see verse 11). But he also assures us it is profitable. It produces "a harvest of righteousness and peace." The purpose of God's discipline is not to punish us but to transform us. He has already meted out punishment for our sins on Jesus at Calvary: "The punishment that brought us peace was upon him" (Isaiah 53:5). But we must be transformed more and more into the likeness of Christ. That is the purpose of discipline.

The psalmist said, "It was good for me to be afflicted so that

I might learn your decrees" (Psalm 119:71). He is speaking of experiential learning. We can learn God's will for our character intellectually through reading and studying the Scriptures—and we should do that. That is where change begins, as our minds are renewed. But real change—down in the depth of our souls—is produced as the tenets of Scripture are worked out in real life. This usually involves adversity. We may admire and even desire the character trait of patience, but we will never learn patience until we have been treated unjustly and learn experientially to "suffer long" (the meaning of patience) the one who treats us unjustly.

If you stop and think about it, you will realize that most godly character traits can only be developed through adversity. The kind of love that gives freely of itself at great cost to itself can only be learned when we are confronted with situations that call forth a sacrificial love. The fruit of the Spirit that is called joy cannot be learned in the midst of circumstances that produce mere "natural" happiness.

God in His infinite wisdom knows exactly what adversity we need to grow more and more into the likeness of His Son. He not only knows *what* we need but *when* we need it and *how* best to bring it to pass in our lives. He is the perfect teacher or coach. His discipline is always exactly suited for our needs. He never overtrains us by allowing too much adversity in our lives.

GOD NEVER EXPLAINS

Usually when we are being trained by someone in a skill, such as in athletics or music, our teacher or coach will explain to us the purpose of the particular drills he is putting us through. Though these drills may at times be tedious and even painful, we can endure them because we know their purpose and the intended end result.

But God never explains to us what He is doing, or why. There is no indication that God ever explained to Job the reasons for all of his terrible sufferings. As readers, we are taken behind the scenes to observe the spiritual warfare between God and Satan, but as far as we can tell from Scripture, God never told Job about that.

The fact is, God has not really told us, even in Scripture, why He allowed Satan to so afflict Job as he did. On the basis of the truth of Romans 8:28 (which was just as valid for Job as it is for us), we must conclude that God had a much higher purpose in allowing Satan's onslaughts against Job than merely using Job as a pawn in a "wager" between Himself and Satan. Satan's part in the drama seems to slip into oblivion. He is never again mentioned after his two challenges of God in Job 1–2. The story does not conclude with a conversation between God and Satan in which God claims "victory" over Satan.

Rather, the story concludes with a conversation between God and Job in which Job acknowledges that through his trials he has come into a new and deeper relationship with God. He said, "My ears had heard of you but now my eyes have seen you" (Job 42:5). We may conclude that this deeper relationship was one (but probably not all) of the results God had in mind all along.

Sometimes afterward we can see some of the beneficial results of adversity in our lives, but we seldom can see it during the time of the adversity. Joseph could surely see after he had become prime minister of Egypt some of the results of the affliction God had allowed in his life, but he certainly could not see it while going through it. To him the whole painful process must have seemed devoid of any meaning and very contrary to his expectations of the future, as given to him through his dreams.

But whether we see beneficial results in this life or not, we are still called upon to trust God that in His love He wills what is best for us and in His wisdom He knows how to bring it about. I think of a dear friend who for more than thirty years has passed through one adversity after another—incredible physical problems in the family, numerous financial difficulties, and family heartaches. As far as I can tell, no apparent "good" has come out of any of these adversities. There has been no happy ending as in the case of Joseph or Job. Yet, in a letter received from her while this chapter was being written, this friend said, "I know God makes no mistakes: 'As for God, His way is perfect.'"

So we should never ask *why* in the sense of demanding that God explain or justify His actions or what He permits in our lives. Margaret Clarkson said, "We may not demand of a sovereign Creator that He explain Himself to His creatures. . . . God had good and sufficient reasons for His actions; we trust His sovereign wisdom and love."[5]

When I say we should never ask *why*, I am not talking about the reactive and spontaneous cry of anguish when calamity first befalls us or one we love. Rather, I am speaking of the persistent and demanding *why* that has an accusatory tone toward God in it. The former is a natural human reaction; the latter is a sinful human reaction. Three of the psalms begin with *why*: "Why, O LORD, do you stand far off?" "Why have you forsaken me?" "Why have you rejected us forever?" (Psalms 10; 22; 74). But each of those psalms ends on a note of trust in God. The psalm writers did not allow their *why*s to drag on. They did not allow them to take root and grow into accusations against God. Their *why*s were really cries of anguish, a natural reaction to pain.

By contrast, there are sixteen *why*s in the book of Job, according to author Don Baker.[6] Sixteen times Job asked God *why*. He is persistent and petulant. He is accusatory toward God. And, as has been observed by many, God never answered Job's *why*. Instead He answered *who*.

Pastor Baker, in his book on Job, says, "I have long since quit seeking the answer to that question [why?] in my own life. . . . God owes me no explanation. He has the right to do what He wants, when He wants, and how He wants. *Why?* Because He's God. . . . Job didn't need to know why these things happened as they did—he just needed to know Who was responsible and Who was in control. He just needed to know God."[7]

In using Job as an example of asking *why* in a bad or sinful sense, I do not mean to denigrate Job. I know that I have asked that question many times under obviously far less trying circumstances than the calamities that overcame Job. God Himself commended Job's righteousness to us. But God was not only dealing with Job; He recorded those dealings for our benefit that we might learn from them. And it seems clear that one of the lessons God wants us to learn from Job's experience is the lesson Pastor Baker learned: to stop asking *why*.

Just as God has used David's prayer of confession and repentance of his adultery in Psalm 51 to minister to His people down through the centuries, so God has used Job's struggles with doubt about the goodness of God to minister to His people. I still recall my first conscious struggle with the goodness of God some thirty-four years prior to writing this book. It was a passage from the book of Job, where God through Elihu confronts Job with his audacity, that met my need at the time, causing me to realize and repent of my own accusations against God. Though we don't want to be critical of Job, we do want to learn from him about the sinfulness of asking a demanding *why* of God.

But though we should never ask a demanding *why*, we may and should ask God to enable us to understand what He may be teaching us through a particular experience. But even here we must be careful that we are not seeking to satisfy our souls by finding some spiritual "good" in the adversity. Rather we must trust God that He is working in the experience for our good, even when we see no beneficial results. We must learn to trust God when He doesn't tell us why, when we don't understand what He is doing.

GOD'S WAYS ARE INCOMPREHENSIBLE

Sometimes we come to the place where we do not demand of God that He explain Himself, but we try to determine or comprehend for ourselves what God is doing. We are unwilling to live without rational reasons for what is happening to us or those we love. We are almost insatiable in our quest for the *why* of the adversity that has come upon us. But this is a futile as well as an untrusting task. God's ways, being the ways of infinite wisdom, simply cannot be comprehended by our finite minds.

God Himself said through Isaiah,

> "For my thoughts are not your thoughts,
>   neither are your ways my ways,"
>   declares the LORD.
> "As the heavens are higher than the earth,
>   so are my ways higher than your ways
>   and my thoughts than your thoughts."
>
> ISAIAH 55:8-9

In his commentary on Isaiah, Edward J. Young said of this passage, "The implication is that just as the heavens are so high above the earth that by human standards their height cannot be measured, so also are God's ways and thoughts so above those of man that they cannot be grasped by man in their fullness. In other words, the ways and thoughts of God are incomprehensible to man."[8]

The apostle Paul states the same truth in his doxology at the end of Romans 11 when he exclaims in amazement,

Oh, the depth of the riches of the wisdom and
knowledge of God!
How unsearchable his judgments,
and his paths beyond tracing out!

ROMANS 11:33

The Williams translation of the New Testament brings out perhaps even more forcefully the depth of this passage. It says in verses 33 and 34,

How fathomless the depths of God's resources, wisdom, and knowledge! How unsearchable His decisions, and how mysterious [footnote: literally, untraceable] His methods! For who has ever understood the thoughts of the Lord, or has ever been His adviser?[9]

God's wisdom is fathomless, His decisions are unsearchable, His methods are mysterious and untraceable. No one has ever even understood His mind, let alone advised Him on the proper course of action. How futile and even arrogant for us to seek to determine what God is doing in a particular event or circumstance. We simply cannot search out the reasons behind His decisions or trace out the ways by which He brings those decisions to pass.

If we are to experience peace in our souls in times of adversity, we must come to the place where we truly believe that God's ways are simply beyond us and stop asking Him *why* or even trying to determine it ourselves. This may seem like an intellectual "cop-out," a refusal to deal with the really tough issues of life. In fact, it is just the opposite. It is a surrender to the truth about God and our circumstances as it is revealed to us by God Himself in His inspired Word.

C. H. Spurgeon, again in his sermon on divine providence,

said, "Providence is wonderfully intricate. Ah! you want always to see through Providence, do you not? You never will, I assure you. You have not eyes good enough. You want to see what good that affliction was to you; you must believe it. You want to see how it can bring good to the soul; you may be enabled in a little time; but you can not see it now; you must believe it. Honor God by trusting him."[10]

In Job's final response to God, he humbly acknowledges God's unfathomable ways. He says,

> You asked, "Who is this that obscures my counsel
>   without knowledge?"
> Surely I spoke of things I did not understand,
>   things too wonderful for me to know.

JOB 42:3

God's ways, said Job, were too wonderful for him to know or understand. When he saw God in His great majesty and sovereignty, he repented of his arrogant questioning in "dust and ashes." He stopped asking and simply trusted.

David, in a similar manner, bowed to the sovereign purposes and infinite wisdom of God. He said,

> My heart is not proud, O LORD,
>   my eyes are not haughty;
> I do not concern myself with great matters
>   or things too wonderful for me.

PSALM 131:1

The great and wonderful things referred to are the secret purposes of God and His infinite means for accomplishing them. David did not exercise his heart in seeking to understand them. Instead he stilled and quieted his soul in submission and trust toward God. If we are to honor God by trusting Him, and if we are to find peace for ourselves, we must come to the place where we can honestly say, "God, I do not have to understand. I will just trust You."

DON'T INTERPRET, BUT LEARN!

Because God's wisdom is infinite and His ways inscrutable to us, we should also be very careful in seeking to interpret the ways of God in His providence, especially in particular events. Additionally, we need to be cautious of others who offer themselves as interpreters about the why and wherefore of all that is happening. Be wary of those who say, "God let this happen so that you might learn such and such a lesson." The fact is we do not *know* what God is doing through a particular set of circumstances or events.

This does not mean we should not seek to learn from God's providence as well as His revealed will in Scripture. Quite the contrary. As we observed earlier in the chapter, the psalmist learned God's decrees experientially through affliction (see Psalm 119:71). The people of Israel also learned through God's adverse providence in their lives. Deuteronomy 8:3 says,

> He humbled you, causing you to hunger and then feeding you with manna, which neither you nor your fathers had known, to teach you that man does not live on bread alone but on every word that comes from the mouth of the LORD.

God taught the nation through His divine providence—through putting them in a situation where they could not simply go to the cupboard for their daily bread—that they were utterly dependent upon Him. God was leading the nation into a land where material provision would be "naturally" plentiful (see Deuteronomy 8:7-9). He knew they would be tempted by the pride of their own hearts to say, "My power and the strength of my hands have produced this wealth for me" (verse 17). So before they entered the land, God taught them of their dependence through His divine providence.

Some months before writing this chapter, I was invited to speak to a Christian convention on a particular theme. One day in the course of reading through 2 Timothy, the Holy Spirit clearly opened up a passage that spoke so beautifully to the theme of the convention. Scrapping the preparation I had already done, I sat down and quickly prepared three messages, about which I was very excited. But then I subtly became very proud of them. I began to entertain sinful, prideful thoughts of how well-thought-of I would be as a speaker because of these exciting messages. I began to try to usurp some of God's glory for myself.

Shortly before the convention began, I was afflicted with a strange virus I had never had before. I was barely able to speak. I did not enjoy the convention at all. Though I gave the messages, I have no idea if anyone profited from them or not. Through those circumstances I learned experientially what God has said, "I will not give my glory to another" (Isaiah 42:8). I had memorized that verse years before and knew its truth intellectually. But through that adversity I learned it experientially. I could then say with the psalmist, "It was good for me to be afflicted so that I might learn your decrees" (Psalm 119:71).

GOD'S WISDOM IS GREATER THAN OUR ADVERSARIES'

God's wisdom is not only as high above *ours* as the heavens are above the earth, it is also higher than the wisdom and cunning of our adversaries. This should be a great comfort to us. I personally have, at least to this point in my life, found adversity from contrary circumstances easier to bear than that which comes from the hands of other people. David apparently felt the same way. In 2 Samuel 24:14, he said, "I am in deep distress. Let us fall into the hands of the LORD, for his mercy is great; but do not let me fall into the hands of men."

Other people for various reasons may plan and scheme to treat us unjustly, to take advantage of us, or to "use" us for their own selfish ends. But Proverbs 21:30 says, "There is no wisdom, no insight, no plan that can succeed against the LORD." Therefore we can say in the words of Paul, "If God is for us, who can be against us?" (Romans 8:31). Even the most nefarious schemes of our adversaries can only accomplish what God has sovereignly ordained for us and in His infinite wisdom skillfully brings to pass.

Joseph's brothers thought they were getting rid of their brother of whom they were exceedingly envious. But God planned all along to use their scheme to send Joseph ahead of them to be their provider during the seven years of famine. They intended their actions for evil, but God intended them for good.

Saul sought to kill David because David was receiving more praise for his military prowess than was Saul. But God used those months and years, when David was hiding from Saul, to build into David the character that made him a great king and a man after God's own heart. Many of the most meaningful psalms were apparently written during those months. One of my favorites, Psalm 34, was written during a time when David was reduced to acting as an insane man for fear of a heathen king. Yet that is the psalm I most frequently turn to when I struggle with discouragement. What Saul meant for evil, God meant for good.

Satan thought that by getting God to allow him to afflict

Job, he would thereby get Job to curse God to His face. But he succeeded only in being an instrument to bring Job into a deeper and more reverent relationship with God.

Satan was given permission to afflict Paul with a thorn in the flesh to torment him. Satan probably thought he would thereby nullify the effectiveness of Paul's ministry. Instead, he succeeded only in putting Paul in the circumstance where Paul learned experientially the sufficiency of God's grace and that His strength is made perfect in our weakness (see 2 Corinthians 12:9). Think of how many thousands of believers down through the centuries have found God's grace to be sufficient for them through meditating on God's words to Paul at that time.

God's wisdom, then, is greater than the wisdom of any of our adversaries, whether they be other people or the Devil himself. Therefore, we should not fear what they seek to do, or even succeed in doing to us. God is just as much at work in those "things" as He is in the adversities of sickness, death, financial reversal, and ravages of nature.

GOD'S WISDOM IN WORLD AFFAIRS

Going beyond our own personal circumstances, we can also say that God's infinite wisdom, directing His sovereign power, governs the world. As we look around us, it does seem that much of the world is outside of God's control and that much of what happens makes no sense. Why should 109 children suffocate under a mud slide in South Wales, or thousands die from starvation in East Africa? Why do the seemingly more "wicked" nations so frequently prosper in the arena of world affairs? Why do the rich get richer and the poor get poorer? Granted we live in a sin-cursed world, and all these things could simply be attributed to the sinfulness of mankind.

But if we accept that God is sovereign, as we saw in earlier chapters, then we must conclude that God is in control of all these sad circumstances and is guiding them with His infinite wisdom to their appointed purpose. They are not just an assortment of uncontrolled and unrelated events. Rather, they are all part of God's perfect pattern and plan, which will one day be shown to be for both His glory and the good of His church. Professor Berkouwer is again helpful when he writes,

> All facets of life are embraced in God's rule. The plurality of life is brought under one perspective. It is not that there is a confusion of countless atomistic events in all of which God's activity is manifest. There is a pivot, a centrum which unifies the diversity of His activity. The unity includes progress of events from His promise at the time of the fall to the completion of the formation of His holy people.[11]

Just as we should learn to stop asking why, or searching for rational explanations, or seeking to discover what "good" there is in our own adversities, so we must also learn to quiet our hearts in regard to God's government of the universe. We must come to the place where we can say, in the words of David, "I have stilled and quieted my soul" (Psalm 131:2) about all the tragedies that come on mankind around the world.

The Puritan John Flavel wrote,

> Believe firmly that the management of all the affairs of this world, whether public or personal, is in the hands of your all-wise God. . . . Resign up yourselves to the wisdom of God, and lean not to your own understanding. . . . When Melancthon was oppressed with cares and doubts about the distracting affairs of the church in his time, Luther thus chides him

out of his despondency . . . do not thou presume to be the governor of the world, but leave the reins of government in his hands that made it, and best knows how to rule it.[12]

This does not mean we are to become indifferent and callous to the tremendous amount of suffering that goes on around the world. We should pray for the victims of tragedies and, where opportunity permits, respond tangibly to the relief of their sufferings. But we can be compassionate without questioning God about His government of the world.

It is not only an irreverent act to question God's wisdom, it is also spiritually debilitating. We not only besmirch God's glory, we also deprive ourselves of the comfort and peace that comes by simply trusting Him without requiring an explanation. An unreserved trust of God, when we don't understand what is happening or why, is the only road to peace and comfort and joy. God wants us to honor Him by trusting Him, but He also desires that we experience the peace and joy that come as a result.

In researching the subject of God's wisdom among the teachers of previous centuries, I came across the following paragraph, which so beautifully sums up all that I have tried to say on the subject. I append it without further comment, hoping that it will encourage you, as it has me, to trust God in all circumstances, whether private or public, and to believe that He is working all things out for our good as well as for His glory.

It should fill us with joy, that infinite wisdom guides the affairs of the world. Many of its events are shrouded in darkness and mystery, and inextricable confusion sometimes seems to reign. Often wickedness prevails, and God seems to have forgotten the creatures that he has made. Our own path through life is dark and devious, and beset with difficulties and dangers. How full of consolation is the doctrine, that infinite wisdom directs every event, brings order out of confusion, and light out of darkness, and, to those who love God, causes all things, whatever be their present aspect and apparent tendency, to work together for good.[13]

KNOWING GOD'S LOVE

Who shall separate us from the love of Christ? Shall
trouble or hardship or persecution or famine or nakedness
or danger or sword? . . . No, in all these things we are
more than conquerors through him who loved us.

ROMANS 8:35, 37

A friend of mine who spends a good amount of time encouraging others found himself distraught over the spiritual struggles of one of his children. In desperation he cried out, "God, I think I'm doing a better job taking care of Your children than You are of mine." He told me, "As soon as I said it, I repented to the Lord." Nevertheless, his frustrating experience illustrates a point. Most of us are tempted, from time to time, to question God's love for us.

I can identify with my friend. Once when one of our children was going through a series of difficult experiences, I said, "God, I wouldn't treat my child the way You are treating her." I, too, had to repent of my brash words and work through the assurance in the Scriptures that God's love is just as real in times of adversity as it is in times of blessing.

It seems the more we come to believe in and accept the sovereignty of God over every event of our lives, the more we are tempted to question His love. We think, "If God is in control of this adversity and can do something about it, why doesn't He?" Rabbi Kushner chose to believe in a God who is good but not sovereign. Sometimes we are tempted, if only momentarily, to believe in a sovereign God who is not good. Satan, whose very first act toward man was to question the goodness of God, will even plant the thought in our minds that God is up in heaven mocking us in our distress.

But we are not forced to choose between the sovereignty and the goodness of God. The Bible affirms both His sovereignty and His goodness with equal emphasis. References to His goodness and loving-kindness, like His sovereignty, appear on almost every page of Scripture. In our struggles with adversity, we dare not malign the goodness of God. As Philip Hughes said, "That *he cares not* is just as unthinkable as that *he can not*."[1]

The apostle John said, "God is love" (1 John 4:8). This succinct statement, along with its parallel one, "God is light" (1 John 1:5; that is, God is holy), sums up the essential character of God, as revealed to us in the Scriptures. Just as it is impossible in the very nature of God for Him to be anything but perfectly holy, so it is impossible for Him to be anything but perfectly good.[2]

Because God is love, it is an essential part of His nature to do good and show mercy to His creatures. Psalm 145 speaks of His "abundant goodness," of His being "rich in love" and "good to all," of having "compassion on all he has made," and of being "loving toward all he has made" (verses 7-9, 17). Even in His role of Judge of rebellious men, He declares, "I take no pleasure in the death of the wicked" (Ezekiel 33:11).

When we are in the midst of adversity and, as it frequently seems to happen, calamity after calamity seems to be surging in upon us, we will be tempted to doubt God's love. Not only do we struggle with our own doubts, but Satan seizes these occasions to whisper accusations against God, such as, "If He loved you, He wouldn't have allowed this to happen." My own experience suggests that Satan attacks us far more in the area of God's love than either His sovereignty or His wisdom.

We cannot keep from being tempted, but if we are to honor God by trusting Him, we must not allow such thoughts to lodge in our minds. As Philip Hughes again said, "To question the goodness of God is, in essence, to imply that man is more concerned about goodness than is God. . . . To suggest that man is kinder than God is to subvert the very nature of God. . . . It is to deny God; and this is precisely the thrust of the temptation to question the goodness of God."[3]

Let's go back to the two incidents at the beginning of the chapter. In both instances my friend and I questioned the goodness of God. We did just what Philip Hughes warned against. We, even though only momentarily, told God we were more concerned about goodness toward our children than He was; that we were kinder than He is. In our more reasoned moments such thoughts are unthinkable to us, but in times of prolonged adversity, we can begin to entertain such thoughts.

Even righteous Job, who at the beginning of his calamities was able to say, "The LORD gave and the LORD has taken away; may the name of the LORD be praised" (Job 1:21), finally came to the place where he too questioned the goodness of God. He said, "God denies me justice," and "It profits a man nothing when he tries to please God" (Job 34:5, 9).

If God is perfect in His love and abundant in His goodness, how do we take a stand against our own doubts and the temptations of Satan to question the goodness of God? What truths about God do we need to store up in our hearts to use as weapons against temptations to doubt His love?

GOD'S LOVE AT CALVARY

There is no doubt that the most convincing evidence of God's love in all of Scripture is His giving His Son to die for our sins.

> This is how God showed his love among us: He sent his one and only Son into the world that we might live through him. This is love: not that we loved God, but that he loved us and sent his Son as an atoning sacrifice for our sins. 1 JOHN 4:9-10

John said that God is love, and this is how He showed His love, by sending His Son to die for us. Our greatest need is not freedom from adversity. All the possible calamities that could occur in this life cannot in any way be compared with the absolute calamity of eternal separation from God. Jesus said no earthly joy could compare with the eternal joy of our names written in heaven (see Luke 10:20). In like manner, no earthly adversity can compare with that awful calamity of God's eternal judgment in hell.

So when John said that God showed His love by sending His Son, he was saying God showed His love by meeting our greatest need—a need so great that no other need can even come close to it in comparison. If we want proof of God's love for us, then we must look first at the Cross where God offered up His Son as a sacrifice for our sins. Calvary is the one objective, absolute, irrefutable proof of God's love for us.

The extent of God's love at Calvary is seen in both the infinite cost to Him of giving His one and only Son, and in the wretched and miserable condition of those He loved. God could not remove our sins without an infinite cost to both Himself and His Son. And because of their great love for us, both were willing—yes more than merely willing—to pay that great cost, the Father in giving His one and only Son, and the Son in lay-ing down His life for us. One of the essential characteristics of love is the element of self-sacrifice, and this was demonstrated for us to its ultimate in God's love at Calvary.

Consider also the miserable and wretched condition of those God loved. Paul said, "But God demonstrates his own love for us in this: While we were still sinners, Christ died for us" (Romans 5:8): It is sometimes difficult for those of us who grew up in morally upright or Christian homes to appreciate the force of Paul's statement, "while we were still sinners." Because we were generally upright and morally decent people in the eyes of society around us and in our own eyes, it is difficult for us to see ourselves as God saw us, as wretched, miserable, rebellious sinners.

But Paul describes us as being spiritually dead in our transgressions and sins (see Ephesians 2:1). Ezekiel's vision of Israel as a valley of very dry bones (see Ezekiel 37) would be an apt description of all of us before our salvation. One day a friend and I were marveling about the conversion of one of the more notorious white-collar criminals of our time. I said to my friend, "How dead is dead? Weren't we just as spiritually dead before our salvation as he was?" Regardless of how morally upright we had been in our unsaved state, we still appeared to God like the house of Israel, nothing more than a pile of bones, bones that were very dry.

Paul continues in Ephesians 2 with his description of our wretched condition. He says we followed the ways of this world (see verse 2), that is, of the ungodly society around us. Not only did we follow the ways of the ungodly society, we even followed the Devil, whom Paul calls the ruler of the kingdom of the air. Perhaps it was not by a conscious, deliberate choice that we followed the Devil, but we did so because we were under his power and dominion (see Acts 26:18; Colossians 1:13). We were actually servants of the archenemy of God. Further, Paul says that we spent our days gratifying the cravings of our sinful nature, following its desires and thoughts (see Ephesians 2:3). We lived for ourselves, our ambitions, our desires, our pleasures. And then, as Paul continues this description of us in our unsaved state, he concludes with the statement that we were by nature objects of God's wrath. We must not lose sight of the fact that God's wrath is very real and very justified. We have all sinned incessantly against a holy, righteous God. We have rebelled willfully against His commands, defied His moral law, and acted in total defiance of His known will for us. Because of these actions, we were justly objects of His wrath.

Perhaps you wonder why, in a chapter on the love of God in adversity, I have seemingly digressed so extensively about our sinful condition. I have done so for two reasons: First, that we might see the depth of God's love, not only in giving His one and only Son, but in giving Him to die for such people as Paul has described us to be.

But I have dwelt on this point for another reason. When we begin to question the love of God, we need to remember who we are. We have absolutely no claim on His love. We don't deserve one bit of God's goodness to us. I once heard a speaker say, "Anything this side of hell is pure grace." I know of nothing that will so quickly cut the nerve of a petulant, "Why did this happen to me?" attitude as a realization of who we are before God, considered in ourselves apart from Christ.

We see then that God loved us when we were totally unworthy, when there was nothing whatsoever within us that would call forth His love.

Any time that we are tempted to doubt God's love for us, we should go back to the Cross. We should reason somewhat in this fashion: If God loved me enough to give His Son to die for me when I was His enemy, surely He loves me enough to care for me now that I am His child. Having loved me to the ultimate extent at the Cross, He cannot possibly fail to love me in my times of adversity. Having given such a priceless gift as His Son, surely He will also give all else that is consistent with His glory and my good.

Note that I said we should reason. If we are to trust God in adversity, we must use our minds in those times to reason through the great truths of God's sovereignty, wisdom, and love as they are revealed to us in the Scriptures. We must not allow our emotions to hold sway over our minds. Rather, we must seek to let the truth of God rule our minds. Our emotions must become subservient to the truth. This does not mean we do not feel the pain of adversity and heartache. We feel it keenly. Nor does it mean we should seek to bury our emotional pain in a stoic-like attitude. We are meant to feel the pain of adversity, but we must resist allowing that pain to cause us to lapse into hard thoughts about God.

It may seem cold and even unspiritual to seek to reason through the truths of God's love in times of heartache, pain, and disappointment. But it is neither cold nor unspiritual. Paul himself, in one of the most ecstatic passages of Scripture, used a form of reasoning—an argument from the greater to the lesser—when he said, "He who did not spare his own Son, but gave him up for us all—how will he not also, along with him, graciously give us all things?" (Romans 8:32). Paul reasoned that if God loved us so much to give us the greatest conceivable gift, then surely He will not withhold any lesser blessing from us. Or to restate this truth in a way more applicable to our present theme: If God's love was sufficient for my greatest need, my eternal salvation, surely it is sufficient for my lesser needs, the adversities I encounter in this life. If we are going to come to the same heartfelt conviction that Paul had, that no adversity can separate us from the love of God, we must use our minds to reason through the great truths of Scripture even as Paul did.

GOD'S FAMILY LOVE

By God's grace having trusted Christ as our Savior, we who are believers have been brought into the very family of God. He has covenanted with us to be our God, and we to be His people (see Hebrews 8:10). Through Christ He has adopted us as His children and has sent His Holy Spirit to live within us and to testify with our spirit that we are His children. The Holy Spirit bears witness within us to this filial relationship we have with God when He causes us to cry in our hearts, "*Abba*, Father" (Romans 8:15-16). It was said that in the Jewish household, slaves were not allowed to use the word "Abba" to address the head of the family. It was a word reserved for the children. Thus Paul's use of that word is intended to convey to us how deeply the Spirit assures us that we are indeed children of the Most High God, now our heavenly Father.

As our heavenly Father, God loves us, His children, with a very special love, a fatherly love. He calls us His "chosen people, holy and *dearly loved*" (Colossians 3:12, emphasis added). As incredible as it may seem, "He will take great delight in you . . . will rejoice over you with singing" (Zephaniah 3:17). He delights in us as a father delights in his children. As Matthew Henry observed when commenting on Zephaniah 3:17, "The great God not only loves his saints, but he loves to love them." God takes great delight in loving us because we are His very own.

In Psalm 103:11, David speaks of God's fatherly love in this way: "For as high as the heavens are above the earth, so great is his love for those who fear him." In the last chapter, we saw that God's *ways* are higher than our ways, as the heavens are higher than the earth. Here we see that God's love for His own is as high as the heavens are above the earth. Just as God's wisdom, like the height of the heavens, cannot be measured, so God's *love* for us cannot be measured. It is not only perfect in its effect, it is infinite in its extent. No calamity that may come upon us, however great it may be, can carry us beyond the pale of God's fatherly love for us.

GOD'S LOVE IN CHRIST

This infinite, measureless love of God is poured out upon us, not because of who we are or what we are, but because we are in Christ Jesus. Note that in Romans 8:39, Paul says that "[nothing] will be able to separate us from the love of God that is in Christ Jesus our Lord." The love of God flows to us entirely through, or in, Jesus Christ. The term *in Christ* is one Paul uses frequently to refer to our spiritually organic union with Jesus Christ. Jesus speaks of this same union in His metaphor of the vine and its branches in John 15. Just as the branches are organically related to the vine in a life-giving union, so believers, in a spiritual sense, are organically united to Christ. Just as the parts of the body are organically related to its head, so we are spiritually related to Christ in this same way.

It is very important that we grasp this crucial concept that God's love to us is *in Christ*. Just as God's love to His Son cannot change, so His love to us cannot change because we are in union with the One He loves. God's love to us can no more waver than His love to His Son can waver.

We are constantly tempted to look within ourselves to seek to find some reason why God should love us. Such searching is, of course, usually discouraging. We usually find within ourselves reasons why we think God should *not* love us. Such searching is also unbiblical. The Bible is quite clear that God does not look within us for a reason to love us. He loves us because we are in Christ Jesus. When He looks at us, He does not look at us as "stand alone" Christians, resplendent in our own good works, even good works as Christians. Rather, as He looks at us, He sees us united to His beloved Son, clothed in His righteousness. He loves us, not because we are lovely in ourselves, but because we are in Christ.

Here then is another weapon of truth that we should store up in our hearts to use against our doubts and the temptation to question God's love for us. *God's love to us cannot fail any more than His love to Christ can fail.* We must learn to see our adversities in relation to our union with Christ. God does not deal with us as, so to speak, "free standing" individuals. He does deal with us individually, but as individuals united to Christ.

GOD'S SOVEREIGN LOVE

In earlier chapters we look extensively at the sovereignty of God over all of His universe. That sovereignty is exercised primarily for His glory. But because you and I are *in* Christ Jesus, *His* glory and *our* good are linked together. Because we are united with Christ, whatever is for His glory is also for our good. And whatever is for our good is for His glory.

Therefore, we can, with scriptural warrant, say that God exercises His sovereignty on our behalf. Paul says in Ephesians 1:22-23, "God placed all things under his feet and appointed him [Christ] to be head over everything for the church, which is his body, the fullness of him who fills everything in every way." That is, Christ reigns over the entire universe for the benefit of His body, the church. We have already seen that God's sovereignty is absolute over the most awesome earthly or spiritual powers and penetrates to the most mundane and minute details of life. Now we see in Ephesians 1:22-23 that this power is exercised by Christ on behalf of the church, which is His body.

It is because the church is His body that Christ exercises His sovereignty on its behalf. That is, in the words of New Testament commentator William Hendriksen, "since he is so intimately and indissolubly united with [the church] and loves it with such profound, boundless, and steadfast love," Christ's power is being used for the government of the universe. Hendriksen goes on to say,

> It is the closeness of the bond, the unfathomable character of the love between Christ and his church that is stressed by the head-body symbolism. . . . Since the church is Christ's body, with which he is organically united, he loves it so much that *in its interest* he exercises his infinite power in causing the entire universe with all that is in it to co-operate, whether willingly or unwillingly.[4]

We can see that it is our union with Christ that guarantees that God's sovereign power is exercised on our behalf. This, of course, does not mean that, because of our union with Christ, we should not expect any adversity in this life. The Scriptures clearly teach just the opposite. It *does* mean that those adversities are being controlled by God and used by Him only in ways that His wisdom and love dictate.

This idea of God's sovereignty being united with His love for the benefit of His people is expressed in another symbol— the shepherd and his sheep—in Isaiah 40. In verses 10-11, the prophet says,

> See, the Sovereign LORD comes with power,
>   and his arm rules for him. . . .
> He tends his flock like a shepherd:
>   He gathers the lambs in his arms

and carries them close to his heart;
  he gently leads those that have young.

The juxtaposition in this passage of God's sovereign power and His gentle care of His sheep is striking. The arm of the Lord in Scripture is always a symbol of His mighty power and strength; and the title *shepherd*, when used of God, always indicates His tender care and constant watchfulness.

In this passage, God's sovereign power and tender care are united for the benefit of His people. The same arm that is exercised in power over all the universe is used to gather up His lambs and to carry them close to His heart. No more picturesque symbol of God's love for us can be given than that of the faithful and tender Shepherd carrying His lambs close to His heart. And we are carried in the arms of sovereign power.

Alexander Carson said,

God's sovereignty is always to his people in wisdom and in love. This is the difference between sovereignty in God and sovereignty in man. We dread the sovereignty of man, because we have no security of its being exercised in mercy, or even justice: we rejoice in the sovereignty of God, because we are sure it is always exercised for the good of his people.[5]

Professor Berkouwer said, "God's Providence is not only a matter of Divine invincibility and power, but of the invincibility and power of His *love*." And he also said,

This is the comfort, that we stand at the disposal of a merciful heavenly Father to whom we can with confidence abandon ourselves. . . . He makes an eternal covenant of grace with us, and adopts us for His children and heirs, and therefore will provide us with every good thing and avert all evil or turn it to our profit.[6]

The psalmist said, "I have hidden your word in my heart that I might not sin against you" (Psalm 119:11). To murmur against God and to question His goodness is indeed sin. We should work as diligently in trusting God's love as we do in obeying His commands. If we are going to trust God's love, we must store up in our hearts these great truths we have looked at in this chapter—God's love at Calvary, our union with Christ, and the sovereignty of God's love exercised on our behalf.

God's love is an objective truth that cannot be contradicted. But it is truth we must store away in our minds and hearts. Then we must use it in the midst of adversity to deal with our doubts, combat the accusations of Satan, and glorify God by trusting Him.

CHAPTER TEN

EXPERIENCING GOD'S LOVE

For I am convinced that neither death nor life, neither angels nor
demons, neither the present nor the future, nor any powers, neither
height nor depth, nor anything else in all creation, will be able to
separate us from the love of God that is in Christ Jesus our Lord.

ROMANS 8:38-39

In the previous chapter we saw that God's love is sovereign; that His powerful arm is also His arm of tender care. But it seems so often we do not *see* or *sense* God's sovereign love exercised on our behalf. Instead, we see ourselves beset with all kinds of calamities that come rolling in upon us. We see ourselves as the victims of "nature's cruel fate," of the injustices of other people, and of adversities that occur with no rational cause.

It is at times like this that we must take our stand by faith on the assurances of God's love given to us in the Scriptures. We cannot evade one of the basic principles of the Christian life, "We live by faith, not by sight" (2 Corinthians 5:7). Certainly our faith frequently wavers and, just as we may momentarily question the wisdom of God, we will momentarily question the goodness and love of God. We will be like David when he said, "In my alarm I said, 'I am cut off from your sight!'" (Psalm 31:22). That is often our initial reaction when adversity strikes us. We feel cut off from God's face, from His love and tender care.

But we must also learn to say with David, "Yet you heard my cry for mercy when I called to you for help" (Psalm 31:22). God cannot forsake us because we are His children, in blessed union with His Son. We cannot be cut off from His sight. But we can be cut off from the *assurance* of His love when we allow doubt and unbelief to gain a foothold in our hearts.

Isaiah speaks of God's people (called Zion) as questioning God's love: "But Zion said, 'The LORD has forsaken me'" (Isaiah 49:14). But God's response to His people's doubts is forceful:

Can a mother forget the baby at her breast
and have no compassion on the child she has borne?
Though she may forget,
I will not forget you!

ISAIAH 49:15

God uses the tightest human bonding possible, the nursing baby at his mother's breast, to illustrate His love for us. But even the highest illustration of human love is not sufficient to demonstrate God's love for His children. For it is tragically possible for a mother to neglect her nursing child. Mothers are sinful and sometimes their natural love can be overcome by their own selfish interests. The greatest human love may sometimes fail.

But God's love cannot fail. Edward J. Young says about this passage, "Not merely will God not forget, He cannot forget. This is one of the strongest, if not the strongest expression of God's love in the Old Testament." Young then quotes Calvin, "In a word, the Prophet here describes to us the inconceivable carefulness with which God unceasingly watches over our salvation, that we may be fully convinced that he will never forsake us, though we may be afflicted with great and numerous calamities."[1]

In Lamentations 3, the author of the book, traditionally

146

accepted to be Jeremiah, personifies the nation of Judah after its destruction by the Babylonian army. If anyone could have felt cut off from God's face, it was that nation, and justly so because of its vileness and idolatry. But the writer does more than just personify the nation. You get the impression that he *personally* feels the apparent alienation from God. You are not sure if he is merely using a literary device or allowing his own personal feelings to come out. Anyone who has ever felt cut off from the Lord's face and forsaken by Him can ponder with great feeling the misery this author depicts in Lamentations 3:1-20. The section ends with this statement:

> I remember my affliction and my wandering,
>   the bitterness and the gall.
> I well remember them,
>   and my soul is downcast within me.

LAMENTATIONS 3:19-20

The writer has reached the bottom of the barrel emotionally and spiritually. But then the mood changes completely, as the writer says in verse 21, "Yet this I call to mind and therefore I have hope." There follows one of the greatest passages in all of the Bible—a passage that has brought hope and encouragement to countless believers down through the centuries:

> Because of the LORD's great love we are not consumed,
>   for his compassions never fail.
> They are new every morning;
>   great is your faithfulness.

LAMENTATIONS 3:22-23

What was it that caused such a dramatic mood change in the heart of the writer? He turns from the circumstances at hand to the Lord. He was not cut off from God. Even the nation in the depth of its sin was not cut off from God's love. God disciplined the nation severely, but He did not cease to love it. We, too, if we would speak of the Lord's great faithfulness, must turn from our circumstances to the Lord. We must see our circumstances through God's love instead of, as we are prone to do, seeing God's love through our circumstances.

How did the writer turn to the Lord? He reflected on the love, the compassion, and the faithfulness of God. We must do that, too. That is why we need to store up in our hearts some of these great passages on the love of God. We must have them ready to use when adversity strikes and when doubts and temptations to unbelief arise in our hearts.

GOD'S LOVE IN DISCIPLINE

The Bible's assurance of the sovereignty and constancy of God's love does not mean that we should not expect adversity. On the contrary, the author of Hebrews assures us that discipline, in the form of adversity, is a proof of His love:

> My son, do not make light of the Lord's discipline,
>   and do not lose heart when he rebukes you,
> because the Lord disciplines those he loves,
>   and he punishes everyone he accepts as a son.

HEBREWS 12:5-6

We mistakenly look for tokens of God's love in happiness. We should instead look for them in His faithful and persistent work to conform us to Christ. As Philip Hughes has observed, "Discipline is the mark not of a harsh and heartless father but of a father who is deeply and lovingly concerned for the well-being of his son."[2]

The author of Hebrews concedes that the divine discipline is painful. It is intended to be. It would not accomplish its purpose if it were not. But God in His infinite wisdom and perfect love will never over-discipline us; He will never allow any adversity in our lives that is not ultimately for our good. We may be sure that we never suffer needlessly. As Lamentations 3:33 states, "For he does not willingly bring affliction or grief to the children of men."

God disciplines us with reluctance, though He does it faithfully. He does not delight in our adversities, but He will not spare us that which we need to grow more and more into the likeness of His Son. It is our imperfect spiritual condition that makes discipline necessary.

This is not to say that every adversity that occurs in our lives is related to some specific sin we have committed. The issue God is dealing with in our lives is not so much what we *do*, but what we *are*. All of us tend to underestimate the remaining sinfulness in our hearts. We fail to see the extent of pride, fleshly self-confidence, selfish ambitions, stubbornness, self-justification, lack of love, and distrust of God that He does see. But adversity brings these sinful dispositions to the surface just as the refiner's fire brings impurities to the surface of the molten gold.

We cannot always discern what specific spiritual good is being brought about in our lives through a particular adversity. Of course, often, we do see God dealing with some obvious character need, but we may not see *all* that God is doing in us. But God is at work through our adversities, working in us what is pleasing to Him (see Hebrews 13:21).

I alluded briefly to Romans 8:28 in a previous chapter and pointed out that the "good" Paul speaks of there is defined in verse 29 as being conformed to the likeness of God's Son. But now let's look more closely at verse 28. The text says, "And we know that in all things God works for the good of those who love him." Many of the "things" Paul has in mind are evil in themselves. There is nothing inherently good about birth defects, natural calamities, and the host of other adversities we may encounter. And when evil is perpetrated against us by someone else, there certainly is no inherent good in it. But in God's infinite wisdom and love, He takes all the events of our lives—both good and bad—and blends them together so that they work together ultimately for our good, the good that He intends.

While growing up in Texas, I enjoyed my mother's buttermilk biscuits made from "scratch" every morning for breakfast. But there was not a single ingredient in those biscuits that I would have enjoyed by itself. And even after they were mixed together, I would not have cared for the raw biscuit dough. Only after they were mixed together in the right proportions by my mother's skillful hands and then subjected to the fire of the oven were they ready to be enjoyed for breakfast.

The "things" of Romans 8:28 are like the ingredients of the biscuit dough. By themselves they are not tasteful to us. We shun them. And we certainly shun the heat of the oven. But when God in His infinite skill has blended them all together and cooked them properly in the oven of adversity, we shall one day say it is good.

As we consider God's discipline through adversity, we must also be careful that we do not equate a certain amount of adversity with a certain level of sinfulness in either our own or someone else's life. Some of the most Christlike people I have known seem to experience the most adversity. And we have only to look at Job to see this truth in the Bible. God Himself said of Job, "There is no one on earth like him; he is blameless and upright, a man who fears God and shuns evil" (Job 1:8). Yet I know of no one, except the Lord Jesus Christ, who has ever experienced the total calamity that Job experienced.

One of my friends has described the theme of the book of Job as "God making a good man better." So if you feel that you experience more than your "fair share" of adversity, do not let a supposed link between adversity and sin discourage you. God may have other things in mind than corrective discipline. There seems to be little doubt, for example, that Joseph's brothers needed corrective discipline far more than he did, yet none of them suffered as he suffered.

GOD'S UNFAILING LOVE

A very frequent expression in the Psalms is God's *unfailing love*. For example, Psalm 32:10 says, "The LORD's unfailing love surrounds the man who trusts in him." Think of what that means. God's love cannot fail. It is steadfast, constant and fixed. In all the adversities we go through, *God's love is unfailing*. As He says to us in Isaiah 54:10,

> "Though the mountains be shaken
>   and the hills be removed,
> yet my unfailing love for you will not be shaken
>   nor my covenant of peace be removed,"
>   says the LORD, who has compassion on you.

And because His love cannot fail, He will allow into our lives only the pain and heartache that is for our ultimate good.

Even the grief that He Himself brings into our lives is tempered with His compassion. "Though he brings grief, he will show compassion, so great is his unfailing love" (Lamentations 3:32). The assurance here is that God will *show* compassion. It is not enough to say that He *is* compassionate, but He will *show* compassion. That is, even the fires of affliction will be tempered by His compassion, which arises out of His unfailing love. Our afflictions are always accompanied with the compassion and consolation of God.

Paul experienced God's compassion in the midst of his grief. To prevent pride in his life, God gave him a thorn in his flesh. What the thorn was we do not know, but we know it was a severe affliction for Paul. On three occasions he pleaded with the Lord to take it away, but God said no. Instead, God said, "My grace is sufficient for you" (2 Corinthians 12:9). God brought grief into Paul's life for his good, but he also showed compassion. He gave grace, in this case divine strength, to bear the grief. He did not leave Paul to bear the thorn in his flesh alone. In His compassion, He provided the divine resources to meet the trials. So eventually Paul came to rejoice in his affliction, because through it he experienced God's overcoming power.

Paul received grace when he needed it. God does not give us all the divine strength we need for the Christian life the day we trust Christ. Rather, David speaks of God's goodness, which is stored up for those who fear Him (see Psalm 31:19). Just as we are to store up (the meaning of "hidden" in Psalm 119:11) God's Word in our hearts against a time of temptation, so God stores up goodness or grace for our times of adversity. We do not receive it before we need it, but we never receive it too late.

I think of a physician whose son was born with an incurable birth defect, leaving him crippled for life. I asked the father how he felt when he, who had dedicated his life to treating the illnesses of other people, was confronted with an incurable condition in his own son. He told me his biggest problem was the tendency to capsule the next twenty years of his son's life into that initial moment when he learned of his son's condition. Viewed that way, the adversity was overwhelming. God does not give twenty years of grace today. Rather, He gives it day by day. As the song says, "Day by day, and with each passing moment, strength I find to meet my trials here; trusting in my Father's wise bestowment, I've no cause for worry or for fear."[3]

GOD'S PRESENCE WITH US

God's love is unfailing, His grace is always sufficient. But there is even more good news. He is *with us* in our troubles. He does not merely send grace from heaven to meet our trials. He Himself comes to help us. He says to us, "Do not be afraid . . . for I myself will help you" (Isaiah 41:14).

In Isaiah 43:2, God says,

> When you pass through the waters,
>   I will be with you;
> and when you pass through the rivers,
>   they will not sweep over you.
> When you walk through the fire,
>   you will not be burned;
>   the flames will not set you ablaze.

God promises specifically to be *with us* in our sorrows and afflictions. He will not spare us from the waters of sorrow and the fires of adversity, but He will go through them with us.

Even when the waters and the fires are those that God Himself brings into our lives, He still goes through them with us. Most of the gracious promises of God to be with us were given first to the nation of Judah during times of national spiritual declension. God, through His prophets, continually warned the people of coming judgment; yet in the midst of those warnings, we find these incredible promises of His being with them. God judged His people, but He did not forsake them. Even in their judgments, He was with them. As Isaiah said, "In all their distress he too was distressed" (Isaiah 63:9).

So regardless of the nature or the cause of our adversities, God goes through them with us. He says, "I will strengthen you and help you; I will uphold you with my righteous right hand" (Isaiah 41:10). It is often in the very midst of our adversities that we experience the most delightful manifestations of His love. As Paul said in 2 Corinthians 1:5, "For just as the sufferings of Christ flow over into our lives, so also through Christ our comfort overflows."

Christ identifies with us in our distresses. When He confronted Saul on the road to Damascus, He said, "Saul, Saul, why do you persecute me?" And in answer to Saul's question, "Who are you, Lord?" He replied, "I am Jesus, whom you are persecuting" (Acts 9:4-5). Because His people were in union with Him, to persecute them was to persecute Him. This truth is no different today. You are in union with Christ, just as surely as the disciples were in the time of the book of Acts. And because you are in union with Christ, He shares your adversities.

In whatever way we view our adversities, we find God's grace is sufficient, His love adequate. Nothing can separate us from His love. In the words of Paul, "Neither height nor depth, nor anything else in all creation, will be able to separate us from the love of God that is in Christ Jesus our Lord" (Romans 8:39).

God's unfailing love for us is an objective fact affirmed over and over in the Scriptures. It is true whether we believe it or not. Our doubts do not destroy God's love, nor does our faith create it. It originates in the very nature of God, who is love, and it flows to us through our union with His beloved Son.

But the *experience* of that love and the comfort it is intended to bring is dependent upon our believing the truth about God's love as it is revealed to us in the Scriptures. Doubts about God's love, allowed to harbor in our hearts, will surely deprive us of the comfort of His love. Nineteenth-century Scottish commentator John Brown has a helpful comment on this truth. He said,

> The only way in which the "sufferings of the present
> time" may seem to come between the Christian and the

love of God and Christ, is when he falls before them as a temptation, or in unbelief sinks under them. Then a cloud comes between him and the light of his Father's countenance. But the cloud is not the affliction, but the sin; and it is a merciful arrangement that it is so. The want of comfort tells him that something is wrong.[4]

It is true that we are just as dependent upon the Holy Spirit to enable us to trust in God's love as we are dependent upon Him to enable us to obey His commands. But just as we are responsible to obey in confidence that He is at work in us, so we are responsible to trust Him in that same attitude of dependence and confidence. Many times in our distress we may have to do as one man did before Jesus when he "cried out, and said with tears, Lord, I believe; help thou mine unbelief" (Mark 9:24, KJV).

We will almost always struggle with doubts about God's love during our times of adversity. If we never had to struggle, our faith would not grow. But we must engage in the struggle with our doubts; we must not let them overwhelm us. During seemingly intolerable times, we may feel like David, who said at a time of great distress:

How long, O LORD? Will you forget me forever?
How long will you hide your face from me?
PSALM 13:1

David had his doubts; he struggled with them. In fact, in the next verse he continues his struggle as he asks, "How long must I wrestle with my thoughts?" He felt God had, at least for a time, forgotten him. But David, by the enabling power of God, won his struggle. He overcame his doubts. He could then say,

But I trust in your unfailing love;
>   my heart rejoices in your salvation.
I will sing to the LORD,
>   for he has been good to me.

PSALM 13:5-6

You and I, like David, must wrestle with our thoughts. With God's help we, too, can come to the place, even in the midst of our adversities, where we will be able to say, "I trust in Your unfailing love."

CHAPTER ELEVEN

TRUSTING GOD FOR WHO YOU ARE

For you created my inmost being;
you knit me together in my mother's womb. . . .
All the days ordained for me were written in your book
before one of them came to be.

PSALM 139:13, 16

I can still remember trying to play baseball as a youngster in elementary school. I could neither bat nor catch well because I could not tell where the ball was or judge how fast it was coming to me. I did not know until years later that my inability to play baseball was due to my having monocular vision—the ability to focus only one eye at a time. Depth perception is based on binocular vision, the ability to focus both eyes together to produce a stereoscopic or three-dimensional effect.

I've had this problem all my life, or at least since infancy. Even today I experience apprehension each time I go to renew my driver's license. I wonder if the examiner will not renew my license because I cannot pass the depth perception part of the eye exam. I cannot play tennis, and I would not dare step into a handball or racquetball court for fear I would be hit right in the face with the ball.

But as a youngster I didn't understand why I couldn't play baseball with the other boys. I just knew that I felt shame and rejection because I was not like they were. Of course, many people have physical or mental impairments that are much worse than mine. But whether they are major or minor, these disabilities often cause childhood heartache and then, later on, difficulty with self-acceptance as an adult. When we become Christians, we may begin to struggle with God over the disabilities and limitations we have.

Other people who have no disabilities struggle with problems of physical appearance. Their ears are too big or their nose is too long or their body in some way does not match normal proportions. Still other people have difficulty with temperament or emotional traits. Others struggle with unavoidable environmental and hereditary factors over which they had no control.

Whatever the problem, many people struggle to accept themselves as they are. For them life is just a continuous adversity, not from outside circumstances, but from who they are. Their greatest need in trusting God may be to "trust God for who I am." For those with this need, Psalm 139:13-16 has some very important and helpful things to say.

GOD MADE ME WHO I AM

Psalm 139:13-16 teaches us that we are who we are because God Himself created us the way we are—not because of an impersonal biological process. Notice in verse 13 that David says to God, "You knit me together in my mother's womb." He pictures God as a master weaver at work in our mother's womb, creating us as directly as He created Adam out of the dust of the earth.

Obviously David was aware of the biological process that God used to bring him into this world. He does not deny that. Rather he teaches us that God so superintends that biological process that He is directly involved in fashioning each one of us into the person He wants us to be.

The first part of verse 13 says, "For you created my inmost being." The Hebrew word for "inmost being" is literally *kidneys*, a word used by the Jews to express the seat of longings and desires. The *New International Version Study Bible* says the word was used in Hebrew idiom for "the center of emotions and of moral sensitivity." David, then, is essentially saying, "You created my personality." Not only did God create David's physical body, He also created his personality. David was the person he was because God created him that way, physically, mentally, and emotionally. And just as God was personally involved in the creation of David, so He was directly involved in creating you and me. Rev. James Hufstetler said it well when he said,

> You are the result of the attentive, careful, thoughtful, intimate, detailed, creative work of God. Your personality, your sex, your height, your features, are what they are because God made them *precisely* that way. He made you the way he did because that is the way he wants you to be. . . . If God had wanted you to be basically and creatively different he would have made you differently. Your genes and chromosomes and creaturely distinctives—even the shape of your nose and ears—are what they are by God's design.[1]

Psalm 139:13 is not the only passage in the Bible that speaks of God's direct creation of each of us. Job said,

> Your hands shaped me and made me. . . .
> Remember that you molded me like clay. . . .
> Did you not . . .
> clothe me with skin and flesh
>   and knit me together with bone and sinews?
>
> JOB 10:8-11

The writer of Psalm 119 said, "Your hands made me and formed me" (verse 73). And God said to Jeremiah, "Before I formed you in the womb I knew you" (Jeremiah 1:5).

The application of this truth should be clear to us. If I have difficulty accepting myself the way God made me, then I have a controversy with God. Obviously you and I need to change insofar as our sinful nature distorts that which God has made. Therefore, I do not say that we need to accept ourselves as we are, but as God made us in our basic physical, mental, and emotional makeup.

David, instead of fretting over the way God made him, said, "I praise you because I am fearfully and wonderfully made" (Psalm 139:14). David was a man "with a fine appearance and handsome features" (1 Samuel 16:12). So we could say, "It's well enough for David to praise God because he was handsome, athletic, skilled in war, and a gifted musician. But look at me. I'm very ordinary physically and mentally." In fact, some people feel they don't even measure up to ordinary.

I understand people who feel that way. In addition to my hearing and vision disabilities, I've never been excited about my physical appearance. But God did not give His own Son handsome features in His human body. Isaiah said of Jesus, "He had no beauty or majesty to attract us to him, nothing in his appearance that we should desire him" (Isaiah 53:2). The portrait of the bearded, handsome Jesus that we usually see has no basis in Scripture. Jesus, at best, was apparently nondescript in His physical appearance, and it never bothered Him nor interfered in any way with His carrying out the will of His Father.

David praised God, not because he was handsome, but because *God made him*. We need to dwell on that thought. The eternal God who is infinite in His wisdom and perfect in His love personally made you and me. He gave you the body, the mental abilities, and the basic personality you have because that is the way He wanted you to be. And He wanted you to be just that way because He loves you and wants to glorify Himself through you.

This is the believer's foundation for self-acceptance. I am who I am and you are who you are because God sovereignly and directly created us to be who we are. Self-acceptance is basically trusting God for who I am, disabilities or physical flaws and all. We need to learn to think like George MacDonald, who said, "I would rather be what God chose to make me than the most glorious creature that I could think of; for to have been thought about, born in God's thought, and then made by God, is the dearest, grandest, and most precious thing in all thinking."[2]

If we have physical or mental disabilities or impairments, it is because God in His wisdom and love created us that way. We may not understand why God chose to do that, but that is where our trusting Him has to begin. In an earlier chapter, we saw that God ascribes to Himself the responsibility for physical disabilities. He said to Moses, "Who gave man his mouth? Who makes him deaf or mute? Who gives him sight or makes him blind? Is it not I, the LORD?" (Exodus 4:11).

This truth is admittedly difficult to accept, especially if you or one of your loved ones are the object of such disability. But Jesus also affirmed God's hand in disabilities. When the disciples asked Jesus why a certain man was born blind, He replied, "This happened so that the work of God might be displayed in his life" (John 9:3). Think about what Jesus said. A man was born blind and lived in blindness all the way into adulthood, so that God's work might be displayed in his life. That hardly seems fair, does it? Why should that man suffer blindness all those years merely to be available to display God's work on a certain day? Is God's glory worth a man's being born blind?

Such questions when posed about a Bible character who lived 2,000 years ago seem crass and irreverent. We would probably all agree that the glory of God is worthy of a man's being born blind. But what about our own physical disabilities or inadequacies? Is God's glory worthy of those also? Are we willing to take our physical limitations, our learning disabilities, and even our appearance problems to God and say, "Father, You are worthy of this infirmity in my life. I believe You created me just the way I am because You love me and You want to glorify Yourself through me. I will trust You for who I am"?

This is the path to self-acceptance, learning to trust God for who I am. To do this, though, we must continually keep in mind that the God who created us the way we are is the God who is wise enough to know what is best for us and loving enough to bring it about. Certainly we will sometimes struggle with who we are. Unlike specific incidents of adversity, our disabilities and infirmities are always with us. So we have to learn to trust God in this area continually. To do this we have to learn to say with David, "You created my inmost being; you knit me together in my mother's womb."

James Hufstetler is again helpful to us when he said, "You will never really enjoy other people, you will never have stable emotions, you will never lead a life of godly contentment, you will never conquer jealousy and love others as you should until you thank God for making you the way he did."[3]

As we thank God for who we are, we also need to thank Him for those so-called positive abilities and traits we do have. All of the abilities—physical, mental, personality, talents, and so on—that we do have were given to us by God. Paul's words to the Corinthians apply to all of us: "For who makes you different from anyone else? What do you have that you did not receive?" (1 Corinthians 4:7). All of us received whatever ability, learning, riches, station in life, rank, or influence we have from God to be used by us for His glory. Whether it is an ability or disability, let us learn to receive it from God, to give Him thanks, and to seek to use it for His glory.

TRUSTING GOD FOR WHAT I AM

God created us in our mother's womb exactly as He wanted us to be, in order that we might fulfill His plan for us. God does not act according to whim or impulse but according to His eternal purpose. He had a reason for creating each of us as He did. Psalm 139:16 must be taken along with verses 13-15. It says,

> All the days ordained for me
> were written in your book
> before one of them came to be.

There are two possible meanings that may be given to this verse. The first is that the span of David's lifetime, in other words, the number of days he would live, was divinely ordained by God. Certainly this is a truth stated elsewhere in Scripture. David says in Psalm 31:15, "My times are in your hands." Job said,

> Man's days are determined;
> you have decreed the number of his months
> and have set limits he cannot exceed.

JOB 14:5

And Paul said, "From one man he made every nation of men . . . and he determined the times set for them and the exact places where they should live" (Acts 17:26). God not only created us as He intended us to be, He also sovereignly determines how long we live. This in itself is a glorious truth. Along with David, our times are in His hands. As one line from a song says, "Till He bid, I cannot die."

But it is likely that David had in mind the other meaning in this passage, that all the experiences of his life, day by day, were written down in God's book before he was even born. This refers not simply to God's prior knowledge of what will occur in our lives, but to His plan for our lives. This meaning fits better with the flow of thought in verses 13-15. God created each of us uniquely to fulfill the plan He has ordained for us. Our disabilities as well as our abilities all fit into that plan. Did He create you with an incurable speech impediment? He did so because that particular infirmity uniquely fits you for the life He has planned for you. God's plan for you and His creation of you were consistent. He equipped you to fulfill His purpose for you.

Someone well said that one of the most inspiring of truths is that God has a distinct plan for each one of us in sending us into this world. This plan embraces not only His original creation of us, but also the family and social setting into which we were born. It includes all the vicissitudes of life, all the seemingly chance or random happenings, and all the sudden and unexpected turns of events, both "good" and "bad," that occur in our lives. All these situations and circumstances, though they may appear only as happenstance to us, were written in God's book before one of them came to be.

However, God's plan for us embraces more than merely the events or circumstances that happen to us. It also embraces that which He wants us to *be* and to *do*. The Scriptures teach that God places each believer in the body of Christ as it pleases Him. He sovereignly determines our respective functions in the body and gives us the corresponding spiritual gifts with which to perform those functions (see Romans 12:4-6; 1 Corinthians 12:7-11). Moreover, our spiritual gifts are generally consistent with the physical and mental abilities as well as the temperaments with which God created us.

God does not look us over the day we accept Christ and say, "Let's see, what spiritual gifts shall I give to her?" No, God has planned our days before even one of them came to be. He said to Jeremiah, "Before you were born I set you apart; I appointed you as a prophet to the nations" (Jeremiah 1:5). And Paul speaks of his apostolic call in this manner: "When God, who set me apart from birth [literally, from the womb] and called me by his grace" (Galatians 1:15).

Verses 13 through 16 of Psalm 139 must be taken as a unit. God created our inmost being and fashioned us in our mother's womb so that we might be equipped to fulfill the plan that He set out for us even before we were born. *Who* you are is not a biological accident. *What* you are is not a circumstantial accident. God planned both for you.

Just as we must trust God for who we are, we must also trust Him for what we are—whether it be an engineer or missionary, a homemaker or a nurse. If there is one area of life where the saying "the grass is always greener on the other side of the fence" applies, surely it is in the area of vocational calling and station in life. Someone has estimated that as many as eighty percent of our work force are dissatisfied with the jobs they are in. For many of us that may be due to a reluctance to be what God planned for us to be.

Although I studied engineering in college, I soon left that vocation because I thought God wanted me to be an overseas missionary. But God never allowed me to become an overseas missionary. Instead, I became an administrator in a missions organization. At first I thought of administration as a temporary interlude on the way to the mission field. Then one day I had to face the fact that God had gifted me both by talent and temperament for administration, and that was probably what He had called me to do. For a time I thought of myself as a reluctant administrator, as one who would rather be out in the so-called "ministry." But I realized that to think such thoughts was to say I was reluctant to accept God's plan for me. I had to realize He created me a certain way to fulfill the plan He had ordained even before I was born.

God called me to be a missions administrator instead of a missionary. Most people are not to be either. God is the God of society as well as the church, and He determines the course of our lives in the natural realm as well as in the church. He ordained days for plumbers just as much as He did for pastors.

That thought should give meaning to the most humdrum of vocations. In fact, no vocation should be considered humdrum if God has ordained it for us. In the words of J. R. Miller, "The question of small or great has no place here. To have been thought about at all, and then fashioned by God's hands to fill any place, is glory enough for the grandest and most aspiring life. And the highest place to which anyone can attain in life is that for which he was designed and made."[4]

This is not to deny that work, along with all other aspects of creation, is under the curse of sin. God's words to Adam, "By the sweat of your brow you will eat your food" (Genesis 3:19), should be taken in their broadest meaning to indicate the laboriousness and frequent futility that often accompanies any work. Becoming a Christian does not remove that curse from our respective jobs, but it should give us a new perspective about those jobs. We should begin to view them, not as a necessary evil through which we eat our daily bread, but as the place where God has placed us to serve Him by serving society.

Paul wrote to the slaves in the Colossian church, "Whatever you do, work at it with all your heart, as working for the Lord, not for men" (Colossians 3:23). Undoubtedly many of those believing slaves were assigned to tasks that were irksome and wearisome. Some were probably in jobs far beneath their abilities or training. But they were to work at their tasks with enthusiasm because they were working for the Lord. They were doing the things ordained for them before they were born.

The fact that God ordained our days for us should also give meaning to every day, not just the special or exciting days of our lives. Every day is important for us because it is a day ordained by God. If we are bored with life there is something wrong with our concept of God and His involvement in our daily lives. Even the most dull and tedious days of our lives are ordained by God and ought to be used by us to glorify Him.

The realization that God has planned our days for us should not lead us to a fatalistic acceptance of the status quo. If we have an opportunity to improve our situation in a way that will honor God, we should do so. Even to believing slaves Paul wrote, "If you can gain your freedom, do so" (1 Corinthians 7:21). But immediately before that statement Paul had written, "Were you a slave when you were called? Don't let it trouble you." There has to be in our lives a delicate balance between godly efforts to improve our situation and godly acceptance of those situations that cannot be changed by us.

For most of us, there are many seemingly adverse details of our lives that will not be changed regardless of our efforts or our prayers. They are simply part of God's plan for us. In these situations, we need to take comfort from the words of God to the Jewish captives in Babylon, when He said in Jeremiah 29:11:

"For I know the plans I have for you," declares the LORD, "plans to prosper you and not to harm you, plans to give you hope and a future."

Although those words were given by God to a specific group of people, the captives, they reveal the heart of God for all His children. Just as He planned only good for the captives, so He plans only good for you and me. The plan God ordained for you and wrote down in His book even before you were born is a good plan. It is a plan to prosper you and not to harm you. I readily acknowledge there are many aspects of His plan for each of us that do seem harmful, that do seem calculated to take away hope. But here again, we are called upon to walk by faith, to trust God in the face of these adversities that will not go away.

TRUSTING GOD FOR GUIDANCE

The realization that God has ordained our days for us leads logically to the thought, "Can I trust God to guide me in that plan? What if I make a mistake and miss the way?" In answering such questions, I find it helpful to distinguish between God's guidance and that which has come to be called by such terms as "finding the will of God."

David said of God, "He *leads* me beside quiet waters. . . . He *guides* me in the paths of righteousness for his name's sake" (Psalm 23:2-3, emphasis added). The imagery is that of the shepherd leading his sheep. The initiative is with the shepherd. He is the one who determines the watering places and guides the flock as he thinks best. As our shepherd, God has committed Himself to guiding us in the ways that He knows to be best for us. God sovereignly guides our lives so that we do indeed live out in our daily experiences all the days ordained for us.

The subject of discovering God's will in a particular matter (or as some prefer to state it, making wise decisions) is a different, though somewhat related, subject. It usually refers to a "fork in the road" type of decision. Much has been written on that subject, and there are several divergent views. I do not propose to enter that discussion here.

What I want to do is draw our attention to God's initiative

and God's faithfulness in guiding us, so that we do fulfill the plan He has ordained for us. We think so much about our responsibility to discover God's will in a situation or to make wise decisions in life's choices, but the biblical emphasis seems to be on God's guiding us.

Consider the book of Acts. The only reference to the disciples seeking to determine the will of God occurs in the choosing of Matthias to succeed Judas. From that point onward, it is a record of God's guiding His people. In Acts 16, for example, Paul and his companions were moving ahead in their missionary journey in a logical progression. Twice, however, they are stopped by the Holy Spirit and then, as a result of Paul's vision, they concluded God was calling them to Macedonia. As they moved ahead, the Spirit guided them, stopping them in two places and calling them to another. The account doesn't tell us *how* the Spirit guided, it simply says that He did.

God did have a plan for Paul and his team that was more specific than the Great Commission to make disciples of all nations. The provinces of Asia and Bithynia that Paul was prevented from entering were just as needy as Macedonia. But it was God's plan that Paul should take the gospel to Macedonia and then to the entire Grecian peninsula. God did not leave it to Paul to seek His will. Rather, as Paul moved along, God took the initiative to guide him.

God does have a plan for each of us. He has given each of us different gifts, abilities, and temperaments and has placed each of us in the body of Christ according to His will. To place us in the body obviously denotes far more than leaving the choice to us. It means actually putting us there. It includes all the providential circumstances that are brought to bear upon us to insure that we do find our rightful place in the body and fulfill the functions He has given us to do.

We do have a responsibility to make wise decisions or to discover the will of God, whichever term we may prefer to use. But God's plan for us is not contingent upon our decisions. God's plan is not contingent at all. God's plan is sovereign. It includes our foolish decisions as well as our wise ones.

For most of us, many of life's more crucial decisions are made before we have enough spiritual wisdom to make wise decisions. When I was a senior in college I interviewed for and was offered a job to become effective upon completion of my required military service. At that time I didn't know anything about the will of God or about making wise spiritual decisions. However, for some reason, I turned down the job. Looking back now I can see that God was guiding me, keeping me available for His later call to The Navigators' ministry.

God's means of guidance are infinite. As I look back over thirty-nine years of my Christian life, I am amazed at the many and diverse ways by which God has guided me. I am inclined to say with David, "How precious to me are your thoughts, O God! How vast is the sum of them!" (Psalm 139:17). God is at work guiding all the details of my life.

Like most Christians, I have struggled over the right choice at some of those "fork in the road" decision points, which we encounter from time to time. I may have made some wrong decisions, I do not know. But God in His sovereignty has faithfully guided me in His paths through right decisions and wrong ones. I am where I am today, not because I have always made wise decisions or correctly discovered the will of God at particular points along the way, but because God has faithfully led me and guided me along the path of His will for me.

God's guidance is almost always step-by-step; He does not show us our life's plan all at once. Sometimes our anxiousness to know the will of God comes from a desire to "peer over God's shoulder" to see what His plan is. What we need to do is learn to trust Him to guide us.

Of course, this does not mean that we put our minds into neutral and expect God to guide us in some mysterious way apart from hard and prayerful thinking on our part. It does mean, as Dr. James Packer has said, "God made us thinking beings, and he guides our minds as we think things out in his presence."[5]

I believe Dr. Packer has expressed it so well: God guides our minds as we think. But the important truth for this study is that *God does guide*. He does not play games with us. He does not look down from heaven at our struggles to know His will and say, "I hope you make the right decision." Rather, in His time and in His way He will lead us in His path for us.

Many years ago Fanny J. Crosby penned these words, which are so appropriate to this topic of trusting God for guidance:

All the way my Savior leads me
What have I to ask beside?
Can I doubt His tender mercy,
Who through life has been my guide?
Heavenly peace, divinest comfort,
Here by faith in Him to dwell!
For I know, whate'er befall me,
Jesus doeth all things well.

All the way my Savior leads me—
O the fullness of His love!
Perfect rest to me is promised
In my Father's house above.
When my spirit, clothed immortal,
Wings its flight to realms of day,
This my song through endless ages:
Jesus led me all the way.[6]

We *can* trust God to guide us. He *will* lead us all the way. And when we stand before His throne we will not be singing about successfully discovering the will of God. Rather with Fanny Crosby we, too, will sing, "Jesus led me all the way."

CHAPTER TWELVE

GROWING THROUGH ADVERSITY

*Consider it pure joy, my brothers, whenever you face trials of
many kinds, because you know that the testing of your faith
develops perseverance. Perseverance must finish its work so that
you may be mature and complete, not lacking anything.*

JAMES 1:2-4

One of the many fascinating events in nature is the emergence
of the Cecropia moth from its cocoon—an event that occurs
only with much struggle on the part of the moth to free itself.
The story is frequently told of someone who watched a moth
go through this struggle. In an effort to help—and not realizing
the necessity of the struggle—the viewer snipped the shell of
the cocoon. Soon the moth came out with its wings all crimped
and shriveled. But as the person watched, the wings remained
weak. The moth, which in a few moments would have stretched
those wings to fly, was now doomed to crawling out its brief
life in frustration of ever being the beautiful creature God created it to be.

What the person in the story did not realize was that the
struggle to emerge from the cocoon was an essential part of
developing the muscle system of the moth's body and pushing
the body fluids out into the wings to expand them. By unwisely
seeking to cut short the moth's struggle, the watcher had actually crippled the moth and doomed its existence.

The adversities of life are much like the cocoon of the Cecropia moth. God uses them to develop the spiritual "muscle system" of our lives. As James says in our text for this chapter, "The testing of your faith [through trials of many kinds] develops perseverance," and perseverance leads to maturity of our character.

We can be sure that the development of a beautiful Christlike character will not occur in our lives without adversity. Think of those lovely graces that Paul calls the fruit of the Spirit in Galatians 5:22-23. The first four traits he mentions—love, joy, peace, and patience—can only be developed in the womb of adversity.

We may think we have true Christian love until someone offends us or treats us unjustly. Then we begin to see anger and resentment well up within us. We may conclude we have learned about genuine Christian joy until our lives are shattered by an unexpected calamity or grievous disappointment. Adversities spoil our peace and sorely try our patience. God uses those difficulties to reveal to us our need to grow, so that we will reach out to Him to change us more and more into the likeness of His Son.

However, we shrink from adversity and, to use the terms from the moth illustration, we want God to snip the cocoon of adversity we often find ourselves in and release us. But just as God has more wisdom and love for the moth than its viewer did, so He has more wisdom and love for us than we do for ourselves. He will not remove the adversity until we have profited from it and developed in whatever way He intended in bringing or allowing it into our lives.

Both Paul and James speak of rejoicing in our sufferings (see Romans 5:3-4; James 1:2-4). Most of us, if we are honest with ourselves, have difficulty with that idea. Endure them, perhaps, but rejoice? That often seems like an unreasonable expectation. We are not masochistic; we don't enjoy pain.

But Paul and James both say that we should rejoice in our trials because of their beneficial results. It is not the adversity considered in itself that is to be the ground of our joy. Rather, it is the expectation of the results, the development of our character, that should cause us to rejoice in adversity. God does not ask us to rejoice because we have lost our job or a loved one has been stricken with cancer or a child has been born with an incurable birth defect. But He does tell us to rejoice because we believe He is in control of those circumstances and is at work through them for our ultimate good.

The Christian life is intended to be one of continuous growth. We all want to grow, but we often resist the process. This is because we tend to focus on the events of adversity themselves, rather than looking with the eye of faith beyond the events to what God is doing in our lives. It was said of Jesus that He "for the joy set before him endured the cross, scorning its shame" (Hebrews 12:2). Christ's death on the cross, with its intense physical agony and infinite spiritual suffering of bearing God's wrath for our sins, was the greatest calamity to ever come upon a human being. Yet Jesus could look beyond that suffering to the joy set before Him. And, as the writer of Hebrews said, we are to fix our eyes on Him and follow His example. We are to look beyond our adversity to what God is doing in our lives and rejoice in the certainty that He is at work in us to cause us to grow.

GOD WORKS THROUGH ADVERSITY

Fortunately God does not ask us how or when we want to grow. He is the Master Teacher, training His pupils when and how He deems best. He is, in the words of Jesus, the Gardener who prunes the branches of His vineyard. The healthy vine requires both nourishment and pruning. Through the Word of God we are nourished (see Psalm 1:2-3), but through adversity we are pruned. Both the Hebrew and Greek languages express discipline and teaching by the same word. God intends that we grow through the disciplines of adversity as well as through instruction from His Word. The psalmist joins adversity and instruction together in God's training process when he says, "Blessed is the man you discipline, O LORD, the man you teach from your law" (Psalm 94:12).

God is at work in each of His children, regardless of how aware of it we may be. One of the most encouraging passages in the Bible is Philippians 1:6: "Being confident of this, that he who began a good work in you will carry it on to completion until the day of Christ Jesus." God is at work in us, and He will not fail to carry on to completion that which He has begun. He will "work in us what is pleasing to him" (Hebrews 13:21).

Horatius Bonar, a nineteenth-century Scottish pastor, wrote,

> He who is carrying it on is not one who can be baffled and forced to give up His design. He is able to carry it out in the unlikeliest circumstances and against the most resolute resistance. Everything must give way before Him. This thought is, I confess, to me one of the most comforting connected with the discipline. If it could fail! If God could be frustrated in His designs after we have suffered so much, it would be awful![1]

But God cannot be frustrated. He will carry on to completion that which He has begun. As Bonar also wrote, "God's treatment *must* succeed. It cannot miscarry or be frustrated even in its most arduous efforts, even in reference to its minutest objects. It is the mighty power of God that is at work within us and upon us, and this is our consolation. . . . All is love, all is wisdom, and all is faithfulness, yet all is also power."[2]

That God cannot fail in His purpose for adversity in our lives, that He will accomplish that which He intends, is a great encouragement to me. Sometimes I do fail to respond to difficulties in a God-honoring way. But my failure does not mean God has failed. Even my painfully sharp awareness of failure may be used of God, for example, to help me grow in humility. And perhaps that was God's intention all along.

God knows what He is doing. Again in the words of Bonar, "He knows exactly what we need and how to supply it. . . . His training is no random work. It is carried on with exquisite skill."[3] God knows us better than we know ourselves. What we think may be our greatest need may not be at all. But God unerringly knows where we need to grow. He carries on His work with a skill that far exceeds that of the most expert physician. He correctly diagnoses our need and applies the most sure remedy.

Every adversity that comes across our path, whether large or small, is intended to help us grow in some way. If it were not beneficial, God would not allow it or send it, "For he does not willingly bring affliction or grief to the children of men" (Lamentations 3:33). God does not delight in our sufferings. He brings only that which is necessary, but He does not shrink from that which will help us grow.

WE LEARN FROM ADVERSITY
Because God is at work in our lives through adversity, we must learn to respond to what He is doing. As we have already seen in previous chapters, God's sovereign work never negates our responsibility. Just as God teaches us through adversity, we must seek to learn from it.

There are several things we can do in order to learn from

adversity and receive the beneficial effects that God intends. First, we can *submit* to it—not reluctantly as the defeated general submits to his conqueror, but voluntarily as the patient on the operating table submits to the skilled hand of the surgeon as he wields his knife. Do not try to frustrate the gracious purpose of God by resisting His providence in your life. Rather, insofar as you are able to see what God is doing, make His purpose your purpose.

This does not mean we should not use all legitimate means at our disposal to minimize the effects of adversity. It means we should accept from God's hand the success or failure of those means as He wills and at all times seek to learn whatever He might be teaching us.

Sometimes we will perceive quite clearly what God is doing, and in those instances we should respond to God's teaching in humble obedience. At other times we may not be able to see at all what He is doing in our lives. At those times, we should respond in humble faith, trusting Him to work out in our lives that which we need to learn. Both attitudes are important, and God wants one at one time and the other at another time.

Second, to profit most from adversity, we should *bring the Word of God to bear upon the situation*. We should ask God to bring to our attention pertinent passages of Scripture and then, in dependence on Him to do so, look for those passages. My first great lesson on the sovereignty of God is still stamped indelibly on my mind after many years. It came as I was desperately searching the Scriptures to find some kind of an answer to a severe time of testing.

As we seek to relate the Scriptures to our adversities, we'll find we will not only profit from the circumstances themselves, but we will gain new insight into the Scriptures. Martin Luther reportedly said, "Were it not for tribulation I should not understand the Scriptures." Although we may be going to the

Scriptures to learn how to respond to our adversities, we find those adversities in turn help us to understand the Scriptures. It is not that we will learn from adversity something different than what we can learn from the Scriptures. Rather, adversity enhances the teaching of God's Word and makes it more profitable to us. In some instances it clarifies our understanding or causes us to see truths we had passed over before. At other times it will transform "head knowledge" into "heart knowledge" as theological theory becomes a reality to us.

The Puritan Daniel Dyke said,

> The word, then, is the storehouse of all instruction.
> Look not for any new diverse doctrine to be taught thee
> by affliction, which is not in the word. For, in truth,
> herein stands our teaching by affliction, that it fits and
> prepares us for the word, by breaking and sub-dividing
> the stubbornness of our hearts, and making them pliable,
> and capable of the impression of the word.[4]

We might say, then, that the Word of God and adversity have a synergistic effect as God uses both of them together to bring about growth in our lives that neither the Word nor adversity would accomplish by itself.

Third, in order to profit from our adversities we must *remember* them and the lessons we learned from them. God wants us to do more than simply endure our trials, even more than merely find comfort in them. He wants us to remember them, not just as trials or sorrows, but as His disciplines—His means of bringing about growth in our lives. He said to the Israelites,

> Remember how the LORD your God led you all the way
> in the desert these forty years, to humble you and to test
> you. . . . He humbled you, causing you to hunger and then

feeding you with manna . . . to teach you that man does not live on bread alone but on every word that comes from the mouth of the LORD.   DEUTERONOMY 8:2-3

The "word that comes from the mouth of the LORD" in this passage is not the Word of Scripture but the word of God's providence (see Psalms 33:6, 9 and 148:5 for similar usage). God wanted to teach the Israelites that they were dependent upon Him for their daily bread. He did this—not by incorporating this truth into the law of Moses, but by bringing adversity in the form of hunger into their lives. But in order to profit from this lesson they must *remember* it. We, too, if we are to profit from the painful lessons God teaches us, must remember them.

I referred in an earlier chapter to a rather painful lesson I learned when I tried to subtly usurp some of God's glory for my own reputation. God holds me responsible to remember that lesson. Every time I come across Isaiah 42:8, "I will not give my glory to another," in either my Bible reading or my Scripture memory review, I should remember that painful circumstance and let the lesson sink more deeply into my heart. Every time I stand up to teach God's Word I should remember that lesson and purge my heart of any desire to enhance my own reputation. This is the way adversity becomes profitable to us.[5]

Thus far we have considered profiting from adversity in a general way, looking first at God's working in our lives through trials and then at how we should respond to them. Now it will be helpful to consider some specific ends God has in mind when He allows adversity in our lives. Of course, we cannot cover all the lessons God intends to teach us through adversity, but these are some specifically mentioned or implied in the Bible. Through studying these specific objectives, we should be encouraged to believe that God always has a reason for bringing or allowing particular difficulties in our lives, even when we cannot discern what His reason is.

PRUNING

Jesus said that "every branch that does bear fruit [God] prunes so that it will be even more fruitful" (John 15:2). In the natural realm, pruning is important for fruit bearing. An unpruned vine will produce a great deal of unproductive growth but little fruit. Cutting away unwanted and useless growth forces the plant to use its life to produce fruit.

In the spiritual realm, God must prune us. Because even as believers we still have a sinful nature, we tend to pour our spiritual energies into that which is not true fruit. We tend to seek position, success, and reputation even in the body of Christ. We tend to depend upon natural talents and human wisdom. And then we are easily distracted and pulled by the things of the world—its pleasures and possessions.

God uses adversity to loosen our grip on those things that are not true fruit. A severe illness or the death of someone dear to us, the loss of material substance or the tarnishing of our reputation, the turning aside of friends or the dashing of our cherished dreams on the rocks of failure, cause us to think about what is really important in life. Position or possessions or even reputation no longer seem so important. We begin to relinquish our desires and expectations—even good ones—to the sovereign will of God. We come more and more to depend on God and to desire only that which will count for eternity. God is pruning us so that we will be more fruitful.

HOLINESS

We have already seen in a previous chapter that another intended result of adversity is to cause us to grow in holiness: "God disciplines us [through adversity] for our good, that we may share in his holiness" (Hebrews 12:10). But what is the connection between adversity and holiness?

For one thing, adversity reveals the corruption of our sinful nature. We do not know ourselves or the depths of sin remaining in us. We agree with the teachings of Scripture and assume that agreement means obedience. At least we intend to obey. Who of us does not read that list of Christian virtues called the fruit of the Spirit—love, joy, peace, patience, kindness, goodness, faithfulness, gentleness, and self-control (see Galatians 5:22-23)—and agree we want all those traits in our lives? We even begin to think we are making good progress in growing in them.

But then adversity comes. We find we are unable to love, from the depths of our hearts, the person who is the instrument of the adversity. We find we don't want to forgive that person. We realize we are not disposed to trust God. Unbelief and resentment surge within us. We are dismayed at the scene. The growth in Christian character we thought had occurred in our lives seems to vanish like a vapor. We feel as if we are back in spiritual kindergarten again. But through this experience God has revealed to us some of the remaining corruption within us.

Jesus said, "Blessed are the poor in spirit. . . . Blessed are those who mourn. . . . Blessed are those who hunger and thirst for righteousness" (Matthew 5:3-4, 6). All of these descriptions refer to the believer who has been humbled over his sinfulness, who mourns because of it, and yearns with all his heart for God to change him. But no one adopts this attitude without being exposed to the evil and corruption of his own heart. God uses adversity to do this.

In making us holy, God goes deeper than just specific sins we may be conscious of. He wants to get at the root cause: the corruption of our sinful nature manifested in the rebellion of our wills, the perversity of our affections, and the spiritual ignorance of our minds. God uses adversity to enlighten our minds about our own needs as well as the teachings of Scripture. He uses adversity to rein in our affections that have been drawn out to unholy desires and to subdue our stubborn and rebellious wills.

But we often resist God's work in our lives. We shrink from the rod of God's discipline instead of seeking to profit from it. We are more desirous of relief from the adversity than we are of its profit unto holiness. But as we look to God to use His discipline in our lives, we may be sure it will in due time produce "a harvest of righteousness and peace for those who have been trained by it" (Hebrews 12:11).

DEPENDENCE

Another area of our lives that God must continually be at work on is our tendency to rely on ourselves instead of on Him. Jesus said, "Apart from me you can do nothing" (John 15:5). Apart from our union with Christ and a total reliance upon Him, we can do nothing that glorifies God. We live in a world that worships independence and self-reliance. "I am the master of my fate; I am the captain of my soul" is the motto of society around us. Because of our own sinful nature, we can easily fall into the world's pattern of thinking. We tend to rely on our knowledge of Scripture, our own business acumen, our ministry experience, and even our goodness and morality.

God has to teach us through adversity to rely on Him instead of ourselves. Even the apostle Paul said of his difficulties, which he described as "far beyond our ability to endure," that they occurred so "that we might not rely on ourselves but on God, who raises the dead" (2 Corinthians 1:8-9). God allowed Paul and his band of men to be brought into a situation so desperate that they despaired even of life itself. They had no place to turn except to God.

Paul had to learn dependence on God in the spiritual as well as the physical realm. Whatever his thorn in the flesh was, it was an adversity that Paul desperately wanted to be rid of. But God let it remain, not only to curb any tendency for pride in Paul's heart, but also to teach him to rely on God's strength. Paul had to learn that it was not his strength but God's grace—God's enabling power—that he must depend on.

Paul was one of the most brilliant men in history. At least one theologian has said that if Paul had not become a Christian and had instead gone into philosophy that he might well have surpassed Plato. God gave Paul an abundance of natural intellect, and God gave him divine revelations, some of which were of such glory that Paul was not permitted to tell about them. But God never permitted Paul to depend on either his intellect or his revelations. Paul had to depend on God's grace just like you and me. And he learned this through severe adversity.

I am a person of many weaknesses and few natural strengths. My physical limitations, though not apparent to most people, prevent my relating to other men through golf, tennis, or other recreational sports. I feel this keenly, and for some years I struggled frequently with God about it. But I have at last concluded that my weaknesses are actually channels for *His* strength. After many years, I think I am finally at the point where I can say with Paul, "I delight in weaknesses. . . . For when I am weak, then I am strong" (2 Corinthians 12:10).

It does not matter whether you are predominantly a person of strengths or weaknesses on the natural level. You may be the most competent person in your field, but you can be sure that if God is going to use you, He will cause you to feel keenly your dependence on Him. He will often blight the very thing we feel confident in, so that we will learn to depend on Him, not on ourselves. According to Stephen, "Moses was educated in all the wisdom of the Egyptians and was powerful in speech and action" (Acts 7:22). Moreover he "thought that his own people would realize that God was using him to rescue them" (verse 25). But when Moses attempted to take matters into his own hands, God so frustrated his efforts that Moses had to flee for his life. Forty years later Moses still had no confidence in his own abilities and even had difficulty believing that God could use him.

Paul experienced a thorn in the flesh. Moses saw his efforts to do something for God utterly frustrated and turned into disaster. Each of these men of God experienced an adversity that caused him to realize his own weakness and his dependence on God. Each adversity was different, but each had a common goal of bringing these men to a place of greater dependence on God. If God is going to use you and me, He will bring adversity into our lives so that we, too, may learn experientially our dependence on Him.

PERSEVERANCE

The recipients of the letter to the Hebrews were experiencing a great deal of adversity. The writer of that letter acknowledged that they stood their ground in the face of suffering, that sometimes they were publicly exposed to insult and persecution, and that they joyfully accepted the confiscation of their property because they knew they had better and lasting possessions (see Hebrews 10:32-34).

To these people, who were experiencing such persecution and hardship for their faith in Christ, the writer wrote, "You need to persevere so that when you have done the will of God, you will receive what he has promised" (Hebrews 10:36). And, "Let us run with perseverance the race marked out for us" (12:1).

Perseverance is the quality of character that enables one to pursue a goal in spite of obstacles and difficulties. It is one thing to simply bear up under adversity. This in itself is commendable. But God calls us to do more than simply bear the load of adversity. He calls us to persevere (to press forward) in the face of it. Note how the writer of Hebrews focuses on reaching the goal: "When you have *done* the will of God" and "*run* . . . the race marked out for us." The Christian life is meant to be active, not passive. The Christian is called to pursue with diligence the will of God. To do this requires perseverance.

We saw in the first chapter one writer's comment that life is difficult. It is really a series of difficulties of different kinds and varying degrees, usually experienced over a period of many years. It has often been observed that the Christian life is not a sprint but a marathon. But even those metaphors fail to adequately express reality. The Christian life could better be described as an obstacle course of marathon length. Think of a race course just over twenty-six miles in length. Add to it walls to climb over, streams to forge, hedges to jump across, and an endless variety of other *unexpected* obstacles. That is the Christian life. It is no wonder that someone has observed "few Christians finish well."

But God wants all Christians to finish well. He wants us to run with perseverance. He wants us to persist in doing His will whatever the obstacles might be. William Carey, often called the father of modern missions, is a famous example of one who persevered. Despite a succession of unbelievable obstacles (including an unsympathetic wife who later became insane), he translated all or parts of the Bible into forty languages and dialects of India. And William Carey's sister is equally an example of one who persevered. Almost totally paralyzed and bedridden, she lay on her bed in London and prayed for all the details and struggles of her brother's work in far-off India.

Few people can identify with the perseverance of William Carey in either the incredible obstacles he faced or the amazing tasks he accomplished. But we should identify with the perseverance of Carey's sister. She persevered in doing the will of God in her invalid state. She could not do much (at least what we tend to think of as much), but she persevered in doing what she could, in doing the will of God for her. And because she persevered in prayer, her brother was strengthened and enabled to persevere in his missionary labors in India. Carey's sister did more than bear cheerfully her paralysis; she persevered in doing the will of God in spite of it.

You and I are also called to persevere. Each of us has been given a race to run, a will of God to do. All of us encounter innumerable obstacles and occasions for discouragement. To run the race and finish well we must develop perseverance. How can we do it?

Both Paul and James give us the same answer. Paul said, "We know that suffering produces perseverance," and James said, "The testing of your faith develops perseverance" (Romans 5:3; James 1:3). We see here a mutually enhancing effect. Adversity produces perseverance, and perseverance enables us to meet adversity. A good analogy is found in weight training. Lifting weights develops muscle, and the more one's muscles are developed, the heavier the weight one can lift.

Though perseverance is developed in the crucible of adversity, it is energized by faith. Again, consider the analogy of weight training. Although the weights on a bar provide the resistance needed to develop muscle, they do not provide the energy. That must come from within the athlete's body. In the case of adversity, the energy must come from God through faith. It is God's strength, not ours, that enables us to persevere. But we lay hold of His strength through faith.

We have already noted the writer's call to perseverance in Hebrews 10:36 and 12:1. Sandwiched between those two calls to perseverance is the well-known chapter on faith, Hebrews 11. The writer is actually calling us to persevere *by faith*. His eleventh chapter is a motivational chapter, as he gives example after example of people who persevered in doing the will of God by faith.

The sequence of putting *dependence* before *perseverance* in this chapter was deliberately chosen. We cannot grow in perseverance until we have learned the lesson of dependence. You may, for example, drive a dog sled to the North Pole purely by a self-energized indomitable spirit, but you cannot run the Christian race that way. If you are going to run God's race, doing God's will, then you must run it with His strength. Jesus said, "Apart from me you can do nothing," and Paul said, "I can do everything through him who gives me strength" (John 15:5; Philippians 4:13). Jesus and Paul state two sides of the same truth: Without His strength we can do nothing, but with it we can do all we need to do. We are called to persevere—to do God's will despite the obstacles and discouragements—but in His strength and His alone.

SERVICE

God also brings adversity into our lives to equip us for more effective service. All that we have considered so far—pruning, holiness, dependence, and perseverance—contributes to making us useful instruments in God's service. God could have brought Joseph directly to Pharaoh's palace without taking him through prison. And He certainly did not need to leave Joseph to languish in prison for two more years after he had interpreted the cupbearer's dream. Joseph's difficult circumstances were not necessary just for him to be in the right place at the right time. They were necessary to make him into the right kind of person for the responsibilities God would give him.

The apostle Paul wrote that "[God] comforts us in all our troubles, so that we can comfort those in any trouble with the comfort we ourselves have received from God" (2 Corinthians 1:4). Everyone faces times of adversity, and everyone needs a compassionate and caring friend to come alongside to comfort and encourage during those times. As we experience God's comfort and encouragement in *our* adversities, we are equipped to be His instrument of comfort and encouragement to others. We pass on to others what we have received from God ourselves. To the extent we are able to lay hold of the great truths of the sovereignty, wisdom, and love of God and find comfort and encouragement from them in our adversities, we will be able to minister to others in their times of distress.

In commenting on Paul's ministry of comforting, I have deliberately used the expression "comfort and encourage." The Greek word translated as *comfort* in our Bibles may mean admonition, encouragement, or comfort depending on the context. Because God the Father is called here "the Father of compassion and the God of all comfort," it seems our English translators have done well to choose the word *comfort* to express God's compassion. If we are to minister to others in their times of adversity, we must first of all show compassion, the deep feeling of sharing in the suffering of another and the desire to relieve that suffering.

If we are to really help another person in his or her time of adversity, we must also encourage that person. To encourage is to fortify another with the spiritual and emotional strength to persevere in times of adversity. We do this by pointing that person to the trustworthiness of God as it is revealed to us in

Scripture. Only to the extent that we ourselves have been comforted and encouraged by the Holy Spirit through His Word will we be able to comfort and encourage others. Adversity in our own lives, rightly responded to, enables us to be instruments of comfort and encouragement to others.

THE FELLOWSHIP OF SUFFERING

The apostle John, writing to the persecuted believers of the seven churches in Asia, identified himself as "your brother and companion in the suffering . . . that [is] ours in Jesus" (Revelation 1:9). The Greek word that is translated as *companion* means a "fellow sharer." It is a form of the word *koinonia* from which we get our word *fellowship*.

John identified himself as one who shared together with his readers in the sufferings they were enduring. He could understand their afflictions since he was at that time also suffering for the sake of Jesus. John was a partaker with them in their suffering, and it was important to the effective communication of his message that they understand that fact. In this verse, then, John introduces us to yet another way in which we profit from adversity: the privilege of entering into a special fellowship with other believers who are also in the throes of adversity.

Trials and afflictions have a leveling effect among believers. It has often been said that "the ground is level at the foot of the cross." That is, regardless of our wealth or power or station in life, we are all alike in our need for a Savior. In the same way, we are all alike subject to adversity. It strikes the rich and the poor, the powerful and the weak, the superior and the subordinate, all without distinction. In times of adversity we tend to set aside such notions of "vertical" relationships and relate to one another on a horizontal level as brothers and fellow sufferers. John could have rightly identified himself as an apostle of

Jesus Christ, as one in a position of spiritual authority over the suffering believers in Asia. Instead he chose to identify himself as a brother and companion in their suffering.

Trials and afflictions also have a mutual drawing effect among believers. They tend to break down barriers between us and dissolve any appearance of self-sufficiency we may have. We find our hearts warmed and drawn toward one another. We sometimes worship together with another person, pray together, and even serve together in the ministry without ever truly feeling a bond of fellowship. But then, in a strange way, adversity strikes us both. Immediately we sense a new bond of fellowship in Christ, the fellowship of suffering.

There are many elements that go into the total concept of fellowship, as it is described in the New Testament, but the sharing together in suffering is one of the most profitable. It probably unites our hearts together in Christ more than any other aspect of fellowship. I'm reminded of one believer with whom I had a friendship for many years, but we were never close. Then adversity struck us both. Our circumstances were different, and his adversity was far worse than mine, but in our efforts to care for one another our hearts were drawn together in a new and deeper way.

This chapter has dealt with various ways in which we profit from adversity. Prior to this section, we have considered ways in which we profit as individual believers, but in the fellowship of suffering we are looking at a way in which we profit as members of the whole body of Christ. The Christian life is not meant to be lived privately in isolation from other believers. It is to be lived as members of the body of Christ. God wants to use our times of adversity to deepen our relationship with other members of the body—to create a greater sense of sharing together the life we have in Christ.

RELATIONSHIP WITH GOD

Perhaps the most valuable way we profit from adversity is in the deepening of our relationship with God. Through adversity we learn to bow before His sovereignty, to trust His wisdom, and to experience the consolations of His love, until we come to the place where we can say with Job, "My ears had heard of you but now my eyes have seen you" (Job 42:5). We begin to pass from knowing *about* God to knowing God Himself in a personal and intimate way.

We have just considered the fellowship of suffering among believers. In Philippians 3:10, Paul speaks of the fellowship of sharing in the sufferings of Jesus Christ, that is, of believers sharing with our Lord in His sufferings. The passage reads as follows:

> I want to know Christ and the power of his resurrection and the fellowship of sharing in his sufferings, becoming like him in his death.

This verse has given expression to the deepest heart cry of believers down through the centuries: the desire to know Christ in an ever-increasing intimate, personal way. I can remember as a young Christian being challenged to "know Christ and to make Him known," and I can remember praying, because of Philippians 3:10, that God would enable me to know Christ more and more.

I have to confess, though, that down deep inside it always bothered me a bit that Paul not only wanted to know Christ Himself but also wanted to experience the fellowship of His sufferings. To know Christ in a more intimate way and to experience the power of His resurrection in my life appealed to me, but not the suffering. I shrank from that.

But I have come to see that the message of Philippians 3:10 is a "package deal." Part of coming to know Christ in a more intimate way is through the fellowship of His sufferings. If we are to truly grow in knowing Christ, we can be sure we will to some degree experience the fellowship of His sufferings. If we are to experience the power of His resurrection, we can also be sure we will experience the fellowship of His sufferings.

It will help us to appreciate the truth that Paul is teaching in Philippians 3:10 if we understand that the suffering Paul envisions is not limited to persecution for the sake of the gospel. It includes all adversity that overtakes the believer and that has as its ultimate purpose his conformity to Christ, described here by Paul as "becoming like him in his death."

Repeatedly in the Bible, we see men and women of God drawn into a deeper relationship with God through adversity. There is no doubt that all the circumstances in the long delay of the birth of Isaac and then the experience of taking his only son up to the mountain to offer as a sacrifice brought Abraham into a much deeper relationship with God. The psalms are replete with expressions of ever-deepening knowledge of God as the psalmists seek Him in times of adversity (see, for example, Psalms 23; 42; 61; 62).

You and I obviously do not seek out adversity just so we can develop a deeper relationship with God. Rather God, through adversity, seeks us out. It is God who draws us more and more into a deeper relationship with Him. If we are seeking Him, it is because He is seeking us. One of the strong cords with which He draws us into a more intimate, personal relationship with Him is adversity. If, instead of fighting God or doubting Him in times of adversity, we will seek to cooperate with God, we will find that we will be drawn into a deeper relationship with Him. We will come to know Him as Abraham and Job and David and Paul came to know Him.

We have seen some of the ways we may profit from adversity.

Obviously we have not covered all the uses God makes of adversity in our lives, nor have we more than scratched the surface of those areas we have considered. Sometimes we will be able to see how we are profiting, at other times we will wonder what God is doing. One thing we may be sure of, however: For the believer all pain has meaning; all adversity is profitable.

There is no question that adversity is difficult. It usually takes us by surprise and seems to strike where we are most vulnerable. To us it often appears completely senseless and irrational, but to God none of it is either senseless or irrational. He has a purpose in every pain He brings or allows in our lives. We can be sure that in some way He intends it for our profit and His glory.

CHAPTER THIRTEEN

CHOOSING TO TRUST GOD

When I am afraid, I will trust in you.
In God, whose word I praise,
in God I trust; I will not be afraid.
What can mortal man do to me?

PSALM 56:3-4

While this book was being written, my first wife, who is now with the Lord, was found to have a large malignant tumor in the abdominal cavity. After eight weeks of radiation therapy and another month of waiting, the doctor ordered a CAT scan to determine if the tumor had been successfully resolved. The day before she was to learn the results of the CAT scan, my wife found herself apprehensive and anxious over the news she would hear the next day.

For some days she had been turning to Psalm 42:11 for assurance during this difficult time. The verse says,

> Why are you downcast, O my soul?
>   Why so disturbed within me?
> Put your hope in God,
>   for I will yet praise him,
>   my Savior and my God.

Turning to Psalm 42:11 that day, she said, "Lord, I choose not to be downcast, I choose not to be disturbed, I choose to put my hope in You." She told me later, as she recounted this to me, that her feelings did not change immediately, but after a while they did. Her heart was calmed as she deliberately chose to trust God.

David, in his times of distress, also chose to trust God. In Psalm 56:3-4, our text for this chapter, David admitted he was afraid. David was not cocky or arrogant. Despite the fact that he was a warrior of great skill and courage, there were times when he was afraid. The heading of Psalm 56 indicates the occasion of David's writing: "When the Philistines had seized him in Gath." The historical narrative of that incident says that he "was very much afraid of Achish king of Gath" (1 Samuel 21:12).

But despite David's fear, he said to God, "I will trust in you. . . . I will not be afraid." Repeatedly in the psalms we find the determination to trust God—choosing to trust Him despite all appearances. David's declaration in Psalm 23:4, "I will fear no evil," is equivalent to "I will trust in God in the face of evil." In Psalm 16:8 he says,

I have set the LORD always before me.
Because he is at my right hand, I will not be shaken.

To set the Lord before me is to recognize His presence and His constant help, but this is something we must choose to do.

God is always with us. He has said, "Never will I leave you; never will I forsake you" (Hebrews 13:5). There is no question of His presence with us. But we must *recognize* His presence; we must set Him always before us. We must choose whether or not we will believe His promises of constant protection and care.

Margaret Clarkson, in speaking of how we may arrive at a place of acceptance of adversity in our lives, said, "Always it is initiated by an act of will on our part; we set ourselves to believe in the overruling goodness, providence, and sovereignty of God and refuse to turn aside no matter what may come, no matter how we feel."[1]

For many years in my own pilgrimage of seeking to come to a place of trusting God at all times—I am still far from the end of the journey—I was a prisoner to my feelings. I mistakenly thought I could not trust God unless I *felt* like trusting Him (which I almost never did in times of adversity). Now I am learning that trusting God is first of all a matter of the will and is not dependent on my feelings. I choose to trust God, and my feelings eventually follow.

Having said that trusting God is first of all a matter of the will, let me qualify that statement to say that, first of all, it is a matter of knowledge. We must *know* that God is sovereign, wise, and loving—in all the ways we have come to see what those terms mean in previous chapters. But having been exposed to the knowledge of the truth, we must then choose whether to believe the truth about God, which He has revealed to us, or whether to follow our feelings. If we are to trust God, we must choose to believe His truth. We must say, "I will trust You though I do not feel like doing so."

BE WILLING TO BELIEVE

To trust God in times of adversity is admittedly a hard thing to do. I do not mean to suggest in my emphasis on choosing to trust God that the choice is as easy as choosing whether or not I will go to the store, or even choosing whether or not I will do some sacrificial deed. Trusting God is a matter of faith, and faith is the fruit of the Spirit (see Galatians 5:22). Only the Holy Spirit can make His Word come alive in our hearts and create faith, but we can choose to look to Him to do that, or we can choose to be ruled by our feelings of anxiety or resentment or grief.

John Newton, author of the hymn "Amazing Grace," watched cancer slowly and painfully kill his wife over a period of many months. In recounting those days, John Newton said:

> I believe it was about two or three months before her death, when I was walking up and down the room, offering disjointed prayers from a heart torn with distress, that a thought suddenly struck me, with unusual force, to this effect—"The promises of God must be true; surely the Lord will help me, if I am willing to be helped!" It occurred to me, that we are often led . . . [from an undue regard of our feelings], to indulge that unprofitable grief which both our duty and our peace require us to resist to the utmost of our power. I instantly said aloud, "Lord, I am helpless indeed, in myself, but I hope I am willing, without reserve, that thou shouldest help me."[2]

John Newton was helped in a remarkable way. During those remaining months he tended to his usual duties as an Anglican minister and was able to say,

> Through the whole of my painful trial, I attended all my stated and occasional services, as usual; and a stranger would scarcely have discovered, either by my words or looks, that I was in trouble. [The long affliction] did not prevent me from preaching a single sermon, and I preached on the day of her death. . . . I likewise preached three times while she lay dead in the house. . . . And after she was deposited in the vault, I preached her funeral sermon.[3]

How was John Newton helped? First he chose to be helped. He realized it was his duty to resist "to the utmost of our power" an inordinate amount of grief and distraction. He realized it was sinful to wallow in self-pity. Then he turned to the Lord, not even asking, but only indicating his *willingness* to be helped. Then he said, "I was not supported by lively sensible consolations, but by being enabled to realize to my mind some great and leading truths of the word of God."[4] The Spirit of God helped him by making needed truths of Scripture alive to him. He chose to trust God, he turned to God in an attitude of dependence, and he was enabled to realize certain great truths of Scripture. Choice, prayer, and the Word of God were the crucial elements of his being helped to trust God.

The same David who said in Psalm 56:4, "In God I trust; I will not be afraid" said in Psalm 34:4, "I sought the Lord, and he answered me; he delivered me from all my fears." There is no conflict between saying, "I will not be afraid" and asking God to deliver us from our fears. David recognized it was his responsibility to choose to trust God but also that he was dependent upon the Lord for the ability to do it.

Whenever I teach on the subject of personal holiness, I always stress that we are *responsible* to obey the will of God, but that we are *dependent* upon the Holy Spirit for the enabling power to do it. The same principle applies in the realm of trusting God. We are responsible to trust Him in times of adversity, but we are dependent upon the Holy Spirit to enable us to do so.

Again, let me emphasize that trusting God does not mean we do not experience pain. It means we believe that God is at work through the occasion of our pain for our ultimate good. It means we work back through the Scriptures regarding His sovereignty, wisdom, and goodness and ask Him to use those Scriptures to bring peace and comfort to our hearts. It means, above all, that we do not sin against God by allowing distrustful and hard thoughts about Him to hold sway in our minds. It will often mean that we may have to say, "God I don't understand, but I trust You."

GOD IS TRUSTWORTHY

The whole idea of trusting God is, of course, based upon the fact that God is absolutely trustworthy. That is why we spent twelve chapters of this book studying the sovereignty, wisdom, and love of God. We must be firmly grounded in those scriptural truths if we are to trust Him.

We must also lay hold of some of the great promises of His constant care for us. One such promise we will do well to store up in our hearts is Hebrews 13:5: "Never will I leave you; never will I forsake you." The Puritan preacher Thomas Lye remarked that in this passage the Greek has five negatives and may thus be rendered, "I will not, not leave thee; neither will I not, not forsake thee."[5] Five times God emphasized to us that He will not forsake us. He wants us to firmly grasp the truth that whatever circumstances may indicate, we must believe, on the basis of His promise, that He has not forsaken us or left us to the mercy of those circumstances.

We may sometimes lose the *sense* of God's presence and help, but we never lose them. Job, in his distress, could not find God. He said:

> But if I go to the east, he is not there;
>   if I go to the west, I do not find him.
> When he is at work in the north, I do not see him;
>   when he turns to the south, I catch no glimpse
>   of him.
> But he knows the way that I take;
>   when he has tested me, I will come forth as gold.

JOB 23:8-10

In previous chapters we have seen lessons from some of Job's struggles to trust God. Job apparently wavered, as we do, between trust and doubt. Here we see a strong affirmation of trust. He couldn't find God anywhere. God had completely withdrawn from Job the comforting sense of His presence. But Job believed, though he couldn't see Him, that God was watching over him and would bring him through that trial as purified gold.

You and I will sometimes have the same experience as Job—perhaps not in the same kind or intensity of sufferings—but in the seeming inability to find God anywhere. God will seem to hide Himself from us. Even the prophet Isaiah said to God on one occasion, "Truly you are a God who hides himself, O God and Savior of Israel" (Isaiah 45:15). We should learn from Job and Isaiah, so that we are not totally surprised and dismayed when, in the time of our distress, we can't seem to find God. At these times we must cling to His bare but inviolate promise, "Never will I leave you; never will I forsake you."

The apostle Paul speaks of "God, who does not lie" (Titus 1:2). This is the God who has promised, "Never will I leave you; never will I forsake you." He may hide Himself from our sense of His presence, but He never allows our adversities to hide us from Him. He may allow us to pass through the deep waters and the fire, but He will be with us in them (see Isaiah 43:2).

Because God will never leave you nor forsake you, you are invited in the words of Peter to "cast all your anxiety on him because he cares for you" (1 Peter 5:7). This is a passage of Scripture that is very familiar to many of us, in fact it seems too familiar. Some passages of Scripture like this one seem so familiar, and consequently so elementary, that we often pass right by them. It is almost like knowing that one plus one equals two. That's for first graders! But it also happens to be the most foundational truth in mathematics. Without that truth we couldn't have algebra, calculus, and all higher forms of mathematics.

Let's go back then and take a deeper look at 1 Peter 5:7. God cares for you! Not only will He never leave you—that's the negative side of the promise—but He cares for you. He is not just there with you, He cares for you. His care is constant—not occasional or sporadic. His care is total—even the very hairs of your head are numbered. His care is sovereign—nothing can touch you that He does not allow. His care is infinitely wise and good so that again in the words of John Newton, "If it were possible for me to alter any part of his plan, I could only spoil it."[6]

We must learn to cast our anxieties on Him. Dr. John Brown says of this verse, "The figurative expression 'cast,' not lay, seems to intimate that the duty enjoined is one that requires an effort; and experience tells us it is no easy matter to throw off the burden of carefulness."[7] So we are back to the matter of choice. We must by an act of the will in dependence on the Holy Spirit say something such as, "Lord, I choose to cast off this anxiety onto You, but I cannot do this of myself. I will trust You by Your Spirit to enable me to, having cast my anxiety on You, not to take it back upon myself."

Trust is not a passive state of mind. It is a vigorous act of the soul by which we choose to lay hold on the promises of God and cling to them despite the adversity that at times seeks to overwhelm us.

Several years ago I encountered a series of related difficulties within a few days. Not major calamities, but of a nature as to cause me great distress. At the outset, the verse Psalm 50:15 came to my mind, "Call upon me in the day of trouble; I will deliver you, and you will honor me." I began to call upon God asking Him to deliver me, but it seemed the more I called, the more the difficulties came.

I began to wonder if God's promises had any real meaning. Finally one day I said to God, "I will take You at Your Word. I will believe that in Your time and in Your way, You will deliver me." The difficulties did not cease, but the peace of God did quiet my fears and anxieties. And then, in due time, God did deliver me from those troubles, and He did it in such a way that I knew He had done it. God's promises are true. They cannot fail because He cannot lie. But, to realize the peace they are intended to give, we must choose to believe them. We must *cast* our anxieties upon Him.

PITFALLS IN TRUSTING

As difficult as it is to trust God in times of adversity, there are other times when it may be even more difficult to trust Him. These would be times when circumstances are going well, when, to use David's expression, "The boundary lines have fallen . . . in pleasant places" (Psalm 16:6). During times of temporal blessings and prosperity, we are prone to put our trust in those blessings, or even worse, in ourselves as the providers of those blessings.

During times of prosperity and favorable circumstances, we show our trust in God by acknowledging Him as the provider of all those blessings. We have already seen that God caused the nation of Israel to hunger in the desert and then fed them with manna from heaven in order to teach them "that man does not live on bread alone but on every word that comes from the mouth of the LORD" (Deuteronomy 8:3).

So how about us with our cupboards and refrigerators filled with food for tomorrow's meals? We are just as dependent upon God as the Israelites were. God rained down manna for them each day. For us He may provide a regular paycheck and plenty of food at the supermarket ready for us to buy. He provided the

Israelites' food through a miracle. He provides our food through a long and complex chain of natural events in which His hand is visible only to the eye of faith. But it is still His provision just as much as was the manna from heaven.

How often are our expressions of thanksgiving at mealtimes hardly more than a perfunctory ritual with little genuine feeling? How often do we stop to acknowledge God's hand of provision and to thank Him for other temporal blessings such as the clothes we wear, the house we live in, the car we drive, the health we enjoy? The extent to which we genuinely thank God for the blessings He does provide is an indicator of our trust in Him. We ought to be as earnest and frequent in our prayers of thanksgiving when the cupboard is full as we would be in our prayers of supplication if the cupboards were bare. That is the way we show our trust in times of prosperity and blessing.

Solomon said,

When times are good, be happy;
  but when times are bad, consider:
God has made the one
  as well as the other.

ECCLESIASTES 7:14

God makes the good times as well as the bad times. In adversity we tend to doubt God's fatherly care, but in prosperity we tend to forget it. If we are to trust God, we must acknowledge our dependence upon Him at all times, good times as well as bad times.

Another pitfall we need to watch for is the tendency to trust in God's instruments of provision rather than in God Himself. In the usual course of events in our lives, God provides for our needs through human means rather than directly. He provides for our financial needs through our vocations and gives us medical personnel to treat us when we are ill. But these human instruments are ultimately under the controlling hand of God. They succeed or prosper only to the extent God prospers them. We must be careful to look beyond the means and human instrumentalities to the God who uses them.

In Proverbs 18:10-11, there is a very interesting and instructive contrast drawn between the righteous and the rich. The passage says:

> The name of the LORD is a strong tower;
> the righteous run to it and are safe.
> The wealth of the rich is their fortified city;
> they imagine it an unscalable wall.

The contrast is not between the righteous and the rich in an absolute sense, as there are many people who are both righteous and wealthy. Rather we should see the contrast drawn between the two primary objects of man's trust: God and money. Those who trust in the Lord *are* safe; while those who trust in their wealth only *imagine* they are safe.

There is a much wider principle for us in this passage. All of us tend to have our fortified cities. It may be an advanced college degree with its ticket to a guaranteed position or our insurance policies or our financial nest egg for retirement years. For our nation, it is our military build-up. Anything other than God Himself that we tend to trust in becomes our "fortified city" with its imagined unscalable walls.

This does not mean we are to disregard the usual means of supply God has provided. It means we must not trust in them. Earlier we saw that the psalmist said, "I do not trust in my bow" (Psalm 44:6), but he did not say, "I have thrown it away." To put the use of ordinary means and a trust in God into proper perspective is to look in trust to God to *use* the means He has provided. At the time of this writing, my wife is experiencing some physical pain, possibly an outgrowth of her bout with cancer. While we are seeking an expert medical diagnosis as to the cause of the pain, we are looking to God that, according to His will, He will give wisdom and guidance to the doctors. Though we respect the medical skill of the physicians, we know God has given them that skill and that only He can prosper that skill in any given situation. So we respect and appreciate the doctors, but we trust in God.

Human means and instrumentalities can be depended upon only insofar as we recognize and honor God in them. Philip Bennett Power, a nineteenth-century Anglican minister, wrote, "We cannot expect God to prosper anything which intrudes itself into His place, and detracts from His honour. . . . [We must] make God the great object of our trust, *even though the usual human instrumentality of help may be at hand.*"[8]

We should also keep in mind that God is able to work with or without human means. Though He most often uses them, He is not dependent upon them. Furthermore, He will frequently use some means altogether different from that which we would have expected. Sometimes our prayers for deliverance from some particular strait are accompanied by faith to the extent we can foresee some predictable means of deliverance. But God is not dependent upon means that we can foresee. In fact, it seems from experience that God delights to surprise us by His ways of deliverance to remind us that our trust must be in Him and Him alone.

Still another pitfall to trusting God, which we are prone to fall into, is to turn to God in trust in the greater crisis experiences of life while seeking to work through the minor difficulties ourselves. A disposition to trust in ourselves is part of our sinful nature. It sometimes takes a major crisis, or at least a moderate one, to turn us toward the Lord. A mark of Christian maturity is to continually trust the Lord in the minutiae of daily life. If we learn to trust God in the minor adversities, we will be better prepared to trust Him in the major ones.

Quoting again from Philip Bennett Power:

> The daily circumstances of life will afford us opportunities enough of glorifying God in Trust, without our waiting for any extraordinary calls upon our faith. Let us remember that the extraordinary circumstances of life are but few; that much of life may slip past without their occurrence; and that if we be not faithful and trusting in that which is little, we are not likely to be so in that which is great. . . . Let our trust be reared in the humble nursery of our own daily experience, with its ever recurring little wants, and trials, and sorrows; and then, when need be, it will come forth, to do such great things as are required of it.[9]

I once asked a dear saint of God who has experienced much adversity whether she found it as difficult to trust God in the minor difficulties of life as in the major ones. She replied that she found the minor ones more difficult. In times of major crisis she readily realized her utter dependence on God and quickly turned to Him, but she often tried to work through the more ordinary adversities herself. Let us learn from her experience and seek to trust God in the ordinary circumstances of life.

But whether the difficulty is major or minor, we must choose to trust God. We must learn to say with the psalmist, "When I am afraid, I will trust in you."

CHAPTER FOURTEEN

GIVING THANKS ALWAYS

Give thanks in all circumstances,
for this is God's will for you in Christ Jesus.

1 THESSALONIANS 5:18

Because God is sovereign, wise, and good, we can trust Him. If we are to honor Him in our times of adversity, we *must* trust Him. In our trusting God, there is more at stake than experiencing peace in the midst of difficulties or even deliverance from them. The honor of God should be our chief concern. Therefore, our primary response to the trustworthiness of God should be, "I will trust God." But there are some corollary responses to trusting God that are also important. They provide tangible evidence that we are in fact trusting God.

THANKSGIVING

In our chapter text Paul said to "give thanks in all circumstances." We are to be thankful in bad times and good times, for adversities as well as for blessings. *All* circumstances whether favorable or unfavorable to our desires are to be occasions for thanksgiving.

Thanksgiving is not a natural virtue; it is a fruit of the Spirit, given by Him. The unbeliever is not inclined to give thanks. He may welcome circumstances that are in accord with his wishes and complain about those that are not, but it never occurs to him in either case to give thanks. If he sees life as anything beyond chance, he may congratulate himself for his successes and blame others for his failures, but he never sees the hand of God in his life. One of the most indicting statements in the Bible about natural man is Paul's charge that "although they knew God, they neither glorified him as God nor gave thanks to him" (Romans 1:21).

Thanksgiving is an admission of dependence. Through it we recognize that in the physical realm God "gives [us] life and breath and everything else" (Acts 17:25), and that in the spiritual realm, it is God who made us alive in Christ Jesus when we were dead in our transgressions and sins. Everything we are and have we owe to His bountiful grace. "For who makes you different from anyone else? What do you have that you did not receive?" (1 Corinthians 4:7).

As God's children we are to give Him thanks in *all* circumstances, both the good and the bad. In his gospel, Luke tells the story of ten lepers who were healed by Christ (see Luke 17:11-19). All ten cried out to be healed, all ten actually experienced Christ's healing power, but only one came back to Jesus to thank Him. How prone we are to be as the other nine, quick to ask for God's help but forgetful to give Him thanks. In fact, our problem is far deeper than mere forgetfulness. We are imbued with a spirit of ingratitude because of our sinful nature. We must cultivate a new spirit, the spirit of gratitude, which the Holy Spirit has implanted within us at our salvation.

Now we all can see the logic in the story of the ten lepers: They all should have returned to give Jesus thanks. We may even acknowledge that many times we have been like the nine forgetful men, when we should have been like the one. We have no trouble with the theology of the story, even if we often fail in the application. In this sense, we have no problem accepting Paul's directive to give thanks in all circumstances.

The time when we have difficulty accepting Paul's instruction to give thanks in all circumstances is when those circumstances are bad. Suppose one person is healed from a dreadful disease while another contracts one. Paul's theology is that both, as believers, should give thanks to God.

The basis for giving thanks in the difficult circumstances is all that we have been learning about God in this book: His sovereignty, wisdom, and love, as they are brought to bear upon all the unexpected and sudden shifts and turns in our lives. In short, it is the firm belief that God is at work in all things—all our circumstances—for our good. It is the willingness to accept this truth from God's Word and rely upon it without having to know just how He is working for our good.

We can see a very close connection between the promise of Romans 8:28 and the command of 1 Thessalonians 5:18, when we understand that the literal translation of the words *in all circumstances* is "in everything." In the Greek, as in the English language, the words and meanings are very, very close. We are to give thanks in *everything* because we know that *in all things* God is at work for our good.[1]

To derive the fullest comfort and encouragement from Romans 8:28—and thus to give thanks in all circumstances—we must realize that God is at work in a preactive, not reactive, fashion. That is, God does not just respond to an adversity in our lives to make the best of a bad situation. He knows before He initiates or permits the adversity exactly how He will use it for our good. God knew exactly what He was doing before He allowed Joseph's brothers to sell him into slavery. Joseph recognized this when he said to his brothers, "So then, it was not you who sent me here, but God. . . . You intended to harm me, but God intended it for good" (Genesis 45:8; 50:20).

Therefore, Paul commands us to "give thanks in all

circumstances, *for this is God's will for you in Christ Jesus*" (emphasis added). Once before in his first letter to the Thessalonian church, Paul had spoken of God's will. In chapter 4, verse 3, he says, "It is God's will that you should be sanctified: that you should avoid sexual immorality." We all recognize the moral imperative in this verse. God commands that we be holy, and holiness includes sexual purity. The imperative is no less strong in chapter 5, verse 18. Giving thanks in all circumstances is as much a part of the moral will of God as is abstaining from sexual immorality. This is not to say that failure to give thanks and indulging in sexual immorality are *equally* sinful in God's sight. But it is to say that giving thanks in all circumstances is part of God's moral will for us, and thus is not an option to the one seeking to please and honor Him.

Thanksgiving in all circumstances, whether favorable or unfavorable, then, is another response to the trustworthiness of God. If we trust Him to work in all our circumstances for our good, then we should give Him thanks in all those circumstances—not thanksgiving for the evil considered in itself, but for the *good* that He will bring out of that evil through His sovereign wisdom and love.

WORSHIP

Another response to the trustworthiness of God is to worship Him in times of adversity. When the initial disaster struck Job, the Scripture says,

> He fell to the ground in worship and said:
>
> "Naked I came from my mother's womb,
>   and naked I will depart.
> The LORD gave and the LORD has taken away;
>   may the name of the LORD be praised."

JOB 1:20-21

Instead of reacting against God in the time of his calamity, Job worshiped Him. Instead of raising his fist in the face of God, he fell down before Him. Instead of defiance, there was a humble recognition of God's sovereignty—God in His sovereignty had given and God in His sovereignty had a right to take away.

Worship involves a two-directional view. Looking upward we see God in all His majesty, power, glory, and sovereignty as well as His mercy, goodness, and grace. Looking at ourselves we recognize our dependence upon God and our sinfulness before Him. We see God as the sovereign Creator, worthy to be worshiped, served, and obeyed, and we see ourselves as mere creatures, unworthy sinners who have failed to worship, serve, and obey Him as we should.

We deserve nothing from God but eternal judgment. We are continuous debtors, not only for His sovereign mercy in saving us, but for every breath we draw, every bite of food we eat. We have no rights before God. Everything is of His grace. Everything in heaven and earth belongs to Him, and He says to us in the words of the landowner to the workers in his vineyard, "Don't I have the right to do what I want with my own money?" (Matthew 20:15).

This is another dimension of God's sovereignty. We saw earlier that God's sovereignty involves His absolute power to do whatever pleases Him and His absolute control over the actions of all His creatures. But God's sovereignty also includes His absolute *right* to do as He pleases with us. That He has chosen to redeem us and to send His Son to die for us, instead of sending us to hell, is not due to any obligation toward us on His part. It is solely due to His sovereign mercy and grace. As He said to Moses, "I will have mercy on whom I will have mercy, and I will have compassion on whom I will have compassion"

(Exodus 33:19). By that statement God was saying, "I am under obligation to no one."

Worship from the heart in times of adversity implies an attitude of humble acceptance on our part of God's right to do as He pleases in our lives. It is a frank acknowledgment that whatever we have at any given moment—health, position, wealth, or anything else we may cherish—is a gift from God's sovereign grace and may be taken away at His pleasure.

But God does not act toward us in bare sovereignty, wielding His power oppressively or tyrannically. God has already acted toward us in love, mercy, and grace, and He continues to act that way toward us as He works to conform us to the likeness of Christ.

As we bow in worship before His almighty power, we can also bow in confidence that He exercises that power for us, not against us. So we should bow in an attitude of humility, accepting His dealings in our lives, but we can also bow in love, knowing that those dealings, however severe and painful they may be, come from a wise and loving heavenly Father.

HUMILITY

The immediate connection of the thoughts in 1 Peter 5:6-7 should be encouraging to us in times of adversity. The two verses say:

> Humble yourselves, therefore, under God's mighty hand, that he may lift you up in due time. Cast all your anxiety on him because he cares for you.

On the one hand we are to humble ourselves under God's mighty hand—an expression equivalent to submitting with a spirit of humility to God's sovereign dealings with you. And on the other hand, we are to cast our anxieties on Him knowing that He cares for us. The anxieties, of course, arise out of the adversities that God's mighty hand brings into our lives. We are to accept the adversities but not the anxieties.

Our tendency is just opposite. We seek to escape from or resist the adversities but all the while cling to the anxieties that they produce. The way to cast our anxieties on the Lord is through humbling ourselves under His sovereignty and then trusting Him in His wisdom and love.

Humility should be both a response to adversity and a fruit of it. The apostle Paul was very clear that the primary purpose of his thorn in the flesh was to curb any tendency of pride in him. He said, "To keep me from becoming conceited because of these surpassingly great revelations, there was given me a thorn in my flesh, a messenger of Satan, to torment me" (2 Corinthians 12:7). If Paul had a tendency to pride, surely we do also. Therefore, we can put it down as a principle: Whenever God blesses us in any way that might engender pride in us, He will along with the blessings give us a "thorn in the flesh" to oppose and undermine that pride. We will be made weak in some way through one or more adversities in order that we might recognize that our strength is in Him, not in ourselves.

We can choose how we will respond to such a thorn in the flesh. We can chafe under it, often for months or even years, or we can accept it from God, humbling ourselves under His mighty hand. When we truly humble ourselves before Him, we will in due time experience the sufficiency of His grace, for "God opposes the proud but gives grace to the humble" (James 4:6).

FORGIVENESS

Adversity often comes to us through the actions of other people. Sometimes those hurtful actions are deliberately directed at us. At other times we may be the victim of another person's irresponsible actions that, though not deliberately aimed at us, nevertheless affect us seriously. How are we to respond to those who are the instruments of our adversity? The answer, of course, is with love and forgiveness.

Our tendency is to blame the other person, to harbor resentment, and to even desire revenge. I have found that two truths help me forgive others. First, I myself am a sinner, forgiven by the grace of God and the shed blood of His Son. I have hurt others, perhaps not so often deliberately but unconsciously through an uncaring spirit or selfish actions.

Ecclesiastes 7:21-22 says, "Do not pay attention to every word people say, or you may hear your servant cursing you—for you know in your heart that many times you yourself have cursed others." While there is a rich direct application in this passage, there is also a broader principle that speaks to the subject of forgiveness. We can see it by restating the idea of the passage as follows: "Do not resent other people who are the instruments of adversity in your life, for you know in your heart that you have sometimes been the instrument of adversity in the lives of others."

God tells us to forgive each other, just as in Christ He forgave us (see Ephesians 4:32). If I want God to forgive me when I have hurt others, then I must be willing to forgive those who are instruments of pain in my life.

Second, I seek to look beyond the person who is only the instrument to see God who has purposed this adversity for me. "Who can speak and have it happen if the Lord has not decreed it?" (Lamentations 3:37). If God has ordained to allow this trial in my life, it is because He has in His infinite wisdom deemed it to be good for me. Through the adversity, wrought by the other person, God is doing His work in my life. One part of humbling myself under His mighty hand is to resist any tendency of bitterness or resentment in my heart toward the other person.

Though his actions may be sinful in themselves, God is using those actions in my life for my good.

PRAYER FOR DELIVERANCE

A spirit of humble acceptance toward God or forgiveness toward others does not mean we should not pray for deliverance from the adversities that come upon us. Scripture teaches just the opposite. A number of the psalms, for example, contain very fervent prayers for deliverance from troubles of various sorts. Most of all, we have the example of the Lord Jesus Himself, who prayed, "My Father, if it is possible, may this cup be taken from me. Yet not as I will, but as you will" (Matthew 26:39).

As long as the ultimate outcome of an adversity is in doubt (for example, in the case of sickness or a spiritually rebellious child), we should continue to pray, asking God to change the situation. But we should pray this in the same spirit as Jesus did—not as we will but as God wills. We certainly must never demand of God that He will change the situation.

We should also pray for deliverance from the attacks of Satan. As we have already seen, Satan's attacks, like the injuries of other people or the calamitous events of nature, are under the sovereign control of God. Satan cannot attack us without the permission of God or go beyond the limits that God has set (see Job 1:12; 2:6; Luke 22:31). We do not know why, in a specific instance, God allows Satan to attack us. But sometimes the reason is that we may engage in spiritual warfare—that we may "resist the devil" (James 4:7).

We should pray for deliverance, and we should learn to resist the attacks of Satan in the power of Jesus Christ. But we should always pray in an attitude of humble acceptance of that which is God's will. Sometimes God's will is deliverance from the adversity; sometimes it is the provision of grace to accept the adversity. Trusting God for the grace to accept adversity is as much an act of faith as is trusting Him for deliverance from it.

SEEKING GOD'S GLORY

Above all else, our response to adversity should be to seek God's glory. We see this attitude illustrated in the life of the apostle Paul during his imprisonment in Rome. Not only was he imprisoned, but there were men, supposedly fellow ministers of the gospel, who were actually trying to add to his troubles by their preaching (see Philippians 1:14-17).

What was Paul's response? He said, "But what does it matter? The important thing is that in every way, whether from false motives or true, Christ is preached. And because of this I rejoice" (Philippians 1:18). Essentially Paul said, "It really doesn't matter what happens to me or how I am affected by all of this, the important thing is what happens to the gospel."

Most of us have probably not progressed that far in our Christian maturity. We have not attained to the degree of self-less spirit that Paul had. It still does matter what happens to us. But this should be our goal, and if we watch for opportunities to grow in that direction, we will see them.

Perhaps you have a certain position of responsibility in your church or a ministry organization. What if someone comes along who is more gifted than you, and you are asked (perhaps not very graciously) to step aside in favor of that person? How will you respond? Here is your opportunity to grow in the direction of being concerned only for God's glory. If you will respond to God in this and humble yourself under His mighty hand, you will experience His grace enabling you to be concerned primarily—if not entirely—with His glory. You will have grown more into the likeness of Jesus, who laid aside His glory to die for you.

Above all, you must see the hand of God in this event, knowing that He, who does all things well, intends this only for your good.

One last quotation from the pen of Alexander Carson will help us to not only see this typical event in its proper perspective, but also to draw together all the gracious truths we have learned in these studies:

> Nothing can be more consoling to the man of God, than the conviction that the Lord who made the world governs the world; and that every event, great and small, prosperous and adverse, is under the absolute disposal of him who doth all things well, and who regulates all things for the good of his people. . . . The Christian will be confident and courageous in duty, in proportion as he views God in his Providence as ruling in the midst of his enemies; and acting for the good of his people, as well as for his own glory, even in the persecution of the Gospel.[2]

CAN YOU TRUST GOD?

We have seen that God is trustworthy. He is absolutely sovereign over every event in the universe, and He exercises that sovereignty in an infinitely wise and loving way for our good. In that sense we have answered the main question raised by this book. You can *trust* God. He will never fail you nor forsake you.

But what about the second way we can ask that question? Can *you* trust God? Is your total relationship with God one on which you can build a bulwark of trust against the attacks of adversity? You cannot trust God in isolation from all other areas of your life. To grow in your ability to trust God in times of adversity, you must first lay a solid foundation of a daily personal relationship with Him. Only as you know Him intimately and seek to obey Him completely will you be able to establish a trust relationship with God.

And then, to that foundation of a life lived in communion with God, we must add what we have learned about God in this book—about His sovereignty, wisdom, and love. We must lay hold of these great truths in the little trials as well as the major calamities of life. As we do this in dependence upon the enabling power of His Holy Spirit, we will be able more and more to say, "I can trust God."

DISCUSSION
GUIDE

HOW TO USE THIS
DISCUSSION GUIDE

Many Christians wish to develop a deeper trust in God. This discussion guide is designed to be used in conjunction with the book *Trusting God*. The guide will help you apply the truths of the book to your personal experience and give you a chance to interact with relevant Scripture passages. The guide can be used for individual or group study.

Please notice that the lessons in this discussion guide don't correspond directly to the chapters in the book. Some of the book chapters are combined in the lessons. We created the discussion guide this way so as to compress the lessons into a shorter amount of time (twelve weeks, if you do one per week) than the book would allow (fourteen chapters).

Preparing the Lesson
Each lesson has four sections.

Central Idea. This section states the main point of the lesson. It will be helpful to keep this in mind while preparing the study, as well as during discussions with a group.

Examining Trust. This section is representative of the chapters in *Trusting God*. The discussion guide can be used alone, but reading the chapters in *Trusting God* is strongly encouraged. Members of a group should read this section before meeting.

Developing Trust. These questions should be answered by group members before the group meeting. Some questions are based on Scripture verses; others, on the section "Examining Trust." The better prepared group members are, the better the discussion will be. Ask the Holy Spirit to bring to mind experiences you have had that you can use to better understand the truths taught in certain questions. Past experiences and lessons learned can be shared without revealing confidential details. If you have no personal experience that relates to a particular question, think about a person you know who has had a relevant experience and try to draw on his or her experience.

Trust in Action. Make a personal commitment to do at least one thing from this section each week. You should read this section early in the week so that you have plenty of time for whatever you decide to do. Be ready to share your experiences with your group.

Leading a Group

Groups vary, and the leader must be sensitive to the needs of his or her group. It is a good idea to dedicate each meeting to the Lord with an opening prayer. The leader can ask for a volunteer to open in prayer or can ask a specific person ahead of time. Having different people open with prayer will give many members this privilege and will lend some variety.

If you have someone who can lead a time of singing, this is a good way to worship together. During this singing time you may want to share Scripture verses that members have been memorizing. The verses can be shared before the singing or between songs in a mood of worship. Members should not feel pressured to memorize Scripture but should have the opportunity to share what they have learned.

Next, move into the material to be covered. If your group has prepared ahead of time, you can go right into the questions. If not, you will want to read the "Examining Trust" section together. Leaders should decide which questions to cover during group time. You probably will not have time to discuss all questions in depth. Focus on the ones that are most important for your group. When a question is about a Scripture passage, it will be helpful to read the passage together. When there are a number of passages, decide which ones to discuss during group time.

Keep your group focused on understanding and applying the truths presented each week. You can minimize controversy by avoiding detailed discussions of conflicting viewpoints. Emphasize what members agree on and accept differences of opinion without contention.

Close your time together with prayer. The leader is responsible to watch the time and to save enough time for prayer. This time is the "heart" of any group and will bind a group together more than anything else. It is better to cut discussion short than to neglect prayer. To avoid spending all your prayer time taking requests, ask members to bring up requests during prayer, explaining important details as they pray. You can talk later about what you have prayed for. Encourage spontaneous prayer. Ask people to pray for one request at a time and to feel free to pray several times. Vary your group prayer time. For instance, you can introduce subjects of prayer with verses from your study and let people pray as they are led.

LESSON ONE

CAN YOU TRUST GOD?

(Preface and Chapter 1)

CENTRAL IDEA

God is completely sovereign, infinite in wisdom, perfect in love, and therefore worthy of our trust. God's desire for us is that we learn to trust Him.

Examining Trust

Learning to trust God has been a slow and difficult process for me. It is a process that is still under way. But several years ago, in an effort to strengthen my own trust in God, I began a lengthy Bible study on the subject of God's sovereignty in the affairs of His people. That study has helped me immeasurably, and it is the fruit of that study I now share with you. This is written from the perspective of a brother and companion to all those who are tempted at times to ask, "Can I really trust God?"

Adversity is difficult even when we know God is in control of our circumstances. In fact, that knowledge sometimes tends to aggravate the pain. "If God is in control," we ask, "why did He allow this to happen?"

All of us experience adversity at different times and in varying degrees throughout our lives. As the Scripture says, "Man is born to trouble as surely as sparks fly upward" (Job 5:7). Adversity and its accompanying emotional pain come in many forms. Some pain is sudden, traumatic, and devastating. Other adversities are chronic, persistent, and seemingly designed to wear down our spirits over time. Even those whose lives are free from major pain still experience the frequently frustrating or anxiety-producing events of daily life, which momentarily grab our attention and rob us of our peace of mind. It is in the crucible of even this minor level of adversity that we are tempted to wonder, "Can I trust God?"

I have spent a good portion of my adult life encouraging people to pursue holiness, to obey God. Yet, I acknowledge it often seems more difficult to trust God than to obey Him. The moral will of God given to us in the Bible is rational and reasonable. The circumstances in which we must trust God often appear irrational and inexplicable. The law of God is readily recognized to be good for us, even when we don't want to obey it. The circumstances of our lives frequently appear to be dreadful and grim or perhaps even calamitous and tragic. Obeying God is worked out within well-defined boundaries of God's revealed will. Trusting God is worked out in an arena that has no boundaries. We are always coping with the unknown.

It is just as important to trust God as it is to obey Him. When we disobey God we defy His authority and despise His holiness. But when we fail to trust God we doubt His sovereignty and question His goodness. In both cases we cast aspersions upon His majesty and His character. God views our distrust of Him as seriously as He views our disobedience.

The Scriptures teach us three essential truths about God—

truths we must believe if we are to trust Him in adversity. They are:

- God is completely sovereign.
- God is infinite in wisdom.
- God is perfect in love.

Someone has expressed these three truths as they relate to us in this way: "God in His love always wills what is best for us. In His wisdom He always knows what is best, and in His sovereignty He has the power to bring it about."

The sovereignty of God is asserted, either expressly or implicitly, on almost every page of the Bible. Rather than being offended over the Bible's assertion of God's sovereignty in both good and calamity, believers should be comforted by it. Whatever our particular calamity or adversity may be, we may be sure that our Father has a loving purpose in it. As King Hezekiah said, "Surely it was for my benefit that I suffered such anguish" (Isaiah 38:17). God does not exercise His sovereignty capriciously, but only in such a way as His infinite love deems best for us.

God's sovereignty is also exercised in infinite wisdom, far beyond our ability to comprehend. God's plan and His ways of working out His plan are frequently beyond our ability to fathom and understand. We must learn to trust when we don't understand.

Developing Trust

1. Do you have a harder time trusting God in the major trials of your life or in relatively minor things? Explain why you think this is the case.

2. Do you think Christians struggle more with questions and uncertainties in the midst of adversity than nonbelievers? Why or why not?

3. a. According to Proverbs 27:1, what should be our perspective on the future?

   b. How does this affect our need to trust God?

4. God desires that we learn to trust Him. What do you learn about trust from these verses?

   • Psalm 32:10

• Proverbs 3:5

• John 14:1

5. a. What is the difference between trusting God and obeying Him?

   b. How are trusting God and obedience related?

   c. Is it easier for you to trust God or to be obedient? Explain why.

   d. Describe a situation in your life where obedience and trusting were both important.

e. Describe a time when trusting God made it easier to be obedient.

6. Read Psalm 78:9-22.

a. What attitude did the Israelites reveal in the desert?

b. What was God's reaction to their attitude?

c. Describe a time when your attitude was similar to that of the Israelites.

d. How do you think God felt about your attitude? (See Hebrews 11:6 and Philippians 2:14.)

e. What in your life indicated how God felt?

7. According to Isaiah 55:9 and Romans 11:33, why is it important for us to trust God even when we don't understand what He is doing?

8. a. What do these verses say about our privilege of knowing God?

    • Psalm 9:10

    • Jeremiah 9:23-24

    • Philippians 3:8-11

b. Knowing God is more than simply knowing facts about Him. What does it mean to know God?

c. What are you doing to get to know God better?

d. Do you need to make or renew your commitments to these actions?

e. Write a prayer in which you express your desire to know God more intimately.

Trust in Action

Choose one or more of these ideas to work on. Groups may want to allow time each week to share experiences from this section.

1. Keep a journal while studying this book. Record all the circumstances in which you see God's control and

guidance in your life. Beginning this log now will help you see concrete evidence for truths discussed in later chapters.

2. Memorize Psalm 32:10.

3. Make a commitment to memorize Romans 8:18-39. This may seem like an overwhelming task, but if the passage is broken down into small sections, it can be memorized fairly easily. The rewards of having this amazing passage memorized will be more than worth the effort.

4. Think of a relationship in which you have trusted another person. Write a letter to this person and share your thoughts from this lesson. Tell this person how much you value his or her trustworthiness.

5. Ask God for the opportunity to share something about His trustworthiness with an unbeliever. Watch for the opportunity and take advantage of it.

IS GOD IN CONTROL?

(Chapters 2 and 3)

CENTRAL IDEA

God is in control. He has a purpose and a plan for you, and He has the power to carry out that plan.

Examining Trust

God is sovereign (all powerful), and He is good. God's providence is a term we often use in Christian parlance to acknowledge God's seeming intervention in our affairs. There are two things wrong, however, with the way in which we refer to the providence of God. For one, we almost always use the expression "the providence of God" in connection with apparently "good" events. God controls both the good and the bad. God has not looked the other way or been caught by surprise when adversity strikes us. He is in control of the adversity, directing it to His glory and our good.

The second problem with our popular use of the expression "the providence of God" is that we either unconsciously or deliberately imply that God intervenes at specific points in our lives but is largely only an interested spectator most of the time.

God's providence is His constant care for and His absolute rule over all His creation for His own glory and the good of His people. Note the twofold objective of God's providence: His glory and the good of His people. These two objectives are never antithetical; they are always in harmony with each other.

The Bible teaches that God not only created the universe but that He upholds and sustains it day by day, hour by hour. Scripture says, "The Son is . . . sustaining all things by His powerful word" (Hebrews 1:3), and "in him all things hold together" (Colossians 1:17).

The Bible also teaches that God governs the universe, not only inanimate creation but also the actions of all creatures, both men and animals. He is called "the ruler of all things" (1 Chronicles 29:12) and "the blessed and only Ruler" (1 Timothy 6:15).

Randomness, luck, chance, fate. This is modern man's answer to the age-old question, "Why?" Even many Christians who accept the concept of God's sovereignty believe that He chooses not to exercise His sovereignty in the daily affairs of our lives. Christians are often unwilling to accept the fact that God is working because they don't understand *how* He is working. They have chosen to substitute the doctrine of chance for the doctrine of divine providence.

I admit that we are often unable to reconcile God's sovereignty and goodness in the face of widespread tragedy or personal adversity, but I believe that, although we often do not understand God's ways, He is sovereignly at work in all of our circumstances.

If there is a single event in all of the universe that can occur outside of God's sovereign control, then we cannot trust Him. His love may be infinite, but if His power is limited and His purpose can be thwarted, we cannot trust Him. He permits, for reasons known only to Himself, people to act contrary to and in defiance of His revealed will. But He never permits them to act contrary to His sovereign will.

One of our problems with the sovereignty of God is that it frequently does not appear that God is in control of the circumstances of our lives. It is difficult to see God working through secondary causes and frail, sinful human beings. But it is the ability of God to so arrange diverse human actions to fulfill His purpose that makes His sovereignty marvelous and yet mysterious.

No one can act and no circumstances can occur outside the bounds of God's sovereign will. But this is only one side of His sovereignty. The other side, which is just as important to our trusting Him, is that no plan of God's can be thwarted. God has an over-arching purpose for all believers: to conform us to the likeness of His Son, Jesus Christ (see Romans 8:29). He also has a specific purpose for each of us that is His unique, tailor-made plan for our individual life (see Ephesians 2:10).

I readily admit it is difficult to believe God is in control when we are in the midst of anxiety, heartache, or grief. We must learn to obey God one choice at a time; we must also learn to trust God one circumstance at a time. Trusting God is not a matter of my feelings but of my will. That act of the will must be based on belief, and belief must be based on truth.

We must believe the truth that God carries out His own good purposes without ever being thwarted, and He so directs and controls all events and all actions of His creatures that they never act outside of His sovereign will. That which should distinguish the suffering of believers from unbelievers is the confidence that our suffering is under the control of an all-powerful and all-loving God; our suffering has meaning and purpose in

God's eternal plan, and He brings or allows to come into our lives only that which is for His glory and our good.

Developing Trust
1. a. What is God's providence? (The "Examining Trust" section may help you answer these questions.)

   b. What is the purpose or objective of God's providence?

   c. Describe a situation in your life when God's will and your best interests seemed to be in conflict.

   d. How was this conflict resolved?

2. What do the following verses say about God's providence?

- Psalm 31:15

- Psalm 147:8-9

- Acts 17:24-28

- 2 Corinthians 9:10

3. What specific evidence of God's sustaining presence in the universe is most dramatic to you? (Illustrations from science would be appropriate here.)

4. a. In what ways do people see God's providence as limited?

   b. Do you think of God's providence as limited? Explain.

   c. In what ways do you act as though God's providence is limited even though you may believe that it isn't?

5. a. Restate Matthew 10:29-31 in your own words.

   b. Think about a person who sees chance or randomness as the explanation for all that happens. How would this philosophy affect his or her life?

   c. What would such a person value?

d. How does Matthew 10:29-31 refute such a perspective?

6. a. Do you believe that God is active in the daily affairs of your life?

b. What evidence do you see, from your past or present, for His involvement in your life? (If you have begun keeping a journal, it may help you answer this question.)

7. There is an invisible war being waged between God and Satan, and our lives are often the battleground. What do the following passages say about Satan's ability to touch us?

• Job 1:12; 2:6

• Luke 22:31-32

8. God never permits people to act contrary to His sovereign will. How do the following verses support this statement?

- Proverbs 16:9

- Proverbs 19:21

- Lamentations 3:37

- James 4:13-15

(For additional study see Proverbs 21:30; Ecclesiastes 7:13; and Revelation 3:7.)

9. What conclusions about God and what He does can you draw from these verses?

- Job 42:2

- Psalm 115:3

- Isaiah 46:10

- Daniel 4:34-35

(For additional verses see Isaiah 14:27; 43:13; and Ephesians 1:11-12.)

10. In his book *When Bad Things Happen to Good People*, Rabbi Harold Kushner concludes that God cannot be both sovereign and good, so Kushner chooses to believe in a God who is good.

   a. What do you think about Rabbi Kushner's conclusion?

   b. How do you reconcile God's goodness and His sovereignty? That is, if God is able to prevent evil, and if He is committed to good, then why doesn't He prevent evil?

11. We need to be very sensitive in teaching others about the sovereignty of God and encouraging them to trust God when they are in the midst of problems or pain. It is much easier to trust in the sovereignty of God when it is the other person who is hurting. We need to be like Jesus, of whom it was said, "A bruised reed he will not break" (Matthew 12:20). Job lost his children, his wealth, and his health. His friends preached to him about God's sovereignty. Read Job's response to his friends in Job 6:14-27.

a. What did Job's friends do wrong? How did they "bruise" him?

b. If you had a friend in Job's position, how would you deal with him when he questioned God's sovereignty and goodness?

Trust in Action

1. Choose one of the following Bible characters and read his or her story. Briefly summarize how God guided the events in this person's life. Remember that these stories were given to us for encouragement (see Romans 15:4). What God did for these people He will do for you.

   • Joseph: Genesis 37; 39–45

   • Esther: Esther

   • Ruth: Ruth

2. Think of someone you know who is in a difficult situation. Express God's love to him or her in a tangible way (prepare a meal, write a note of encouragement, offer to help with household repairs, and so forth).

3. Memorize Romans 8:28-29.

GOD'S SOVEREIGNTY OVER PEOPLE

(Chapter 4)

CENTRAL IDEA

God works in the hearts of people to move them to fulfill His purposes. Any treatment, good or bad, that we receive from another can be seen as part of God's plan for us.

Examining Trust

We are, from a human point of view, often at the mercy of other people and their decisions or actions. Sometimes those decisions or actions are benevolent and good; sometimes they are wicked or careless. Either way they do affect us, often in a significant way. How are we to respond when we find ourselves seemingly in the hands of someone else, when we desperately need a favorable decision or a favorable action on that person's part? Can we trust God that He can and will work in the heart of that individual to bring about His plan for us?

Or consider the instance when someone is out to harm us, to ruin our reputation, or to jeopardize our career: Can we trust God to intervene in the heart of that person so that he does not carry out his evil intent? According to the Bible, the answer in both instances is yes.

Perhaps the clearest biblical statement that God does sovereignly influence the decisions of people is found in Proverbs 21:1: "The king's heart is in the hand of the LORD; he directs it like a watercourse wherever he pleases." The stubborn will of the most powerful monarch on earth is directed by God as easily as the farmer directs the flow of water in his irrigation canals. The argument, then, is from the greater to the lesser—if God controls the king's heart, surely He controls everyone else's.

God can and does move in the hearts of people to show favor to us when that favor will accomplish His purpose. Furthermore, when necessary, God restrains people from decisions or actions that would harm us. Of course, God does not always restrain the wicked and harmful actions of others toward His people. We do not know why God sometimes allows our enemies to prevail and sometimes restrains them. It is enough to know that God can and does restrain the harmful acts of others toward us when that is His sovereign will.

You can trust God in all the areas of your life where you are dependent upon the favor or frown of another person. God will move in that person's heart to carry out His will for you.

The Bible asserts both God's sovereignty and people's freedom and moral responsibility, but it never attempts to explain their relationship. For one thing, God is infinite in His ways as well as His being. A finite mind simply cannot comprehend an infinite being beyond what He has expressly revealed to us. Because of this, some things about God will forever remain a mystery to us. The relationship of the sovereign will of God to the freedom and moral responsibility of people is one of those mysteries.

We must also keep in mind that God is never the author of sin. Though people's sinful intents and actions serve the sovereign purpose of God, we must never conclude that God has induced anyone to sin. God judges people for the very sins that He uses to carry out His purpose.

The Bible consistently portrays people as making real choices of their own will. The choices people make are moral choices; that is, people are held accountable by God for the choices they make. God works without violating or coercing people's will; rather He works in His mysterious way through their wills to accomplish His purposes.

There are some cautions we need to consider, lest we wrongly use the doctrine of God's sovereignty over people.

First, we should never use the doctrine as an excuse for our own shortcomings.

Second, we should not allow the doctrine of God's sovereignty to cause us to respond passively to the actions of other people that affect us. The doctrine of God's sovereignty should never be used to promote passivity.

Third, we must never use the doctrine of God's sovereignty to excuse our own sinful actions or decisions that hurt another person.

Developing Trust

1. Examine the following Scriptures for evidence of God's work in the hearts of believers and unbelievers. Record the key words used to describe His working.

   • Ezra 1:1, 5; 6:22

- Proverbs 21:1

- Daniel 1:9

- 2 Corinthians 8:16-17

- Deuteronomy 2:30

- Joshua 11:20

2. Read Exodus 4:21 and 8:15.

   a. Who is given the responsibility for Pharaoh's hard heart in each of these verses?

b. How do these verses, taken side by side, help us see the relationship between man's responsibility and God's work in our hearts?

3. God's restraining influence on people's actions and decisions is seen in the following verses. Complete the chart.

Scripture	What action did God prevent?	What emotion did God influence?
Gen 20:1-7		
Gen 35:5		
Exod 34:23-24		

4. According to the following verses, how do the sinful actions of man affect God's purposes?

• Genesis 50:20

• Acts 4:27-28

- Revelation 17:15-18

5. Do you agree that a finite mind cannot comprehend an infinite Being beyond what He has expressly revealed? Why or why not?

6. a. God can and does work in the minds and hearts of people to accomplish His will. How should that truth affect your attitude?

   b. How should that truth affect the way you pray about your job or other concerns?

7. Why should confidence in God's sovereignty in the lives of people keep us from becoming resentful and bitter when we are treated unjustly or maliciously by others?

8. a. Describe a time when you were treated unfairly.

   b. How did you react?

   c. To what extent did your reaction show trust in God?

   d. Would you like your response to be different next time? If so, how?

   e. What was the end result of the situation?

f. What good, if any, came from this situation?

9. What are some specific things you can pray for in your own life this week, knowing that God can work in people's hearts?

10. a. Describe a time recently when you were affected by someone else's decision or action.

b. At the time how did you feel about the situation?

c. How do you feel now about the outcome of the situation?

d. Does your study of God's sovereignty in the hearts of people affect your perspective on what happened? How?

Trust in Action

1. Memorize Deuteronomy 29:29 or Proverbs 21:1.

2. Think of three people you know who need to turn to the Lord. Ask the Lord to work in their hearts.

3. Are there people who have treated you unfairly whom you have not forgiven? Spend some time with the Lord, asking Him to cleanse you of all bitterness toward others. Pray Psalm 51:10.

GOD'S RULE OVER THE NATIONS

(Chapter 5)

CENTRAL IDEA

God is in control of all nations, shaping events and decisions to fulfill His purposes.

Examining Trust

As we trace the sovereignty of God through the Bible, one of the most frequent references to it concerns His sovereignty over nations and governments. God is Lord over all of human history, and He is working out all the details of that history, as Paul said in Ephesians 1:11, "in conformity with the purpose of his will." That is, God makes all events of history; all the decisions of rulers, kings, and parliaments; and all the actions of their governments, armies, and navies serve His will.

The fact that God is sovereign over our rulers is usually not evident to us as we view their decisions and actions on a human plane. For the most part, governmental officials and legislative bodies do their work quite apart from any intent to carry out the will of God. We see this amply demonstrated in the life and death of Jesus Christ.

Caesar Augustus issued a decree that a census should be taken. This required Joseph and Mary to go to the town of Bethlehem to register at just the right time for the Messiah to be born in Bethlehem in fulfillment of Micah's prophecy (see Micah 5:2). Caesar certainly did not intend to be an instrument to fulfill any Jewish prophecy, yet that is exactly what he was.

We should likewise see in those affairs reported in our daily paper the sovereign hand of God just as much as we see it in the Bible. Of course, we don't have the advantage of the divinely revealed explanation of today's events, as we do of those recorded in the Bible, but that does not make God's sovereign rule today any less certain. God recorded in His Word specific instances of His sovereign rule over history in order that we might trust Him in the affairs of history as they unfold before us today.

The Scriptures teach the following specific truths about the sovereignty of God over the nations:

- God in His sovereignty has established government for the good of all people—believers as well as unbelievers (see Romans 13:1-4).
- God determines who rules in those governments (see Daniel 4:17).
- God determines the timing of each leader's rule (see Isaiah 40:23-24).
- God controls the decisions that rulers make (see Proverbs 16:33).
- God rules in the victories and defeats between nations on the battlefield (see Proverbs 21:31).

God sometimes causes government leaders or officials to make foolish decisions in order to bring judgment upon a nation. We should take more seriously our responsibility to pray for the leaders of our government that they will make wise decisions. Although we may suspect that some of the more disastrous decisions are evidence of God's judgment, we do not know that. We do know God has instructed us to pray for leaders. Our duty, then, is to pray for wise decisions, but to trust God when foolish and harmful decisions are made.

As we look around the world today, what do we see? We see over one-half of the world's population living in countries whose governments are hostile to the gospel, where missionaries are not allowed, and where national Christians are severely hindered from proclaiming Christ. As we look at these conditions we must also look at the sovereignty of God and at His promises. He has promised to redeem people from every nation, and He has commanded us to make disciples of all nations. We must, then, trust God by praying. Some will go to those nations as God opens doors, but all of us must pray. We must learn to trust God, not only in the adverse circumstances of our individual lives, but also in the adverse circumstances of the church as a whole.

God is sovereign over the nations. He is sovereign over the officials of our own government in all their actions as they affect us directly. He is sovereign over the officials of government in lands where our brothers and sisters in Christ suffer for their faith in Him. And He is sovereign over the nations where every attempt is made to stamp out true Christianity. In all of these areas, we can and must trust God.

Developing Trust

1. There are many events that took place during the life of Jesus that show how government officials, acting freely, fulfilled the purposes of God. Fill in the following chart.

Scripture	Name of ruler	Official action	Prophecy fulfilled
Matt 2:13-16 (cf. Hosea 11:1)	*Herod*		
Matt 2:17-18 (cf. Jer 31:15)	*Herod*		
Matt 2:21-23 (cf. Isa 9:1)			
Luke 2:1-4 (cf. Micah 5:2)			
Acts 4:27-28 (cf. Isa 53:3-6)			

2. What truths are taught about governments and rulers in the following verses?

• Proverbs 16:9, 33

• Proverbs 21:31

• Isaiah 40:22-24

- Daniel 4:17

- Daniel 4:31-32

- Romans 13:1-4

3. What responsibilities do we have toward our government?

- Romans 13:1-7

- 1 Timothy 2:1-4

4. a. Describe a time in your life when a governmental decision had an effect on your life (for example, military draft, new tax laws, or zoning regulation).

b. How did you see God's hand in the events at the time?

c. From your present perspective, what do you think God was doing in that situation?

5. a. Read 2 Samuel 15:1-16 and 16:20–17:14. Why did God want Absalom to follow Hushai's advice?

b. What might be God's purpose in allowing rulers to make foolish decisions?

c. Does God protect His people from the consequences of these poor decisions? Why or why not?

6. According to Daniel 9:1-19, what was Daniel's response when he realized Israel's exile in Babylon was almost over?

7. a. What is promised in the following verses?

   • Matthew 28:18-20

   • Revelation 7:9-10

   b. How can you respond to these promises?

8. a. What are your general thoughts about the present world situation?

b. Did the truths in this chapter change your perspective on current events? If so, how?

Trust in Action

1. Spend some time with the Lord doing some soul searching about your role in the political process of your country. Is God prompting you to a deeper involvement?

2. Write your government representatives letting them know what you think about an issue under debate.

3. Choose several world leaders and make a commitment to pray regularly for them. Make an effort to read articles about these leaders and their lives.

4. Choose one group of missionaries and pray regularly for them. Or choose one nation that is currently hostile to the gospel and pray regularly that God will open doors in that country.

5. Memorize Psalm 33:16-17.

GOD'S POWER OVER NATURE

(Chapter 6)

CENTRAL IDEA

God has established certain physical laws for the operation of His universe. Moment by moment those laws operate according to His direct will.

Examining Trust

God has not walked away from the day-to-day control of His creation. Certainly He has established physical laws by which He governs the forces of nature, but those laws continuously operate according to His sovereign will. The Bible teaches that God controls all the forces of nature, both destructive and productive, on a continuous, moment-by-moment basis. All expressions of nature, all occurrences of weather, whether it be a devastating tornado or a gentle rain on a spring day, are acts of God.

Many sensitive Christians struggle over the multitude of large-scale natural disasters around the world—an earthquake in one place, famine in another, typhoons and floods somewhere else. Thousands of people are killed immediately, others slowly starve to death. "Why does God allow all this?," we may ask.

It is not wrong to wrestle with these issues, as long as we do it in a reverent and submissive attitude toward God. Indeed, to fail to wrestle with the issue of large-scale tragedy may indicate a lack of compassion toward others on our part. However, we must be careful not to, in our minds, take God off His throne of absolute sovereignty or put Him in the dock and bring Him to the bar of our judgment.

God brings Himself into these events. He said in Isaiah 45:7,

> I form the light and create darkness,
> I bring prosperity and create disaster;
> I, the LORD, do all these things.

God Himself accepts the responsibility, so to speak, for disasters. He actually does more than accept the responsibility; He actually claims it. In effect, God says, "I, and I alone, have the power and authority to bring about both prosperity and disaster, both weal and woe, both good and bad."

We obviously do not understand why God creates disaster, or why He brings it to one town and not to another. We recognize, too, that just as God sends His sun and rain on both the righteous and the unrighteous, so He also sends the tornado, or the hurricane, or the earthquake on both. God's sovereignty over nature does not mean that Christians never encounter the tragedies of natural disaster.

Illness and physical affliction is another area in which we struggle to trust God. When God called Moses to lead the Israelites out of Egypt, Moses protested his inadequacy, including the fact that he was slow of speech. God's reply to Moses is very instructive to us in this area of physical affliction, for God said, "Who gave man his mouth? Who makes him deaf or mute? Who gives him sight or makes him blind? Is it not I, the LORD?" (Exodus 4:11). Here God specifically ascribes to His own work the physical afflictions of deafness, muteness, and blindness.

Afflictions don't "just happen." They are all within the sovereign will of God. Such a statement immediately brings us into the problem of pain and suffering. Why does a sovereign God who loves us allow such pain and heartache?

Briefly, we know that all creation has been subjected to frustration because of the sin of Adam (see Romans 8:20). So we can say that the ultimate cause of all pain and suffering must be traced back to the Fall. God's weal and woe are not arbitrary or capricious, but His determined response to man's sin. The sovereign God who subjected creation to frustration still rules over it, pain and all.

God never wastes pain. He always uses it to accomplish His purpose. And His purpose is for His glory and our good. Therefore, we can trust Him when our hearts are aching or our bodies are racked with pain.

Developing Trust

1. Summarize in your own words what each of these verses says about God's role in natural phenomena.

• Job 37:3, 6, 10-13

• Psalm 147:8, 16-18

- Jeremiah 10:13; 14:22

- Amos 4:7-9

2. a. What is your usual attitude toward the weather? Do you tend to complain about it? Thank God for it? Feel that God isn't responsible?

   b. Is your attitude generally pleasing to God? Why or why not?

3. a. What is God taking responsibility for in Exodus 4:11 and Isaiah 45:7?

b. What are some possible responses to these passages?

c. Which response do you choose? Why?

4. Read John 9:1-3. Explain in your own words the reason Jesus gives for the man's blindness.

5. a. What does God teach us about the conception of children in these verses?

• Genesis 16:2

• Genesis 29:31

• Judges 13:3

- 1 Samuel 1:5

- Psalm 139:13

b. If a couple is unable to have children, how can these verses help them maintain a trusting attitude toward God?

6. The idea that God claims responsibility for deadly earthquakes, droughts, blindness, and childlessness prompts sensitive people to ask questions. Certainly we can't learn much without asking questions.

a. Are there limits to the kinds of questions we should ask of God? If so, what limits? If not, why not?

b. Can we expect God to answer our questions? Why or why not?

c. What kinds of attitudes are acceptable when questioning God?

d. What kinds of attitudes are unacceptable?

e. Give some possible reasons why God leaves many of our questions unanswered.

7. a. Describe an experience in your life that caused you to doubt God's control and to ask *why*.

b. What answers did you get to your questioning?

c. Did anything good come from that experience? If so, what was it?

8. How can coming to grips with the fact that God is in control of nature affect your daily life, especially your current circumstances?

Trust in Action

1. Read the book of Job in one sitting. What was God's answer to all Job's questionings?

2. Memorize Habakkuk 3:17-19.

3. Get involved in some form of crisis intervention in your community (for example, emergency relief, pregnancy counseling, helping battered women or abused children).

GOD'S SOVEREIGNTY AND OUR RESPONSIBILITY

(Chapter 7)

CENTRAL IDEA

We are responsible for all our actions. We must seek God in prayer, act with prudence at all times, and trust God to work out His good purposes in our lives.

Examining Trust

There is no conflict between trusting God and accepting our responsibility. Our duty is found in the revealed will of God in the Scriptures. Our trust must be in the sovereign will of God, as He works in the ordinary circumstances of our daily lives for our good and His glory.

Knowledge of His sovereignty is meant to be an encouragement to pray, not an excuse to lapse into a sort of pious fatalism. Prayer assumes the sovereignty of God. If God is not sovereign, we have no assurance that He is able to answer our prayers. God's sovereignty, along with His wisdom and love, is the foundation of our trust in Him; prayer is the expression of that trust. God's sovereignty does not negate our responsibility to pray, but rather makes it possible to pray with confidence.

God's sovereignty also does not negate our responsibility to act prudently. To act prudently means to use all legitimate, biblical means at our disposal to avoid harm to ourselves or others and to bring about what we believe to be the right course of events. One of the most basic means of prudence that God has given to us is prayer. We must not only pray for His overruling providence in our lives, but we must also pray for wisdom to rightly understand our circumstances and use the means He has given us. Another means of prudence God has given us is the opportunity to seek wise and godly counsel.

Prayer is the acknowledgment of God's sovereignty and of our dependence upon Him to act on our behalf. Prudence is the acknowledgment of our responsibility to use all legitimate means.

All of our plans, all of our efforts, and all of our prudence are of no avail unless God prospers those means. Psalm 127:1 says,

> Unless the LORD builds the house,
>   its builders labor in vain.
> Unless the LORD watches over the city,
>   the watchmen stand guard in vain.

In this passage there is the concept of both offensive and defensive efforts—of both building for progress and watching against destruction. In a sense, the verse sums up all of our responsibilities in life. Whether it be in the physical, the mental, or the spiritual, we should always be building and watching. And Psalm 127:1 says none of those efforts will prosper unless God intervenes in them.

The psalmist does not say, "Unless God blesses or helps the builders and the watchmen, their efforts are in vain." Rather, he speaks in terms of God Himself building the house and watching over the city. At the same time, there is, of course, no suggestion in the text that God replaces the builders and the watchmen. The obvious meaning is that in every respect we are dependent upon God to enable us and prosper our efforts.

In His infinite wisdom, God's sovereign plan includes our failures and even our sins. God usually works through ordinary events (as opposed to miracles) and the voluntary actions of people. But He always provides the means necessary and guides them by His unseen hand. He is sovereign, and He cannot be frustrated by our failure to act or by our actions, which in themselves are sinful. We must always remember, however, that God still holds us accountable for the very sins that He uses to accomplish His purpose.

There is no conflict in the Bible between His sovereignty and our responsibility. Both concepts are taught with equal force and with never an attempt to "reconcile" them. Let us hold equally to both, doing our duty as it is revealed to us in the Scriptures and trusting God to sovereignly work out His purpose in us and through us.

Developing Trust

1. a. Read Nehemiah 4:6-9. In what two ways did the Israelites respond to the threat of attack?

   b. What does their response indicate about their understanding of the relationship between prayer and prudence?

2. Meditate on Philippians 4:6-7.

    a. Describe a time when you experienced a great deal of anxiety.

    b. When you are anxious, do you pray more or less than usual?

    c. Is this the way it should be? Explain.

3. a. When we are trusting God and have a peace that comes from Him alone, our prayers are different from when our prayers flow out of anxiety. How are they different?

    b. Which way do you pray most often?

c. Choose a difficult situation for which you are presently praying. Write a prayer for that situation from a mindset of trust.

4. a. Since God is in control and His purpose will inevitably prevail, why do we need to pray?

b. Why do we need to make every effort to act with wisdom?

5. Read Acts 4:23-31.

a. What effect do you think this prayer had on the believers who were praying?

b. What specific requests did the believers make?

c. How does Matthew 28:19-20 help explain their confidence in prayer?

d. What specific applications to your own prayer life can you make from the example of this prayer?

6. Read the account of a violent storm, recorded in Acts 27:13-44.

   a. When God revealed that He would deliver Paul and all his shipmates, Paul trusted God and His promise of deliverance. Even so, Paul didn't passively expect God to do the work that He had equipped the sailors to do. Make a list of all the actions that were taken that helped fulfill God's promise that they would all reach land safely.

   b. What relationship does this story show between God's sovereignty and our responsibility?

7. Read Psalm 127:1.

   a. Are you currently involved in building anything?
      (This need not be a physical building; it could be an
      organization, a relationship, or something similar.)
      If so, what is it?

   b. How is the Lord involved in your building?

   c. In what area(s) of your life are you like a watchman
      guarding a city?

   d. How is the Lord involved in your watching?

   e. How do you think you should feel and respond,
      knowing God's involvement in these situations?

8. a. Describe a time when you felt very dependent on God.

   b. What did you do for yourself at the time?

   c. Did any of your efforts make you less dependent on God? Why or why not?

Trust in Action

1. Read through the book of Proverbs in a modern translation, looking for lessons on prudence. Copy into your journal those verses that especially speak to you.

2. Memorize Philippians 4:6-7.

3. Start a prayer notebook with your requests and God's answers. This can be done very simply, with just a few words for each request. From time to time you may want to write out whole prayers to the Lord. The process of writing prayers causes us to think more seriously about what we are saying to God.

4. Before you go to bed tonight, tell God that you entrust
   each of your current concerns to Him. Name them. Ask
   Him to give you wisdom in dealing with each one. Then
   read Psalm 127:1-2, and go to sleep.

LESSON SEVEN

THE WISDOM OF GOD

(Chapter 8)

CENTRAL IDEA

God is infinite in wisdom. He always knows what is best for us, and He knows the best way to bring it about.

Examining Trust

Wisdom is commonly defined as good judgment, or the ability to develop the best course of action, or the best response to a given situation. God's wisdom is intuitive, infinite, and infallible: "His understanding has no limit" (Psalm 147:5).

Nineteenth-century theologian J. L. Dagg said, "God is infinitely wise, because he selects the best possible end of action . . . [and] because he adopts the best possible means for the accomplishment of the end which he has in view."[1] All that God does or allows in all of His creation will ultimately serve His glory.

God's infinite wisdom is displayed in bringing good out of evil, beauty out of ashes. It is displayed in turning all the forces of evil that rage against His children into good for them. But the good that He brings about is often different from the good we envision.

The good that God works for in our lives is conformity to the likeness of His Son. It is not necessarily comfort or happiness but conformity to Christ in ever-increasing measure in this life and in its fullness in eternity. If you stop and think about it, you will realize that most godly character traits can only be developed through adversity.

God in His infinite wisdom knows exactly what adversity we need to grow more and more into the likeness of His Son. He not only knows what we need but when we need it and how best to bring it to pass in our lives.

God never explains to us what He is doing or why. There is no indication that God ever explained to Job the reasons for all of his terrible sufferings. As readers, we are taken behind the scenes to observe the spiritual warfare between God and Satan, but as far as we can tell from Scripture, God never told Job about that.

We should never ask *why* in the sense of demanding that God explain or justify His actions or what He permits in our lives. I am not talking about the reactive and spontaneous cry of anguish when calamity first befalls us or one we love. Rather, I am speaking of the persistent and demanding *why* that has an accusatory tone toward God in it. The former is a natural human reaction; the latter is a sinful human reaction.

Sometimes we come to the place where we do not demand of God that He explain Himself, but we try to determine or comprehend for ourselves what God is doing. We are unwilling to live without rational reasons for what is happening to us or those we love. We are almost insatiable in our quest for the *why* of the adversity that has come upon us. But this is a futile as well as an untrusting task. God's ways, being the ways of infinite wisdom, simply cannot be comprehended by our finite minds. If we are to find peace for ourselves, we must come to the place where we can honestly say, "God, I do not have to understand. I will just trust You."

It is not only an irreverent act to question God's wisdom; it is also spiritually debilitating. We not only besmirch God's glory; we also deprive ourselves of the comfort and peace that comes by simply trusting Him without requiring an explanation. An unreserved trust of God, when we don't understand what is happening or why, is the only road to peace and comfort and joy. God wants us to honor Him by trusting Him, but He also desires that we experience the peace and joy that come as a result.

Developing Trust
1. How do these verses describe God's wisdom?

• Psalm 147:5

• Jeremiah 10:12

• Romans 11:33-34

2. Are there any past or present events in your life that tempt you to doubt God's wisdom? If so, what are they?

3. a. What is the ultimate purpose of all things according to Romans 11:36 and 1 Corinthians 10:31?

   b. What does it mean to glorify God?

   c. In what ways do you think your present circumstances bring glory to God?

4. Our prayers often seem to go unanswered, yet God is still handling us with wisdom. He knows that the very adversity we long to have removed is His means to help us grow. Read Psalm 119:71.

a. Describe a time when adversity was not removed even though you or others prayed that it would be.

b. Did you experience any personal growth through that adversity? If so, what?

5. What is the logical connection between Romans 8:28 and 8:29? (Notice the word *for* at the beginning of 8:29.)

6. a. Do you think we can fully understand God's reason for any particular event? Why or why not?

b. What attitude is expressed in Job 42:1-3 and Psalm 131:1?

c. What happens when we let go of our questions and trust God?

d. Is it hard for you to let go of your unanswered questions? Why or why not?

7. We should focus not on the reasons for our difficulties but on the lessons we can learn from them.

a. Read Deuteronomy 8:2-5. What lesson did the Israelites learn from their experience of getting only one day's food at a time?

b. Why do you think this lesson would be important for them later when they were prosperous in Canaan? (Read Deuteronomy 8:10-18.)

8. As we read in 2 Samuel 24:10-14, David was more afraid of suffering adversity at the hands of men than from God directly.

   a. Why do you think David felt this way?

   b. When we are facing adversity from other people, what comfort do Proverbs 21:30 and Romans 8:31 offer us?

9. a. What would you say to a friend who is struggling with the question *why* in the face of difficult circumstances?

   b. What kinds of things would you be careful not to say?

Trust in Action

   1. Memorize Romans 11:33.

   2. Share with a friend something God has been teaching you through this study.

3. Next time you hear of a disaster or tragedy, take time to pray for the people involved.

4. Tell God about the situations in your life, past or present, that tempt you to doubt that He knows what He is doing. Ask Him to help you fully believe that His reasons are good, even though He hasn't shown you what they are. Tell Him exactly how you feel about this situation; then meditate on Psalm 131.

KNOWING AND EXPERIENCING GOD'S LOVE

(Chapters 9 and 10)

CENTRAL IDEA

We can trust God's love because He loves us with a perfect and infinite love, which was demonstrated on Calvary. Because of our union with Christ, we are secure in that love.

Examining Trust

It seems that the more we come to believe in and accept the sovereignty of God over every event of our lives, the more we are tempted to question His love. We think, "If God is in control of this adversity and can do something about it, why doesn't He?"

There is no doubt that the most convincing evidence of God's love in all of Scripture is His giving His Son to die for our sins. The extent of God's love at Calvary is seen in both the infinite cost to Him of giving His one and only Son, and in the wretched and miserable condition of those He loved.

Any time we are tempted to doubt God's love for us we should go back to the Cross. We should reason somewhat in this fashion: If God loved me enough to give His Son to die for me when I was His enemy, surely He loves me enough to care for me now that I am His child. Having loved me to the ultimate extent at the Cross, He cannot possibly fail to love me in my times of adversity.

If we are to trust God in adversity, we must use our minds in those times to reason through the great truths of God's sovereignty, wisdom, and love as they are revealed to us in the Scriptures. We must not allow our emotions to hold sway over our minds. Rather, we must seek to let the truth of God rule our minds. Our emotions must become subservient to the truth. This does not mean we do not feel the pain of adversity and heartache. We feel it keenly. Nor does it mean we should seek to bury our emotional pain in a stoic-like attitude. We are meant to feel the pain of adversity, but we must resist allowing that pain to cause us to lapse into hard thoughts about God.

The infinite, measureless love of God is poured out upon us, not because of who we are or what we are, but because we are in Christ Jesus. It is very important that we grasp this crucial concept that God's love to us is *in Christ*. Just as God's love to His *Son* cannot change, so His love to *us* cannot change, because we are in union with the One He loves. God's love to us can no more waver than His love to His Son can waver. God does not look within us for a reason to love us. He loves us because we are in Christ Jesus.

God's sovereignty is exercised primarily for *His* glory. But because you and I are in Christ Jesus, His glory and *our* good are linked together. Because we are united with Christ, whatever is for His glory is also for our good. And whatever is for our good is for His glory.

God cannot forsake us because we are His children, in blessed union with His Son. We cannot be cut off from His sight. But we can be cut off from the *assurance* of His love when we allow doubt and unbelief to gain a foothold in our hearts.

The Bible's assurance of the sovereignty and constancy of God's love does not mean that we should not expect adversity. We mistakenly look for tokens of God's love in happiness. We should instead look for them in His faithful and persistent work to conform us to Christ. God in His infinite wisdom and perfect love will never over-discipline us; He will never allow any adversity in our lives that is not ultimately for our good.

God disciplines us with reluctance, though He does it faithfully. He does not delight in our adversities, but He will not spare us that which we need to grow more and more into the likeness of His Son. It is our imperfect spiritual condition that makes discipline necessary.

God's love is unfailing; His grace is always sufficient. But there is even more good news. He is *with us* in our troubles.

God's unfailing love for us is an objective fact affirmed over and over in the Scriptures. It is true whether we believe it or not. Our doubts do not destroy God's love, nor does our faith create it. It originates in the very nature of God, who is love, and it flows to us through our union with His beloved Son.

But the experience of that love and the comfort it is intended to bring is dependent upon our believing the truth about God's love as it is revealed to us in the Scriptures. Doubts about God's love, allowed to harbor in our hearts, will surely deprive us of the comfort of His love.

We are just as dependent upon the Holy Spirit to enable us to trust in God's love as we are dependent upon Him to enable us to obey His commands. But just as we are responsible to obey in confidence that He is at work in us, so we are responsible to trust Him in that same attitude of dependence and confidence.

With God's help we, too, can come to the place, even in the

midst of our adversities, where we will be able to say, "I trust in Your unfailing love."

Developing Trust

1. What observations about God's love can you make from these verses?

   • Psalm 103:11

   • Isaiah 54:10

   • Zephaniah 3:17

   • Romans 8:38-39

2. a. How does God feel about punishing the wicked (see Ezekiel 18:23, 32; 33:11; 2 Peter 3:9)?

    b. Read Lamentations 3:32-33. How does God feel about the afflictions He allows us to suffer when we sin?

3. a. In what event do we see the supreme demonstration of God's love for us? Read 1 John 4:9-10.

    b. Restate Romans 5:6-8 in your own words.

4. a. What experiences in your life have tempted you to doubt God's love?

    b. When you have doubted God's love, what has helped you regain your confidence in His love for you?

5. a. Based on Ephesians 1:3-6, how does being "in Christ" affect God's love for us?

b. How does John 15:1-8 describe our relationship with Jesus?

c. If the Father loves Jesus, then what are the implications for us?

d. What does pruning have to do with love (see John 15:2)?

6. Read Lamentations 3:17-24.

a. What feelings did Jeremiah express in verses 17-20?

b. How did he deal with those feelings (see verses 21-24)?

c. How do you deal with your feelings of discouragement and defeat?

d. What could you learn from Jeremiah about handling these feelings?

7. a. What can we learn from Hebrews 12:5-11 about why God disciplines us?

b. When have you experienced God's discipline? Describe one instance.

c. What lessons did you learn?

d. Did you sense God's love in the process? Explain.

8. God gives us the grace we need each day. We don't have the grace today for the "what ifs" of tomorrow.

   a. Describe a time when it was especially important for you to focus on God's daily grace without looking ahead.

   b. What happened when you tried to look down the road to see how you would cope tomorrow?

9. Summarize what God promises in the following verses.

   • Psalm 32:10

• Isaiah 41:10

• Isaiah 43:2-3

10. Read Psalm 13.

    a. Have you ever felt as David did when he wrote Psalm 13:1-2? If so, describe those feelings in your own words.

    b. How did David end this psalm (see verses 5-6)?

    c. How do you think it is possible to get from the feelings of verses 1-2 to the decision in verses 5-6?

11. a. To what extent do you currently experience God's love?

   b. What do you think is the major barrier keeping you from feeling God's love for you?

   c. How can you start to remove that barrier?

Trust in Action

1. Use a concordance to find other verses about God's love for us. Copy them into your journal.

2. Choose one verse about God's love and memorize it. Use it when Satan tries to convince you that God doesn't really love you.

3. Write a letter to someone who needs to know about God's love for him or her.

4. Write a letter to Jesus thanking Him for His love.

TRUSTING GOD
FOR WHO YOU ARE

(Chapter 11)

CENTRAL IDEA

God created us with all our abilities and disabilities for His glory. We must accept ourselves and trust God's wisdom in creating us the way we are.

Examining Trust

Many people struggle to accept themselves as they are. For them life is just a continuous adversity, not from outside circumstances but from who they are. Their greatest need in trusting God may be to "trust God for who I am." For those with this need, Psalm 139:13-16 has some very important and helpful things to say.

Psalm 139:13-16 teaches us that we are who we are because God Himself created us the way we are—not because of an impersonal biological process. David says to God, "You knit me together in my mother's womb." He pictures God as a master weaver at work in our mother's womb. David also says, "For you created my inmost being." The Hebrew word for "inmost being" is literally *kidneys*, a word used by the Jews to express the seat of longings and desires. The *New International Version Study Bible* says the word was used in Hebrew idiom for "the center of emotions and of moral sensitivity." David, then, is essentially saying, "You created my personality." And just as God was personally involved in the creation of David, so He was directly involved in creating you and me.

If I have difficulty accepting myself the way God made me, then I have a controversy with God. Obviously you and I need to change insofar as our sinful nature distorts that which God has made. Therefore, I do not say that we need to accept ourselves as we are, but as God made us in our basic physical, mental, and emotional makeup.

David praised God not because he was handsome but because God *made him*. The eternal God who is infinite in His wisdom and perfect in His love personally made you and me. He gave you the body, the mental abilities, and the basic personality you have because that is the way He wanted you to be. And He wanted you to be just that way because He loves you and wants to glorify Himself through you.

Self-acceptance is basically trusting God for who I am, disabilities or physical flaws and all. Certainly we will sometimes struggle with who we are. Unlike specific incidents of adversity, our disabilities and infirmities are always with us. So we have to learn to trust God in this area continually.

Psalm 139:16 says, "All the days ordained for me were written in your book before one of them came to be." There are two possible meanings that may be given to this verse. The first is that the span of David's lifetime, in other words, the number of days he would live, was divinely ordained by God. But it is likely that David had in mind the other meaning in this passage: that all the experiences of his life, day by day, were written down in God's book before he was even born. This refers not simply to God's prior knowledge of what will occur in our lives, but to His plan for our lives.

Just as we must trust God for who we are, we must also trust Him for what we are—whether it be an engineer or a missionary, a homemaker or a nurse. The realization that God has planned our days for us should not lead us to a fatalistic acceptance of the status quo. If we have an opportunity to improve our situation in a way that will honor God, we should do so. There has to be in our lives a delicate balance between godly efforts to improve our situation and godly acceptance of those situations that cannot be changed by us.

We do have a responsibility to make wise decisions or to discover the will of God, whichever term we may prefer to use. But God's plan for us is not contingent upon our decisions. God's plan is not contingent at all. God's plan is sovereign. It includes our foolish decisions as well as our wise ones.

I am where I am today, not because I have always made wise decisions or correctly discovered the will of God at particular points along the way, but because God has faithfully led me and guided me along the path of His will for me.

God's guidance is almost always step-by-step; He does not show us our life's plan all at once. Sometimes our anxiousness to know the will of God comes from a desire to "peer over God's shoulder" to see what His plan is. What we need to do is learn to trust Him to guide us.

Of course, this does not mean that we put our minds into neutral and expect God to guide us in some mysterious way apart from hard and prayerful thinking on our part. It does mean, as Dr. James Packer has said, "God made us thinking beings, and he guides our minds as we think things out in his presence."[2] God guides our minds as we think. He does not look down from heaven at our struggles to know His will and say, "I hope you make the right decision." Rather, in His time and in His way He will lead us in His path for us.

Developing Trust

1. What truth is being taught in the following verses?

   • Job 10:8-11

   • Psalm 119:73

   • Psalm 139:13-14

2. a. Do you ever struggle with accepting the way God made you? Explain.

   b. What is your attitude about your physical appearance?

c. What is your attitude about your personality and inner character?

d. Is your attitude pleasing to God? If it is not, how could you change your attitude?

3. a. What characteristics about yourself do you need to learn to accept?

b. What characteristics should you try to change?

c. To what extent is it all right to try to change your physical appearance?

4. In lesson 5, we looked at Exodus 4:11 and John 9:1-3. How can these verses help us to accept our imperfections?

5. How can 1 Corinthians 4:7 help us keep our good qualities in the proper perspective?

6. Restate in your own words the truths taught in these verses.

   • Job 14:5

   • Psalm 31:15

   • Psalm 139:16

- Acts 17:26

7. How can Jeremiah 29:11 encourage you when life seems overwhelming?

8. a. What advice does Paul give to slaves in 1 Corinthians 7:21?

   b. What general truth can we get from this verse?

9. a. According to Psalm 23:2-3, what does God do for us?

   b. Describe a time when you felt God's guidance in your life.

c. List some of the ways God can guide us when we are making a difficult decision.

Scripture; devotionals

d. Reflect on the last major decision you made. What method did you use to seek God's guidance and to make the wisest decision?

10. Read Acts 16:6-10.

a. What specific guidance did Paul and his companions receive?

b. We are not told how the Spirit prevented them from entering Bithynia and the province of Asia, but we know that He did. From these events what do we learn about God's guidance?

c. Does God regularly guide you in such an explicit way? Why do you suppose this is so?

11. a. Which of the daily activities that you are currently involved in do you feel God wants you to be doing?

b. Which, if any, current activities do you think God may not want you to be doing? What makes you think that?

12. If you are discontent with your present position, do you need to accept where you are with a thankful heart, or does God want you to pursue something new?

Trust in Action

1. Take some time, in addition to your regular devotions, to be alone with the Lord and thank Him for creating you just the way you are. If you are angry about the body, the

mind, the skills, the inabilities, or the personality God has given you, confess your anger and ask God to give you gratitude even for the things you don't like.

2. Memorize Psalm 139:13-14.

3. Make a list of the abilities God has given you. Think about how you are presently serving the Lord. Are you using your gifts and abilities? Can you identify new ways to serve that will better suit your abilities?

4. In Psalm 139:16-18 David expressed his praise and thanksgiving for God's guidance. Write a prayer expressing your gratitude for the way God has guided you to this point in your life. Thank Him for specific events that helped change your life.

GROWING THROUGH ADVERSITY

(Chapter 12)

CENTRAL IDEA

Adversity causes us to develop Christlike character. For the believer all pain has meaning; all adversity is profitable.

Examining Trust

One of the many fascinating events in nature is the emergence of the Cecropia moth from its cocoon—an event that occurs only with much struggle on the part of the moth to free itself. The story is frequently told of someone who watched a moth go through this struggle. In an effort to help—and not realizing the necessity of the struggle—the viewer snipped the shell of the cocoon. Soon the moth came out with its wings all crimped and shriveled. But as the person watched, the wings remained weak. The moth, which in a few moments would have stretched those wings to fly, was now doomed to crawling out its brief life in frustration of ever being the beautiful creature God created it to be.

What the person in the story did not realize was that the

struggle to emerge from the cocoon was an essential part of developing the muscle system of the moth's body and pushing the body fluids out into the wings to expand them.

The adversities of life are much like the cocoon of the Cecropia moth. God uses them to develop the spiritual "muscle system" of our lives. We can be sure that the development of a beautiful Christlike character will not occur in our lives without adversity.

Fortunately God does not ask us how or when we want to grow. He is the Master Teacher, training His pupils when and how He deems best. He is, in the words of Jesus, the Gardener who prunes the branches of His vineyard. The healthy vine requires both nourishment and pruning. Through the Word of God we are nourished (see Psalm 1:2-3), but through adversity we are pruned. Both the Hebrew and Greek languages express discipline and teaching by the same word. God intends that we grow through the discipline of adversity as well as through instruction from His Word.

There are several things we can do in order to learn from adversity and receive the beneficial effects that God intends. First, we can submit to it—not reluctantly as the defeated general submits to his conqueror, but voluntarily as the patient on the operating table submits to the skilled hand of the surgeon as he wields his knife.

Second, to profit most from adversity, we should bring the Word of God to bear upon the situation. Martin Luther reportedly said, "Were it not for tribulation I should not understand the Scriptures." We might say, then, that the Word of God and adversity have a synergistic effect as God uses both of them together to bring about growth in our lives that neither the Word nor adversity would accomplish by itself.

Third, in order to profit from our adversities we must remember them and the lessons we learned from them. God wants us to remember them, not just as trials or sorrows, but as His disciplines—His means of bringing about growth in our lives.

It is helpful to consider some of the specific ends God has in mind when He allows adversity in our lives.

Pruning. God uses adversity to loosen our grip on those things that are not true spiritual fruit. In adversity we begin to relinquish our desires and expectations—even good ones—to the sovereign will of God.

Holiness. Adversity causes us to grow in holiness because it reveals the corruption of our sinful nature. What we have mastered in good times may quickly fade in adversity, showing us the need to go deeper in our battle against the rebellion of our wills, the perversity of our affections, and the spiritual ignorance of our minds.

Dependence. God teaches us through adversity to rely on Him instead of ourselves. Apart from our union with Christ and a total reliance upon Him, we can do nothing that glorifies God.

Perseverance. God wants us to learn to do more than simply bear up under adversity. Perseverance is the quality of character that enables one to pursue a goal in spite of obstacles and difficulties.

Service. Adversity equips us for more effective service. It is necessary to make us into people who are fit for the responsibilities that God wants to give us.

The Fellowship of Suffering. Through adversity we have the privilege of entering into a special fellowship with other believers who are also in the throes of adversity. Suffering unites our hearts together in Christ more than any other aspect of fellowship.

Relationship with God. Perhaps the most valuable way we

profit from adversity is in the deepening of our relationship with God. You and I obviously do not seek out adversity just so we can develop a deeper relationship with God. Rather, God, through adversity, seeks us out. It is God who draws us more and more into a deeper relationship with Him.

Developing Trust
1. a. Think about the fruit of the Spirit listed in Galatians 5:22-23. How does adversity encourage each of the following:

• love

• joy

• peace

• patience

- kindness

- goodness

- faithfulness

- gentleness

- self-control

b. Which of these have grown in your own life through adversity?

c. Did the growth you experienced endure after the adversity passed? Explain.

2. a. Read Romans 5:3-5 and James 1:2-4. What should our attitude be in the midst of adversity, and why?

b. How did Jesus maintain this attitude (see Hebrews 12:2)?

c. How can we cultivate this same attitude?

3. What does Philippians 1:6 say about our spiritual growth?

4. a. What happens when we resist God's working in our lives through adversity?

   b. What warning is given to us in Job 36:21?

5. a. Have you been drawn to God's Word in times of adversity? Why or why not?

   b. What portions of Scripture have become especially important to you during trying times?

6. a. According to John 15:2 what is the purpose of God's pruning?

b. Even in the church, Christians sometimes seek things that are not true spiritual fruit, such as position, success, and reputation. What counterfeit fruit have you been tempted to seek?

7. What is the connection between adversity (or discipline) and holiness, as expressed in Hebrews 12:10?

8. Read 2 Corinthians 1:8-9 and 12:10. How does adversity teach us to depend on God?

9. a. Hebrews 10:36 and 12:1 speak of the need to persevere. What is the goal of our perseverance?

b. How can we learn to persevere? (See question 2.)

10. a. Why does suffering deepen the fellowship between believers?

   b. Describe a time when you experienced deeper fellowship through suffering.

11. What does Psalm 34:18 say about how adversity affects our relationship with God?

12. Which of the seven results of suffering—pruning, holiness, dependence, perseverance, service, fellowship, relationship with God—which are discussed under "Examining Trust"—have you personally experienced?

Trust in Action

 1. Memorize James 1:2-4.

 2. Contact someone you know who is suffering. Offer to get together to pray.

3. One of the best ways to remember what God has taught us through different experiences is to write down those lessons while they are fresh. If you haven't started a journal, begin now by recording the lessons God has been teaching you lately. Then, sit down once a month and record your recent discoveries in your walk with God. Over the years this will have a big impact on how well you remember what God has done in your life.

CHOOSING TO TRUST GOD

(Chapter 13)

CENTRAL IDEA

We must choose, by an act of our will, to trust God in major and minor difficulties. We can do this regardless of how we may feel because we know that God is sovereign, wise, and loving.

Examining Trust

For many years in my own pilgrimage of seeking to come to a place of trusting God at all times—I am still far from the end of the journey—I was a prisoner to my feelings. I mistakenly thought I could not trust God unless I felt like trusting Him (which I almost never did in times of adversity). Now I am learning that trusting God is first of all a matter of the will and is not dependent on my feelings. I choose to trust God, and my feelings eventually follow.

Having said that trusting God is first of all a matter of the will, let me qualify that statement to say that, first of all, it is a matter of knowledge. We must know that God is sovereign, wise, and loving—in all the ways we have come to see what those terms mean in previous chapters. But having been exposed to the knowledge of the truth, we must then choose whether to believe the truth about God, which He has revealed to us, or whether to follow our feelings. If we are to trust God, we must choose to believe His truth. We must say, "I will trust You though I do not feel like doing so."

Trusting God is a matter of faith, and faith is the fruit of the Spirit (Galatians 5:22). Only the Holy Spirit can make His Word come alive in our hearts and create faith, but we can choose to look to Him to do that, or we can choose to be ruled by our feelings of anxiety or resentment or grief. We are responsible to trust Him in times of adversity, but we are dependent upon the Holy Spirit to enable us to do so.

The whole idea of trusting God is, of course, based upon the fact that God is absolutely trustworthy. We must also lay hold of some of the great promises of His constant care for us. One such promise we will do well to store up in our hearts is Hebrews 13:5: "Never will I leave you; never will I forsake you." Because God will never leave you nor forsake you, you are invited in the words of Peter to "cast all your anxiety on him because he cares for you" (1 Peter 5:7). He is not just there with you; He cares for you.

There are three pitfalls in trusting God that we must be careful to avoid. First, during times of temporal blessings and prosperity, we are prone to put our trust in those blessings, or even worse, in ourselves as the providers of those blessings. In adversity we tend to doubt God's fatherly care, but in prosperity we tend to forget it. If we are to trust God, we must acknowledge our dependence upon Him at all times, good times as well as bad times.

Another pitfall we need to watch for is the tendency to trust in God's instruments of provision rather than in God Himself. We must be careful to look beyond the means and human instrumentalities to the God who uses them.

The third pitfall is that we are prone to turn to God in trust in the greater crisis experiences of life while seeking to work through the minor difficulties ourselves. A disposition to trust in ourselves is part of our sinful nature. It sometimes takes a major crisis, or at least a moderate one, to turn us toward the Lord. A mark of Christian maturity is to continually trust the Lord in the minutiae of daily life. If we learn to trust God in the minor adversities, we will be better prepared to trust Him in the major ones.

Developing Trust

1. Read Psalm 56:3-4 and 1 Samuel 21:10-15, which is the historical setting for the psalm.

   a. What emotions was David experiencing at the time he wrote this psalm (see 1 Samuel 21:10-12)?

   b. How much trust in God did David show in 1 Samuel 21:13? Why do you think this?

   c. When David chose to trust God, how did his feelings change (see Psalm 56:3-4)?

d. Tradition says that Psalm 34 was written shortly after Psalm 56, after the crisis was over. How do you explain the relationship between David's statements in Psalm 56:4 and Psalm 34:4?

2. a. Have you had an experience in which you chose to trust God despite your emotions? If so, what happened to your emotions after you decided to trust God?

b. Why do you think emotions work that way?

3. a. Why is God worthy of your wholehearted trust?

b. Is it possible for us to be worthy of His trust? Explain.

4. a. What attitude did Job express in Job 23:8-10?

   b. In times of distress we must be careful that our feelings do not mislead us. Do Job's feelings contradict the truth of Hebrews 13:5? Why or why not?

5. Read 1 Peter 5:7. Is learning to trust God and cast our anxieties on Him something we get better at? If so, how? If not, why not?

6. Sometimes when we are anxious, there are things we need to do. Sometimes there is nothing we can do. Make a list of the things you are anxious about at this time in your life. Which things do you need to act on, and which things do you need to leave in the hands of the Lord?

7. a. Do you tend to forget to trust God when things are going well? Explain.

   b. In what ways do we need to trust God in good times?

8. a. What contrast is made in Proverbs 18:10-11?

   b. Do you get your sense of security from your achievements and possessions or from the Lord? How do your actions reflect this?

9. a. What does God promise us in Psalm 50:15?

b. What do we need to do after God answers our call, according to this verse?

c. In what specific ways might you do this?

10. a. Are you more able to trust God now than when you began this study?

b. If so, what has helped you most?

c. What help do you still need?

11. How would you explain to an unbeliever why you choose to trust God?

Trust in Action

1. For the next week keep a record of your anxious thoughts. Decide which thoughts should prompt you to action and which ones you need to leave in God's hands.

2. Memorize Hebrews 13:5 and 1 Peter 5:6-7.

3. Read a biography of a godly Christian leader. Notice especially how this person's trust in God grew through his or her life. A brief list follows. Check with your pastor or church librarian for other suggestions.

Adoniram Judson by Faith Coxe Bailey

A Chance to Die by Elisabeth Elliot (about Amy Carmichael)

Daws by Betty Lee Skinner (about Dawson Trotman)

George Müller: Delighted in God! by Roger Steer

The Hiding Place by Corrie ten Boom with John and Elizabeth Sherrill

Hudson Taylor's Spiritual Secret by Dr. and Mrs. Howard Taylor

Shadow of the Almighty by Elisabeth Elliot (about Jim Elliot)

The Tapestry by Edith Schaeffer (about Francis and Edith Schaeffer)

William Carey by Basil Miller

GIVING THANKS ALWAYS

(Chapter 14)

CENTRAL IDEA

When we face adversity, we can trust God. In fact, we must trust God. In addition, we should respond to adversity with thanksgiving, worship, humility, forgiveness, prayer, and a heart seeking only God's glory.

Examining Trust

Because God is sovereign, wise, and good, we can trust Him. If we are to honor Him in our times of adversity, we must trust Him. In our trusting God, there is more at stake than experiencing peace in the midst of difficulties or even deliverance from them. The honor of God should be our chief concern. Therefore, our primary response to the trustworthiness of God should be, "I will trust God." But there are some corollary responses to trusting God that are also important. They provide tangible evidence that we are in fact trusting God.

The first corollary response we will consider is thanksgiving.

Paul said to "give thanks in all circumstances" (1 Thessalonians 5:18). We are to be thankful in bad times and good times, for adversities as well as for blessings. Thanksgiving is an admission of dependence. Through it we recognize that in the physical realm God "gives [us] life and breath and everything else" (Acts 17:25), and that in the spiritual realm, it is God who made us alive in Christ Jesus when we were dead in our transgressions and sins.

The basis for giving thanks in the difficult circumstances is the firm belief that God is at work in all things—all circumstances— for our good. It is the willingness to accept this truth from God's Word and rely upon it without having to know just how He is working for our good.

We can see a very close connection between the promise of Romans 8:28 and the command of 1 Thessalonians 5:18, when we understand the literal translation of the words *in all circumstances* is "in everything." In the Greek, as in the English language, the words and meanings are very, very close. We are to give thanks *in everything* because we know that *in all things* God is at work for our good.

Another response to the trustworthiness of God is to worship Him in times of adversity. Worship involves a two-directional view. Looking upward we see God in all His majesty, power, glory, and sovereignty as well as His mercy, goodness, and grace. Looking at ourselves we recognize our dependence upon God and our sinfulness before Him.

A third response to adversity is humility. "Humble yourselves, therefore, under God's mighty hand that he may lift you up in due time. Cast all your anxiety on him because he cares for you" (1 Peter 5:6-7). On the one hand we are to humble ourselves under God's mighty hand—an expression equivalent to submitting with a spirit of humility to God's sovereign dealings with us. And on the other hand, we are to cast our anxieties on Him, knowing that He cares for us. The anxieties, of course, arise out of the adversities that God's mighty hand brings into our lives. We are to accept the adversities but not the anxieties.

Our tendency is just opposite. We seek to escape from or resist the adversities but all the while cling to the anxieties that they produce. The way to cast our anxieties on the Lord is through humbling ourselves under His sovereignty and then trusting Him in His wisdom and love. Humility should be both a response to adversity and a fruit of it.

Adversity often comes to us through the actions of other people. Sometimes those hurtful actions are deliberately directed at us. At other times we may be the victim of another person's irresponsible actions that, though not deliberately aimed at us, nevertheless affect us seriously. Therefore, the fourth response to adversity we must consider is forgiveness.

I have found that two truths help me forgive others. First, I myself am a sinner, forgiven by the grace of God and the shed blood of His Son. I have hurt others, perhaps not so often deliberately but unconsciously through an uncaring spirit or selfish actions. Second, I seek to look beyond the person who is only the instrument to see God who has purposed this adversity for me.

A fifth response to adversity is to pray for deliverance. A spirit of humble acceptance toward God or forgiveness toward others does not mean we should not pray for deliverance from the adversities that come upon us. We should pray for deliverance, and we should learn to resist the attacks of Satan in the power of Jesus Christ. But we should always pray in an attitude of humble acceptance of that which is God's will.

Above all else, our response to adversity should be to seek God's glory. We see this attitude illustrated in the life of the apostle Paul during his imprisonment in Rome. Not only was he imprisoned, but there were men, supposedly fellow ministers of the gospel, who were actually trying to add to his troubles by their preaching (Philippians 1:14-17). Paul's response (verse 18) is essentially, "It really doesn't matter what happens to me or how I am affected by all of this. The important thing is what happens to the gospel."

We have seen that God is trustworthy. He is absolutely sovereign over every event in the universe, and He exercises that sovereignty in an infinitely wise and loving way for our good. To the foundation of a life lived in communion with God, we must add what we have learned about God in this book— about His sovereignty, wisdom, and love. We must lay hold of these great truths in the little trials as well as the major calamities of life. As we do this in dependence upon the enabling power of His Holy Spirit, we will be able more and more to say, "I can trust God."

Developing Trust

1. a. Read Luke 17:11-19. What two human responses to a blessing are illustrated in this event?

   b. According to Acts 17:24-25 and 1 Corinthians 4:7, why should we be thankful?

c. Do you have a thankful attitude toward God most of the time, not often enough, or rarely? Explain.

d. Write a prayer asking God to help you have a more grateful spirit.

2. a. What does Romans 8:28 say about God working in our lives?

b. How does Romans 8:28 help us fulfill 1 Thessalonians 5:18?

3. a. What was Job's reaction to the loss of his children and property? Read Job 1:13-21.

b. What is worship? (A Bible dictionary might be helpful.)

c. What specifically helps you to enter into a spirit of worship?

4. a. Read 2 Corinthians 12:7. Why was Paul given a thorn in the flesh?

b. Has God ever used an adversity in your life to counteract your pride? If so, describe the situation.

c. Why does God cherish humility in us (see James 4:6)?

d. What are major sources of pride in your life?

e. How can you change the areas where you are proud into areas of humility?

5. a. How does humility help us deal with mistreatment from other people?

b. Do you have a hard time forgiving others? Explain.

6. a. What sort of attitude is pleasing to God when we pray for deliverance from some adversity?

b. Is there ever a point at which we need to stop praying for deliverance? If so, how do we know when we have reached that point? If not, why not?

7. Of the six responses discussed in "Examining Trust"—
thanksgiving, worship, humility, forgiveness, prayer, and
a heart seeking only God's glory—which one is the most
difficult for you? Why is this so?

8. Look at Isaiah 42:8. How can your actions better show
that glorifying God is your top priority?

9. What are the most important ideas you have gained from
this study?

Trust in Action

1. Write a prayer to God, expressing the ways you hope to
trust Him more fully.

2. If there is someone you need to forgive, or ask forgiveness
from, make a point of doing it this week.

3. Memorize 1 Thessalonians 5:18.

4. Ask a friend to join you for a brief time of worship. You may want to include Scripture readings, prayer, singing, and silence. Discuss what helps each of you to break past the barriers in your heart to enter a time of true worship.

5. Watch your attitude for one week. How often are you in a negative, complaining state of mind, and how often do you have an attitude of thanksgiving? Keep a record in your journal. Share your results with a friend.

HELP FOR LEADERS

The following pages are designed to help a discussion leader guide a group in an edifying time centered on God's truth. You can appoint one person to lead each session, or you can rotate leadership.

Preparation

Your aim as a leader is to create an environment that is conducive to study. You want the group members to feel comfortable with one another and to find the setting congenial. You want the session to be free from distractions.

Personal Preparation. As the group leader, your most important preparation for each session is prayer. You will want to make your prayers personal, of course, but here are some suggestions:

- Pray that group members will be able to attend the discussion. Ask God to enable them to feel free to share their thoughts and feelings honestly and to contribute their unique gifts and insights.

- Pray for group members' private times with God this week. Ask God to be active in nurturing them.
- Ask God to give each of you new understanding and practical applications from the Scriptures as you talk. Pray that God will meet each person's unique needs.
- Ask for the Holy Spirit's guidance in exercising patience, acceptance, sensitivity, and wisdom. Pray for an atmosphere of genuine love in the group, with each member being honestly open to learning and change.
- Pray that your discussion will lead each of you to obey the Lord more closely and demonstrate His presence.
- Pray for insight as you go over the study materials and for wisdom as you lead the group.

After prayer, your most important preparation is to be thoroughly familiar with the material you will discuss with the group. Make sure you have answered all of the questions. You will also find it important to read the chapters in *Trusting God* that are covered by each lesson. Decide which questions you want to discuss as a group. You may not have time to cover all the questions. Think about which questions are most important for your particular group to discuss. When a question is about a Scripture passage, it will be helpful to read the passage together. When there are a number of passages, you may want to choose ahead of time which ones to discuss.

Group Preparation. Choose a time and place to meet that is consistent, comfortable, and relatively free from distractions. Make plans to deal with children, pets, and ringing telephones. Refreshments can help people mingle, but don't let them consume too much of your time.

The First Session

You may want to begin with a potluck supper. In this way, group members can get to know one another in the context of a meal, which is a good way to break down barriers. Then after dinner you can have your first session.

In this session, be sure to set aside adequate time for people to share who they are. It is amazing how much more productive and honest a Bible discussion is if the participants know each other.

At some point in the evening (probably toward the end), go over the following guidelines. They help make a discussion more fruitful, especially when you are dealing with issues that truly matter to people.

Confidentiality. No one should repeat what someone shares in the group unless that person gives express permission. Even then, discretion is imperative. Be trustworthy. Participants should talk about their own feelings and experiences, not those of others.

Attendance. Each session builds on the previous ones, and you need each other. So, ask group members to commit to attending all twelve sessions, unless an emergency arises.

Participation. This is a *group* discussion, not a lecture. It is important that each person participate in some way in the group.

Preparation. Decide as a group whether everyone will read the material and answer the questions before the group meets. Your discussions will be more interesting if group members have prepared in advance. In addition, group members will get far more out of the study if they have spent time thinking about the questions and meditating on the Scriptures before meeting. If group members are prepared it will not be necessary to take group time to read the excerpt or to look up all the Scripture references together.

Honesty. Appropriate openness is a key to a good group. Be who you really are, not who you think you ought to be.

Leading the Group
Each session is designed to take sixty minutes:

- ten minutes for opening prayer and warm-up questions
- forty minutes for discussion of the study questions
- ten minutes for closing prayer time

Work Toward a Relaxed and Open Atmosphere. This may not come quickly, so be a model for the others of acceptance, openness to truth and change, and love. Develop a genuine interest in each person's remarks and expect to learn from them. Show that you care by listening carefully. Be affirming. Sometimes a hug is the best response.

Pay Attention to How You Ask the Questions. Don't ask, "What did you get for number 1?" Instead, by your tone of voice convey:

- your interest and enthusiasm for the question
- your warmth toward the group

The group will adopt your attitude. Read the questions as though you were asking them of good friends.

If the discussion falters:

- Be comfortable with silence. Let the group wrestle to think of answers. Don't be quick to jump in and rescue the group with your answers.
- Reword a question if the group members have trouble understanding it.
- If a question evokes little response, feel free to leave it and move on.

- Feel free to answer questions yourself occasionally. In particular, you should be the first one to answer questions about personal experiences. In this way you will model the depth of openness and thought you hope others will show. You can also model an appropriate length of response. Don't answer every question, but don't be a silent observer.
- If the discussion is winding down on a question, go on to the next one. It's not necessary to push people to see every possible angle.

Ask Only One Question at a Time. Often, participants' responses will suggest a follow-up question to you. Be discerning as to when you are following a fruitful train of thought and when you are going off on a tangent.

Be Aware of Time. Don't spend so much time discussing that you run out of time for application and prayer. Your goal is not to have something to discuss but to become more like Jesus Christ.

Encourage Constructive Controversy. The group can learn a lot from struggling with the many sides of an issue. If you aren't threatened when someone disagrees, the whole group will be more open and vulnerable. Intervene, if necessary, to be sure that people are debating ideas and interpretations of Scripture, not attacking each other's feelings and character. If the group gets stuck in an irresolvable argument, say something like, "We can agree to disagree here," and move on.

Don't Be the Expert. People will stop talking if they think that you are judging their answers or that you think you know best. Let the Bible be the expert, the final say. Let people candidly express their feelings and experiences.

Don't Do for the Group What It Can Do for Itself. With a beginning group, you may have to ask all of the questions, do all of the outside research, plan the applications, etc. But within a few meetings you should start delegating various leadership responsibilities. Let members learn to exercise their gifts. Let them start making decisions and solving problems together. Encourage them to maturity and unity in Christ.

Encourage People to Share Feelings as Well as Facts. There are two dimensions of truth: the truth about how people feel, and the truth about who God is and what is right. People need to face both their real feelings and the real God.

Summarize the Discussion Frequently. Help the group see where the discussion is going.

Let the Group Plan Applications. The group and individual action responses in this guide are suggestions. Your group should adapt them so that they are relevant and life-changing for members. If group members aren't committed to an application, they won't do it. Encourage, but don't force.

End with Refreshments. Have coffee or soft drinks plus some cookies or cake, so that people will have an excuse to stay behind for a few extra minutes and discuss the subject informally. Often the most life-changing conversations occur after the formal session.

After the Discussion
Use these self-evaluation questions each week to help you improve your leadership next time:

1. Did you have the right number of questions prepared? Should you add to the next session's questions, or delete some?

2. Did you discuss the major issues?

3. Did you know your material thoroughly enough to have freedom in leading?

4. Did you keep the discussion from wandering?

5. Did everyone participate? Were people open?

6. Was anyone overtalkative? Undertalkative? Disruptive? Think about how you can handle these problems next week if they occur again.

7. Was the discussion practical? Did it lead to new understanding, new hope, repentance, change?

8. Did you begin and end on time?

9. Did you give the group the maximum responsibility that it can handle?

NOTES

CHAPTER TWO: IS GOD IN CONTROL?

1. Harold S. Kushner, *When Bad Things Happen to Good People* (New York: Avon Books, 1983), 42–43.
2. Kushner, 43.
3. J. I. Packer, "Providence," *The New Bible Dictionary* (London: InterVarsity, 1962), 1050–1051.
4. A. H. Strong quoted in Dallas Willard, *In Search of Guidance* (Ventura, CA: Regal Books, 1984), 91.
5. Augustine quoted in John Blanchard, *Gathered Gold* (Welwyn, England: Evangelical Press, 1984), 332.
6. Philip E. Hughes, *Hope for a Despairing World* (Grand Rapids, MI: Baker, 1977), 40–41.
7. Steven Fink, *Crisis Management: Planning for the Inevitable* (New York: American Management Association, 1986), 1–2.
8. Kushner, 46–48.
9. Kushner, 59.
10. Alvera Mickelson, "Why Did God Let It Happen?" *Christianity Today* (March 16, 1984), 22–24.
11. Margaret Clarkson, *Destined for Glory* (Grand Rapids, MI: Eerdmans, 1983), 6.
12. G. C. Berkouwer, *The Providence of God* (Grand Rapids, MI: Eerdmans, 1983), 23.

CHAPTER THREE: THE SOVEREIGNTY OF GOD

1. Iain H. Murray, *The Life of Arthur W. Pink* (Edinburgh: Banner of Truth, 1981), 4.
2. Andrew Murray, *Every Day with Andrew Murray*, quoted in *Christianity Today* (March 6, 1987), 41.
3. Margaret Clarkson, *Grace Grows Best in Winter* (Grand Rapids, MI: Eerdmans, 1984), 40–41.
4. Alexander Carson, *Confidence in God in Times of Danger* (Swengel, PA: Reiner, 1975), 25.
5. I acknowledge my indebtedness to Alexander Carson and his book *Confidence in God in Times of Danger* for some of the ideas in this analysis of Esther chapter 6.

CHAPTER FOUR: GOD'S SOVEREIGNTY OVER PEOPLE

1. Charles Bridges, *An Exposition of the Book of Proverbs* (Evansville, IN: The Sovereign Grace Book Club, 1959), 364.
2. G. C. Berkouwer, *The Providence of God* (Grand Rapids, MI: Eerdmans, 1983), 90–91.
3. Alexander Carson, *The History of Providence* (Grand Rapids, MI: Baker, n.d.), 96–97.
4. Basil Manly Sr., *Southern Baptist Sermons on Sovereignty and Responsibility* (Harrisonburg, VA: Sprinkle Publications, 1984), 15–16. Manly was both a pastor and educator. He was president of the University of Alabama from 1838 to 1855, and was also one of the founding fathers of the Southern Baptist Convention.
5. Richard Fuller, *Southern Baptist Sermons on Sovereignty and Responsibility*, 112.
6. Berkouwer, 140–141.
7. Alexander Carson, *Confidence in God in Times of Danger* (Swengel, PA: Reiner, 1975), 55.

CHAPTER FIVE: GOD'S RULE OVER THE NATIONS

1. C. H. Spurgeon, *God's Providence* (Choteau, MT: Gospel Mission, n.d.), 18.
2. Alexander Carson, *Confidence in God in Times of Danger* (Swengel, PA: Reiner, 1975), 41.
3. H. B. Dehqani-Tafti, *Design of My World* (New York: Seabury Press, 1982), 30.
4. Margaret Clarkson, *Grace Grows Best in Winter* (Grand Rapids, MI: Eerdmans, 1984), 41.
5. John Newton, *The Works of John Newton* (Edinburgh: Banner of Truth, 1985), 4:429.
6. G. C. Berkouwer, *The Providence of God* (Grand Rapids, MI: Eerdmans, 1983), 91–92.
7. Alexander Carson, *The History of Providence* (Grand Rapids, MI: Baker, n.d.), 154.

CHAPTER SIX: GOD'S POWER OVER NATURE

1. Mike Nichols, "How's the Weather?" *Christian Herald* (July/August 1984), 33.
2. G. C. Berkouwer, *The Providence of God* (Grand Rapids, MI: Eerdmans, 1983), 85.
3. Alexander Carson, *The History of Providence* (Grand Rapids, MI: Baker, n.d.), v.
4. Alexander Carson, *Confidence in God in Times of Danger* (Swengel, PA: Reiner, 1975), 4–5.
5. Edward J. Young, *The Book of Isaiah* (Grand Rapids, MI: Eerdmans, 1984), 3:201.
6. Quoted from a printed copy of a message, "The Sovereignty of God," preached by Dr. Donald G. Barnhouse, n.d., 2.

CHAPTER SEVEN: GOD'S SOVEREIGNTY AND OUR RESPONSIBILITY

NOTES

CHAPTER SEVEN: GOD'S SOVEREIGNTY AND OUR RESPONSIBILITY

1. Thomas Lye, "How Are We to Live by Faith on Divine Providence?" *Puritan Sermons 1659–1689* (Wheaton, IL: Richard Owen Roberts, Publisher, 1981), 1:374. This is a collection of sermons by seventy-five Puritan preachers, originally published at irregular intervals between 1660 and 1691, in London.
2. John Flavel, *The Works of John Flavel* (Edinburgh: Banner of Truth, 1982), 4:336–497.
3. Lye, 1:374.
4. Alexander Carson, *Confidence in God in Times of Danger* (Swengel, PA: Reiner, 1975), no page number.

CHAPTER EIGHT: THE WISDOM OF GOD

1. Brian H. Edwards, *Not by Chance* (Welwyn, England: Evangelical Press, 1982), 14.
2. J. L. Dagg, *Manual of Theology* (Southern Baptist Publication Society, 1857; rpr. Harrisonburg, VA: Gano Books, 1982), 86–87.
3. John Piper, *Desiring God* (Portland, OR: Multnomah, 1986), 23.
4. Quoted from a very old, undated, and unsigned article in the author's file from a British publication, *A Witness and a Testimony.*
5. Margaret Clarkson, *Destined for Glory* (Grand Rapids, MI: Eerdmans, 1983), 19.
6. Don Baker, *Pain's Hidden Purpose* (Portland, OR: Multnomah, 1984), 103.
7. Baker, 103.
8. Edward J. Young, *The Book of Isaiah* (Grand Rapids, MI: Eerdmans, 1984), 3:383.
9. Charles B. Williams, *The New Testament in the Language of the People* (Nashville: Holman Bible Publishers, 1986), 351.
10. C. H. Spurgeon, *God's Providence* (Choteau, MT: Gospel Mission, n.d.), 19.
11. G. C. Berkouwer, *The Providence of God* (Grand Rapids, MI: Eerdmans, 1983), 88.
12. John Flavel, *The Works of John Flavel* (Edinburgh: Banner of Truth, 1982), 3:361.
13. Dagg, 91.

CHAPTER NINE: KNOWING GOD'S LOVE

1. Philip E. Hughes, *Hope for a Despairing World* (Grand Rapids, MI: Baker, 1977), 14.
2. Theologians, in speaking of the goodness of God, usually distinguish between His goodness of excellence (as in, He's a good engineer), and His goodness of benevolence (as in, He's good to His children). In this and the following chapter I use the goodness of God as His benevolence to His people and use it interchangeably with His love.
3. Hughes, *Hope for a Despairing World,* 18.
4. William Hendriksen, *New Testament Commentary: Exposition of Ephesians* (Grand Rapids, MI: Baker, 1967), 102–103.

5. Alexander Carson, *The History of Providence* (Grand Rapids, MI: Baker, n.d.), 313–314.

6. G. C. Berkouwer, *The Providence of God* (Grand Rapids, MI: Eerdmans, 1983), 180, 47.

CHAPTER TEN: EXPERIENCING GOD'S LOVE

1. Edward J. Young, *The Book of Isaiah* (Grand Rapids, MI: Eerdmans, 1984), 3:285.

2. Philip E. Hughes, *A Commentary on the Epistle to the Hebrews* (Grand Rapids, MI: Eerdmans, 1977), 528.

3. Lina Sandell Berg, "Day By Day," translated by Andrew L. Skoog, n.d.

4. John Brown, *Analytical Exposition of the Epistle of Paul the Apostle to the Romans* (1857; rpr. Grand Rapids, MI: Baker, 1981), 269.

CHAPTER ELEVEN: TRUSTING GOD FOR WHO YOU ARE

1. James Hufstetler, "On Knowing Oneself," *The Banner of Truth*, Issue 280 (January 1987), 13.

2. George MacDonald quoted in J. R. Miller, "Finding One's Mission" (Swengel, PA: Reiner Publications, n.d.), 2.

3. Hufstetler, 14.

4. Miller, 2.

5. J. I. Packer, *Your Father Loves You* (Wheaton, IL: Harold Shaw Publishers, 1986), devotional reading for October 13.

6. Fanny J. Crosby, "All the Way My Savior Leads Me."

CHAPTER TWELVE: GROWING THROUGH ADVERSITY

1. Horatius Bonar, *When God's Children Suffer* (New Canaan, CT: Keats Publishing, Inc., 1981, originally published as *Night of Weeping*), 30.

2. Bonar, 31.

3. Bonar, 28–29.

4. Daniel Dyke quoted in C. H. Spurgeon, *The Treasury of David* (Grand Rapids, MI: Baker, 1984), 4:306.

5. One method that helps us to remember God's lessons through adversity is to keep a record of them and review them periodically.

CHAPTER THIRTEEN: CHOOSING TO TRUST GOD

1. Margaret Clarkson, *Grace Grows Best in Winter* (Grand Rapids, MI: Eerdmans, 1984), 21.

2. John Newton, *The Works of John Newton* (Edinburgh: Banner of Truth, 1985), 5:621–622.

3. Newton, 5:622–623.

4. Newton, 5:623–624.

5. Thomas Lye, "How Are We to Live by Faith on Divine Providence?" *Puritan*

Sermons 1659–1689 (Wheaton, IL: Richard Owen Roberts, Publisher, 1981), 1:378.

6. Newton, 5:624.

7. John Brown, *Expository Discourses on 1 Peter* (1848; rpr. Edinburgh: Banner of Truth, 1975), 2:539.

8. Philip Bennett Power, *The "I Wills" of the Psalms* (1858; rpr. Edinburgh: Banner of Truth, 1985), 10, 8.

9. Power, 63.

CHAPTER FOURTEEN: GIVING THANKS ALWAYS

1. There is a discussion among commentators as to whether the wording of the King James Version "all things work together for good" in which the all things is the subject of the verb *work* or whether as in the NIV translation in which the subject is God—"in all things God works"—is the preferred wording. Whichever wording we prefer, the result is the same. If all things work together for our good it is because God has *caused* them to do so. In fact, the New American Standard Bible translates as follows: "God causes all things to work together for good."

2. Alexander Carson, *The History of Providence* (Grand Rapids, MI: Baker, n.d.), 168–169.

DISCUSSION GUIDE

1. J. L. Dagg, *Manual of Theology* (Southern Baptist Publication Society, 1857; rpr. Harrisonburg, VA: Gano Books, 1982), 86–87.

2. J. I. Packer, *Your Father Loves You* (Wheaton, IL: Harold Shaw Publishers, 1986), devotional reading for October 13.

AUTHOR

 Jerry Bridges was a well-known Christian writer and conference speaker. His best known book, *The Pursuit of Holiness*, has sold well over a million copies. A prolific author, he sold over 3.5 million copies of his various books, with several titles translated and published in a variety of foreign languages. He joined the staff of The Navigators in 1955, serving for sixty years as a staff member in various capacities before transitioning to an associate staff position and serving within the collegiate ministry. Jerry passed away in the spring of 2016, leaving behind his wife, Jane; two married children; and seven grandchildren.